THE KINKS

NEVILLE MARTEN & JEFF HUDSON

For Pang

ACKNOWLEDGMENTS

The authors are indebted to the following band members and associates, past and present, who have given freely of their time to assist with this book: Pete Quaife, Deke Arlon, Steve Hammonds, John Gosling, John Dalton, Andy Pyle, Ian Gibbons, Hal Carter, Malcolm Cooke, Doug Hinman, Dave Emlen, Russell Smith, Alison Thomas, Alan Robinson and the entire weight of The Kinks' Fan Club.

And of course to Ray and Dave Davies, both of whose charm and openness in their interviews with the authors over the years have made this book what it is.

As well as our own tome, the authors would direct readers interested in The Kinks to the following volumes which provided essential background in varying degrees: *X-Ray* by Ray Davies, *Kink* by Dave Davies, *Waterloo Sunset* by Ray Davies, *The Sound And The Fury* by Johnny Rogan, *The Kinks – The Official Biography* by Jon Savage, *You Really Got Me: An Illustrated World Discography Of The Kinks 1964-1993* by Doug Hinman, *Down All The Days (To 1992)* by Rob Kopp, *The Kinks – Reflections On Thirty Years Of Music* Edited by Rebecca Bailey, *The Kinks Kronikles* by John Mendelssohn. Dave Emlen's excellent website is also deserving of extra mention (www.kinks.it.rit.edu).

In the compilation of this book many other publications were consulted, among them *Now & Then* – the official Kinks Fan Club magazine, *NME*, *Melody Maker*, *Guitarist* (thanks to Roger Newell), *Mojo*, *Q*, *Rolling Stone*, *Billboard*, *Flatiron*, *Goldmine* and *Hit Parader*, as well as many of the world's various newspapers, listed throughout.

Closer to home, we would also like to thank Sanctuary Publishing for their exemplary taste and sound business acumen in considering this book worthy of publication: Obergruppenführerin, Number One, The Boy Alan, Des Dept, Chris Here, PR Popsie and, our secret weapon, their erstwhile managing editor. Rispec'.

Closer still to home, kudos from JH to FM for use of floor, phone lines and cable TV. And flat. Put it on the slate, Dave.

For information on The Kinks' Fan Club, write to: PO Box 42, Bolton, Manchester BL5 3WW.

CONTENTS

1 JANE, CAROL, SUE, BINT, TART...

"Yeah, you really got me going, you got me so I don't know what I'm doin'…" sang a young Ray Davies on his first tour as a member of The Kinks. With two flop singles behind them, a cover of Little Richard's 'Long Tall Sally' and Ray's own composition 'You Still Want Me', the band were in dire straits and Davies could see the writing on the wall; back to their homes in north London and that would be the end of it. On the tour Ray had been trying out various self-penned songs, one of which would eventually be their first Number One.

Sharing the bill (almost everyone else was higher up it) were The Mojos, who were about to score their first hit with 'Everything's Alright'; heart throb crooner Mark Wynter ('Venus In Blue Jeans'); The Hollies, whose powerful vocal delivery assured them of more '60s hits than anyone bar The Beatles; and The Dave Clark Five, who were currently top of the charts with 'Bits And Pieces' and whose sound was characterised by Clark's battering drum style. It was also Clark's tour. In the face of such success and confidence Ray, his 17-year-old brother Dave on lead guitar, Pete Quaife on bass and Mick Avory on drums seemed a sorry lot. They dressed scruffily, had little or no stage presence, cringed in the face of the spotlight and generally lacked the professionalism needed – even in the so-called talentless world of pop music – to make it to the top.

At this time The Kinks were managed, handled and promoted by a disparate bunch of characters. First were Grenville Collins and Robert Wace, public school types with a yen for the entertainment business. Wace and Collins had become interested in the band (Wace had actually sung in the group for a while) and secured for them various society dates where they wowed the debs and toffs, who viewed their commonness as quaint; this was, after all, the '60s. Then came agent Arthur Howes, who had met the band when they played at a Chinese restaurant in Edgware Road on New Year's Eve 1963. And there was Larry Page, himself a successful singer in the days of Tommy Steele, Cliff Richard and the 2 I's coffee bar; Page had contacts, such as publisher Eddie Kassner and producer Shel Talmy. All these characters would play a role in the making of The Kinks.

The slot on Dave Clark's 1964 spring tour had been arranged by Arthur Howes, but it was Larry Page who appointed troubleshooter Hal Carter to sort the boys out; to tidy up what was in truth a pretty ramshackle performance. Brash Liverpudlian Carter had worked with many British stars of the '50s, and the group's first run-through was, he recalls, quite bad:

"That very first rehearsal, they started playing and it was, 'Oh God no, not another one.' You see, in those days it seemed like every other band wanted to play 'Smokestack Lightnin'' and all that blues kind of stuff, with extended guitar solos all over the place. It was the equivalent of what punk became later on, that same rebellious effect. So I immediately started tearing them apart and they were carping, 'But this is what we do' and I said, 'Not if you want to be successful it's not.'" Carter told them that success meant playing pop music, and this wasn't pop music. "I said, 'If you want to do this stuff then fine, but prepare to stay round here for the rest of your lives.'" He also added, "'There are American bands who do this kind of thing better than you do in their sleep.' Of course at first they knew better; they were thinking, 'What's this old fart doing here telling us what to do?' – and I was all of three or four years older than them."

After a little persuasion from Hal, and a bit of realisation on the part of the band, they decided to co-operate. "And in the end we got along well," says Carter, "especially me and Ray, because I love talent and in him you could spot it a mile away. I thought the group were pretty good too; good musicians for their age and for that time. And after a while they really started to motor."

Hal Carter began to knock the band into shape, but his cocky Scouse manner and his constant references to the big stars of the '50s with whom he had worked caused the immature band a good deal of mirth. To this bunch of youngsters just setting out into adulthood and the quest for their own fame, past successes of a few years earlier seemed like eons ago. Hal had toured with fellow Liverpudlian, the teen idol Billy Fury, as well as the talented Marty Wilde and tried to instil into the lads what true professionalism, such as that displayed by these stars, was all about. "It wasn't just a matter of how they acted on stage," insisted Carter. "It was as important how they behaved off it. And they didn't understand that. I tried to tell them that wherever they were seen, whether it be on stage or off, they always had to look like stars. That was the way you got the kids to come after you; they'd always want your autograph because you looked like a 'somebody'."

But professional was a word The Kinks simply didn't seem to comprehend. "They thought it meant playing for a living and didn't attach any other meaning to it," rues Carter, "like the way you behaved and presented yourself to the world as a whole. Billy and Marty were both very big stars and both completely understood what professionalism was. Of course, if I'd been working with Elvis and had said to them, 'Now Elvis wouldn't do that', they might've been interested and asked how he would have done it. But they didn't have a lot of respect for Billy and Marty because, in their eyes, they were a load of old farts; the geriatrics. But I would say, 'If you want to see someone pacing themselves, look at Marty or Billy, because they actually work an audience; they select the right numbers, even change numbers mid-set, if need be, to make the show go right.' So I would use actual artists to get across to them how I wanted them to behave, but of course they thought that was hilarious. But you know, even though they took the piss mercilessly, I think they did listen because they went on to become very successful and very professional too. This business of creating your own publicity was so important. And in this respect Dave, in particular, was brilliant, because he was so over the top in everything, such an extrovert and so flamboyant that he couldn't help drawing attention, and controversy, to the band. And his campness, prancing around like a right nancy, attracted more women to the stage door than you could imagine."

The Hollies' falsetto singer and rhythm guitarist, Graham Nash, was less impressed with Carter's advice. He liked the band as they were and felt that their unpolished presentation suited the raucous music they were making. Dave Davies recalls a moment that he still remembers with deep satisfaction: "Graham was at the back and had been watching Hal putting us through our paces; he came up to Hal and said, 'Why don't you bloody well leave them alone. They're all right.' And you know, I always remember that; it was important to us that he said it because it made us think, 'Maybe we are okay.' All the people involved with the business side of things were from a different era and they weren't in touch with what was happening."

But Carter's experience soon showed in the group's performance. With new pink hunting jackets, white frilly shirts, black jodhpurs and Chelsea boots purchased by Robert Wace from Monty Berman's theatrical costumiers, they now looked the part, even attracting favourable comments from the other acts; the outspoken Graham Nash in particular saying how at last they looked like The Kinks. Dave Davies: "The fashion at the time was leather and stuff like that, which was in fact what we used to wear, but now we were looked on more as rebels, because of the way we dressed."

The tour was going well for The Kinks, despite being relegated from second to opening slot when their single 'Long Tall Sally' plopped out of the charts (it had reached a paltry 42) and The Mojos' 'Everything's Alright' roared in (it made the Top Ten). They were making fans around the country and Ray was beginning to realise that, despite his less than subtle delivery, Carter was proving good for the group. So he started playing him new songs, looking for comment or criticism from the oracle.

"Funnily enough," recalls Hal, "the song they really used to stop the show with was The Drifters' 'Save The Last Dance For Me'; they tore the place apart with it. But obviously Ray had been writing songs of his own and one day he came to me and played this song and I said, 'Yeah, it's okay, but we can't really use it because it wouldn't fit in anywhere in the show.' And his little face was a picture; his mouth dropped and for all the world it looked like he might burst into tears. So I thought, 'Oh shit...I don't want to kill his enthusiasm, and also I need him to convince the others that I'm right.' So I said, 'Okay, why not shorten it to a couple of minutes and we'll use it as the opener, because then it won't throw the show out by conflicting with what's around it.' What I was really thinking was, 'If we do it first then we can get it out of the way as soon as possible.' So he shortened the song and then played it to me again and I said, 'Fine, we can use it.' Of course it turned out to be 'You Really Got Me'. Even then it wasn't anything like the final recording, but I did get the sense that there was something about that number. After that he would often bring songs to me and I'd say, 'Why don't you try this, that or the other?' And he always listened. But not just to me, he listened to everything. And he was writing all the time and a lot of the stuff I'm sure never saw the light of day. After a while, he'd only let you hear something when it was perfected."

In Ray Davies' autobiography, *X-Ray*, he attributes even more importance to the role of Hal Carter, telling how, just prior to the recording session which fashioned the band's devastating breakthrough single, he came in to offer one final gem of wisdom. Hal thought the opening line, "Yeah, you really got me going", was too impersonal, and went on to offer the singer a tirade of abuse on his apparently ambiguous sexuality, suggesting that he might even be singing the song to another man. He asked Ray to set the record straight, if only for his sake, and start the line with "Jane, Carol, Sue, bint, tart...even just plain 'Girl'." Ray liked "Girl" very much, and went in to sing his song.

2 THE GREEN AMP

Perhaps the differences that sprang up in the brothers Davies and have caused so many squabbles ever since stem from the fact that they lived part of their formative years away from one another. Muswell Hill and Highgate are barely a stone's throw apart, but the distance was enough – with Dave living at sister Rene's and with her son Bob as his best friend, and Ray sometimes at home and other times staying with Uncle Arthur and Auntie Rose and palling up with cousin Terry – for the pair to be more like acquaintances than even close mates. The Davies clan was huge, but the actual family house – which often hosted gatherings of 20 or more revellers – was tiny.

Annie and Frederick Davies had eight children, whose ages spanned almost 30 years. Dave and Ray were the youngest and second youngest respectively; all the other kids were girls and many of them, obviously, considerably older than the brothers – in some respects more like aunties or even surrogate mothers. As Ray pointed out, "When I was five years old, all my sisters were teenagers." The first-born boy was mollycoddled and spoilt, given everything that his adoring mother and sisters could manage. The three-year difference between Ray and Dave may well have separated them as real playmates in any case, but both have commented on palpable feelings of distance during childhood. And Ray has expressed memories of jealousy when the infant interloper entered his life – it was while running out of the house to escape his sisters' new plaything that he fell and smashed his teeth, causing the damage which characterises the crooked smile we recognise today.

Even then Ray could be described as a difficult child; different from the rest; a loner who showed little emotion, but in whom it welled up large, often leaving him in considerable mental turmoil. He believed that somehow he was destined to end up physically deformed and waited in terror for the symptoms to begin to show. Later on he visited a child therapist and went twice weekly to a special educational clinic because of his condition. In his autobiography Davies appears to romanticise his weirdness – telling the therapist at Pembridge Villas in Notting Hill Gate about "orchestras of guitars interpreting his dreams" – but demonstrates all too well the inanity of the average child psychologist, describing such mental challenges as "being given some square pegs to fit into round holes". When his foster family of Arthur, Rose and Terry eventually emigrated to Australia, Ray was devastated; he was grown up by then, already playing in bands, but still ran off to the beach in Redcar, where he was playing, to let his feelings gush out in solitude.

The Davies house in Fortis Green Road, Muswell Hill was a musical place. But in truth many families in post-war Britain were large, close-knit, had pianos in the parlour and family gatherings where people took turns at the "Joanna" and everyone harmonised a song. In the Davies house, everyone would return from the pub a little the worse for wear and set to it – "Mum used to sing when she'd had a few drinks and my dad used to dance," recalled Dave. Ray is more explicit, saying how his dad used to embarrass them at parties with drunken Cab Calloway impersonations. "I now know where that comes from," he has since confessed. So in many respects Annie and slaughterman Fred's home was pretty normal, except that their eldest boy was a little strange and their daughter Peg – who was truly beautiful, according to Ray, but with a tragically withered arm – had done the doubly unthinkable and had an illegitimate child by one of the newly arrived black men in London.

Ray learned a lot about music from his sisters. "My oldest sister went to live in Canada," recalls Ray, "and when she came to visit she brought back rock 'n' roll music; Elvis Presley and things like that." Ray remembers his sisters' parties, to which they brought their boyfriends and he and Dave would listen to the music from upstairs. "I think it had an effect on me," the singer now admits.

Although obviously an intelligent boy – it's often they who feel marginalised and manifest the "loner" symptoms described by Ray – the lad excelled in the non-academic pursuits at William Grimshaw secondary modern school. Track and field events were his forte; he was a promising boxer too, but in the district championships he was unfortunate enough to meet the schools champ of Great Britain and Northern Ireland who punished him severely, adding to the catalogue of injuries and misfortunes that seemed to beset him during his youth. He suffered everything stoically, hardly ever letting on about the almost constant pain and injury that beleaguered him. And he was still awaiting the deformity that was surely just around the corner.

But Ray was also showing an interest in art, and one teacher in particular, Mr Bond, encouraged him in his efforts, so much so that he took the subject at A level (he sat the exam with a finger bent double due to a cricket practice accident) and entered Hornsey Art college. This was not before having managed just six months at his first job, in the art department of an engineering magazine, and a string of even less successful posts.

Then there was Dave. He was the tearaway, the black sheep of the family who smoked and played truant, who was eventually expelled from secondary school for being caught on Hampstead Heath *inflagrante delicto* with a young lady and who generally revelled in rowdiness. Teenage Dave would often get up in the morning, making all the pretences of preparing for school, leave the house on time but scoot straight round to his friend George Harris' house, where the two would listen to George's blues records all day. Of course the errant Davies was always back home dead on half past four. The rowdy tearaway and the troubled one would clash many times, often most violently, in the years to come.

Ray learnt to play the guitar around a year ahead of Dave, on his 13th birthday. He concentrated mostly on the ballads of the day, seemingly unaffected by current trends such as skiffle, instead preferring the American crooners who pervaded the BBC's Light Programme during the 1950s and giving himself a healthy chord vocabulary into the bargain. This knowledge of chords would make itself evident later, in Ray's songwriting. Davies Senior's first guitar was a present from his sister Rene, who showed him a handful of chords on the instrument, went to the local dance for the evening and died the same night from a hole in the heart. Dave: "She knew she was going to die, but she just left and she died the way she wanted to; on the dance floor, which is what she loved the most." Sister Peg's husband, the appropriately named Mike Picker, later assisted Ray in his guitar studies, introducing him to country musicians such as Merle Haggard, Hank Williams and Chet Atkins. Ray developed a good fingerstyle technique, partly due to Mike's classically influenced lessons but also due to the influence of Haggard and Atkins; two of the finest players in the country style. But although Ray appreciated the playing of these musicians and benefited from it, it was the lonesomeness of Hank Williams' songs and singing that attracted him most. The influence of this uneducated but naturally talented loner (did Ray see a comparison?) would surface in some of Davies' more introspective work. By now the boy was proficient enough on his instrument to already be inventing tunes of his own.

Dave was luckier when it came to receiving his first instrument. Although already messing around on Ray's acoustic guitar by the time his eleventh birthday came round, mother Annie put down the incredible sum (in those days) of £7 as a deposit for a 40-pound, American-made Harmony Meteor. The rest was to be paid on hire purchase – the "never never". Dave took to the guitar immediately, the rebellious nature of the instrument as perceived by conservative '50s England doubtless fuelling his desire to succeed with it. Quite the opposite to Ray, who still preferred songs from Rodgers and Hammerstein musicals, Dave hitched his wagon firmly to rock 'n' roll, especially to the likes of the great Eddie Cochran, whose charismatic style was linked to real musical ability. Cochran was a multi-instrumentalist whose tragically short career inspired many young British musicians.

Dave stole every moment he could to practise on his guitar. He copied chords and licks from Gene Vincent's guitarist Cliff Gallup, the inventive Buddy Holly and the rock 'n' roll genius Chuck Berry. Dave was introduced to Berry's music through school mate Johnny Burnette (no relation to the American singing star of the time); both brothers detested the emasculated pap that was beginning to pass for rock music in the aftermath of Presley, and the raw sound of Chuck's gutsy Gibson ES350 guitar was a massive turn-on for the fledgling musician. This was what music was all about. And when Cliff Richard and The Shadows broke through at the turn of the decade, which was to change the lives of the brothers Davies (and those of Pete Quaife and Mick Avory too), the pubescent lad was completely hooked.

Dave was also into blues and would often scour the West End record shops for any records that he could find. Dave: "We'd go to this one shop called Dobell's, which used to be all jazz and blues, and we used to forage out all these old records." The guitarist's blues and rock background has always been self-evident in his playing, and part of the allure of The Kinks' music has always been the juxtaposition of his rough and ready, flashy style, against the melodic chord structures within many of his brother's songs.

The distorted guitar tone that so characterised the group's early recordings came from the Elpico amplifier that Dave bought in a second hand shop before The Kinks proper were even formed. The amp was tiny. Its little valves produced only eight watts' output, whereas modern products often push out a dozen times that. It was also known as "the green amp" because...it was green. Electric guitars played loudly through valve amplifiers produce natural distortion; it's partly the valves and transformers overdriving and partly the speaker being asked to cope with more than it possibly can, but it's a warm tone that's more pleasing to the ear than high pitched clear sounds. The brothers loved the green amp for this ballsiness and Dave even pierced the speaker – Ray says he used his mother's knitting needles but Dave recalls the act being perpetrated with the help of a razor blade – to garner even more distortion from the poor thing. He then re-christened it the "fart box". Later on, Dave would use the fart box linked up to his Vox AC30 amp, in order to retain the tone he held so dear; rumour has it that he repeated the razor blade trick on the Vox because it was just too clean. Legend says that he also chastised a bewildered sound engineer on the TV show *Ready Steady Go* for coming out of the control room and attempting to clean up the sound. "No. That's what I want," he screamed. And Hal Carter recalls how, even in the early days as The Kinks, the brothers' equipment stayed close to them – perhaps more intimately than even they would have liked. Hal: "Because the whole house in Fortis Green Road wasn't much wider than the average living room, the brothers used to sleep in this one little bedroom, with all the amplifiers, guitars and everything. The room was the size of a box and they had these tiny beds in there and all their equipment. When they made it, Ray bought a house more or less over the road – quite a lot bigger, of course."

It was while at secondary school that Ray met Pete Quaife. The two were in the same year and both later wound up at Hornsey Art College. "Everybody was aware that Ray was 'different'," Quaife now confides. "I don't mean that in some 'blaaa blaaa' kind of way; he was just a different type of person, that was all."

However different, they struck up a friendship which would lead to the formation of The Kinks – contrary to the usual account of the band's origins (told by others in this book). "There are a million stories about how the band started," he told us, "and some of them are quite near – if you use light years as a yardstick! It's unfortunate that Ray uses those times to enhance his position as the great God who saved our dismal lives. It's reported that Dave and myself started the group. That's impossible. At school I didn't have the faintest idea who Dave Davies was. He was three or four years behind Ray and myself and you don't associate with younger members of your school. Ray and I formed the genesis of the band.

"The music teacher had asked, after watching us play our guitars, if we would think about forming a 'combo' to play at the school dance. We sniffed, shrugged and went away to see if we could do it. It was then that Ray mentioned his brother – 'a bit young, but he can play guitar all right'. I knew that a friend of mine, John Start, could play the drums so I suggested him. We rehearsed at John's house on Ringwood Avenue (and actually had Rod Stewart in to try out as a singer). Things went better than anyone had thought and we all got very enthusiastic about the group. Rod didn't work out and he left to pursue his own career," Pete laughs, "and we started to look around for work. The rest is history."

By coincidence, the band's first tour manager, Malcolm Cooke, also became aware of their existence at this time. He lived locally and knew Pete, whose parents owned a grocer's shop nearby. But when, several years later, Cooke went to Wigan to meet the latest group he was to look after, he received something of a surprise. Malcolm: "Wigan ABC decided to have pop concerts after a layoff of several years and I was booked as tour manager. I knew I had this new band called The Kinks to open the show – actually they only did three numbers – and there were these three guys I knew – particularly Pete Quaife, because of his parents' shop. Actually I knew them before they were even in a band; I used to see them around Muswell Hill all the time, usually knocking about in the El Toro coffee bar. That day in Wigan I looked up and there was Quaifey and I said, 'What are you doing here?' and he said, 'I'm with The Kinks.' I said, 'Who else is here?' and he said, 'There's Ray, Dave and Mick.' I didn't know Mick, but all the others were art school boys and I said to them, 'Where did you find him?' and Ray said, 'Oh, he just used to mix the paint for us.' At that time on stage they wore these black leather caps on the backs of their heads and high-cut, thick tweed suits in brown. This came from when they used to play society hunt balls, which Grenville Collins and Robert Wace had got them doing, because that was their particular social scene."

But back in 1958, Ray was beginning to be impressed by his brother's progress on the guitar. "I was amazed at how he'd improved," says Davies. "I was the guitarist, the real deep-thinking, serious musician. I went away to college and played in clubs and when I came back there was this crazed kid, with really big hair, playing these amazing guitar licks. I thought, 'He's terrific; I must get in on this.'" Ray was no doubt surprised at his brother sticking at one thing for such a length of time and before long the two were performing at home as a musical duo, although at the time the lead and rhythm roles were reversed, Ray still a far more skilled exponent of the instrument than his brother. Ray tells of how he, Dave and Pete Quaife got a gig at the local dance hall through one of his sisters' boyfriends. But the lads apparently weren't quite ready for stardom – at least a hall full of angry teddy boys didn't think so. The group didn't even have a drummer and all three guitarists were plugged into the green amp, so they were hardly audible to the rowdy crowd. The manager was eventually asked to end everyone's embarrassment and so the bemused trio were dragged off stage – while still playing and while still plugged into the green amp.

Around this time too, Dave's rock influences started rubbing off on his older brother, and while watching a TV programme called *This Wonderful World*, Ray met up with that other, most profound musical form, the blues. The black guitarist and singer Big Bill Broonzy was playing in one short clip of the programme and this affected Ray deeply. Art college friends were also into the blues – late '50s art students were the Bohemians of their day and followed folk, trad jazz and blues trends avidly. Ray joined forces with like minded college souls and formed several blues outfits; he often switched to piano for these sessions but success was not to be theirs. However, during a stint in a blues duo with his friend Geoff Prowse, Ray attended a gig at Hornsey Art College where British blues guru Alexis Korner was performing. Through Korner, Ray would soon join his first band and gain valuable live experience, although not quite enough to gain him entry to the Billy Fury school of stagecraft.

Alexis Korner is often referred to as the Father of British Blues, although many British 40-somethings will remember him on children's TV's *Five O'Clock Club* with presenters Muriel Young and Wally Whyton, ably assisted by glove puppets Pussycat Willum and Ollie Beak. Outside his day job, though, Korner really was a driving force for the music he loved, and became the inspiration for many young musicians to form their own blues and R&B bands. The Rolling Stones would be one such outfit; their eventual drummer, Charlie Watts, was currently holding down that position with Korner.

Ray spoke to the bluesman while he was packing away his guitar after the gig and confessed his desire to get into the blues in a more serious way; he wanted to find a decent, working band, sort of like his hero Broonzy but with a rhythm section behind it. Korner seemed to understand and in characteristically helpful fashion suggested that Ray get in touch with a friend who ran the Scene Club in Piccadilly. Ray dutifully obeyed and was delighted with what he found; having expected more of a one-man, foot-stomping show in the style of Broonzy or Sonny Boy Williamson, he was treated to a curious mixture of blues and jazz. Various names and names-to-be could be found hanging out at the Scene: indeed, Ray met the owner, Giorgio Gomelsky, who would later make his name as producer of The Yardbirds (later to become Led Zeppelin).

Gomelsky set him up with an audition the following week, with The Dave Hunt Band. Trombonist Hunt needed a young guitarist to add flair to his big band style line-up and Ray, having successfully negotiated the tricky chord changes of the jazzy numbers, was offered the gig. Hunt's support act that same night was an embryonic Rolling Stones, and although Hunt referred to the band as "nothing more than a glorified skiffle group", Davies was impressed by their energy and rapport with the young audience as they delivered Chuck Berry's 'Roll Over Beethoven' with genuine gusto. He could see the potential in this primeval, yet completely charismatic style.

Although still at college, Ray accepted the job with Hunt and worked with the band on average three nights a week, often turning up for lectures only four or five hours after getting home from a session. The exhaustion often showed and, combined with Davies' growing disillusionment with all things establishment or "corporate", the writing was, as they say, on the wall. But the writing – at least as far as Ray was concerned – was also on the wall for The Dave Hunt Band. Although the months of work had honed a certain proficiency in his playing, Davies was beginning to find almost everything about the band frustrating. Musically it was not what he really wanted – he'd seen the Stones, remember – and he was beginning to realise that his position in the group was that of crowd puller; he was the token youngster, brought in to keep the college kids happy. But after a while even that was not working; the Stones had signed a deal with Decca Records and the musical mood in London was shifting from trad to R&B. After a frank discussion with the band's tenor sax player, Lol

Coxhill, who suggested he should leave and join a band of his own age, Ray took the plunge and resigned. The desperation in Hunt's voice as he broke the news convinced Davies he was making the right decision.

During Ray's stint with The Dave Hunt Band, his young brother had not been idle. Now a flashy-looking 14-year-old, already gaining something of a reputation with the girls, Dave had hitched up with his older brother's schoolmate, Pete Quaife, and a young drummer called John Start, whose father owned a successful jewellery business. They called themselves The Ravens. Quaife had originally been a guitarist – he'd learnt to play as a sort of physiotherapy following a nasty accident involving a spike – but had lately switched to bass. Ray decided, with the acquiescence of Dave, Pete and John, to make the trio a quartet. Perhaps surprisingly, they didn't alter the spelling of the band's name to The Rayvens.

When John Start's dad demanded that he leave the band to enter the family business (and that the boys repay him for the Marks & Spencer jumpers he had bought them as "stage gear"), Pete Quaife secured a replacement drummer in the form of an older musician, Mickey Willet. Willet didn't really look the part but his experience – along with that of Ray – helped the band sound at least somewhat professional. Dave's lead guitar style was by now well established as a fiery, aggressive, machine-gun-like affair and so the group now had at least two of the basic requirements: a solid rhythm section and a flashy instrumentalist. A singing frontman would have been a godsend, some decent work an added bonus and management...well, that would surely set them on their way. Enter that pair of up-and-coming society toffs, Grenville Collins and Robert Wace.

3 PIMPLE-FACED LIBERACES

The year was 1963, probably best known to those who were there as the year The Beatles had their first Number One (in certain charts) with 'Please Please Me'. And their second with 'From Me To You'. And their third with 'She Loves You'. The fourth was 'I Want To Hold Your Hand' and history will confirm that things continued in pretty much the same vein throughout the next year and indeed the entire decade, although rather less tediously in reality than on paper. Ray would doubtless have heard 'Love Me Do', which had charted the previous year and opened the door for the musical onslaught that changed the world as everyone knew it. This music was radically different to anything that had gone before; not only was it performed by everyday working-class lads – a fact that was definitely not lost on Davies Senior – but word began to spread too that The Beatles had actually written most of it themselves. An unthinkable state of affairs back then. Young musicians throughout Britain began to see the possibility of stardom; not only in the physical sense of being on telly, selling lots of records and having as many girls as they could possibly consume, but also in the intellectual sense of creating something from scratch. Something that would last. Something that really said something about their time.

Although the pop record business in early '60s Britain seemed like a gigantic machine run by moguls and magnates, it was in truth a small world populated by characters who were often there purely by chance, with no real knowledge or musical background. Indeed so much so that a Liverpool sales assistant (okay, so his dad owned the business) managed to bluff his way to becoming the best-known group manager of them all. Brian Epstein was like the fifth Beatle; he was a celebrity in his own right with regular articles written about him in the popular and quality press and features on the nation's radio stations and still primitive television. In the wake of Epstein, young men from all over the country, with perhaps a little more confidence than ability, were aching to get into management.

According to Ray, Mickey Willet (the unsuitable-looking drummer) and Pete Quaife had met Grenville Collins and Robert Wace while drinking in a pub. They got talking about music and it seemed the two factions could form a mutual benefaction society; Wace and Collins were probably thinking they could use the young "innocents" to further their own ends, but there's no doubt the cash registers were ringing just as loud and equally clear in the heads of Pete and Mickey. Grenville fancied himself as a manager and was apparently providing most of the money, and his friend Wace could see his name in lights as the British answer to Sinatra, Presley and Buddy Holly all rolled into one. Robert thought he could sing and Grenville had no reason to doubt him; they were young gentlemen of the highest stock and mixed in the very best circles. And this band that the scruffy urchins said they played bass and drums in could just prove the perfect vehicle for his talents. It was agreed that, in turn for Wace securing well-paid, high-society gigs, the band would play their set of raunchy R&B numbers and then allow Robert to stroll out on stage with great panache and aplomb to captivate the primed and lubricated debs and toffs. It couldn't fail. Robert Wace And The Boll-Weevils were on their way.

Unfortunately, the match was rather less successful than had been expected. For a start, none of the Boll-Weevils made six feet in height and both Grenville and Robert were a good five inches taller. More a case of Gulliver and the Lilliputians than Gerry And The Pacemakers. Secondly, Robert couldn't actually sing, a deficiency which only became apparent after a season of successful West End dates, debutante balls and country manor engagements. These were in front of Robert's own crowd; the swanky set, who were perhaps more interested in each other's diamonds and pearls than in paying much heed to the band. But when Grenville, whose confidence in his management and booking skills had temporarily outgrown them, booked the band to play at an East End youth club, it became a different story. According to Ray, Robert's renditions of the pop tunes of the day sung in an upper-class accent rather missed the point with the cynical working-class kids. A titter sprang up and before long the whole audience was singing – unfortunately in mockery rather than adoration. Robert, his confidence badly shaken, stumbled over his words and missed his notes. He couldn't go on and so left the stage in disarray, leaving Dave – not Ray – and a roadie to finish the set on vocals. The band sounded good – and looked pretty cool in their new pink shirts and blue cord pants, which Grenville had given them money to purchase in Carnaby Street. So all was not lost; in fact things still sounded promising.

With Robert badly shaken and his audience not exactly stirred, he did what any English hero would do and adopted another disguise. He joined forces with Grenville and formed Boscobel Productions (after Boscobel Place, where his father lived) and they decided to manage the band, who had become The Ravens once more. A contract was duly produced – Frederick and Annie Davies had to sign for the brothers, as they were not yet 21 – and the group had management. Ray cites this moment as the only time in his life he wishes he'd seen a lawyer; management, contract and royalty wranglings would dog the band for ever, it seemed. According to Wace, Ray approached him and asked to be managed by Boscobel, whereas Ray suggests in his autobiography that the pressure came from Robert and Grenville.

The Ravens were in the throes of losing Mickey Willet and gaining an even more short-term drummer, Johnny Green. Willet was never particularly enamoured with Wace and Collins; he'd been around a bit and was less impressed by their abilities and contacts than were Pete, Ray and Dave. He also discovered what he believed to be financial discrepancies between what the band were getting and Robert and Grenville's own cut; on one particular gig it appeared that management had received double that of the entire band for their evening's work, although Robert insisted the extra was for other expenses incurred. It also seems unlikely, given the type of people both Wace and Collins were, that they would stoop to cheating the group in this way.

As the oldest, Mickey gained the role of band spokesman and was constantly at odds with The Ravens' management about bookings, schedules and payments. In his turn Wace was intimidated by the drummer's lack of trust and insubordination. In the end it all became too much for Robert, who persuaded Ray that it was time for the drummer to go. Although in some respects Ray was prepared to side with Willet – he was after all one of them, and probably had secured better deals for the band here and there – the pressure was too much and so a clause in the contract was invoked and Willet removed. Although he left The Ravens still on good terms with Ray, Mickey felt hard done by. But the truth of the matter was that, although he was by all accounts a fine drummer who fitted in well musically, he was very much an outsider in other respects and would have parted company with The Ravens sooner or later. Of course Ray would have realised this at the time, too.

Time for another drummer to depart and for the final piece of the jigsaw to fall into place. Dave recalls the perennial difficulty in finding a suitable drummer in the early '60s: "At that time, there weren't any drummers that really slotted into the type of music that we liked; in fact it was very difficult to find a drummer that could play. We auditioned Viv Prince [who later joined The Pretty Things, a band perhaps even more way-out than Ray, Dave and the boys], but he'd never turn up for rehearsals." When Johnny Green decided that showbusiness was not for him, Dave placed an advert in *Melody Maker* saying, "Drummer wanted for a smart, go-ahead group". And so it was that Mick Avory attended a professionally organised audition in a room above the Camden Head pub. Throughout his audition, Avory was subjected to the sharp end of the band's highly developed and rather wry sense of humour. The fact that the drummer had apparently played with Mick Jagger and Brian Jones in an early incarnation of The Rolling Stones cut no ice at all with The Ravens. In fact, had it not been for a fear of losing his day job, Mick may well have become a Stone and pop history might have looked rather different.

The early '60s was a great time for sex scandals; not only was there the Profumo affair, which involved call girls Christine Keeler and

Mandy Rice-Davies and rocked the Conservative cabinet, but the *Lady Chatterley's Lover* obscenity case was all over the press. Add to this a spy scandal involving the homosexual Vassal – homosexuality was still very much underground and indeed illegal then – and it's understandable that sexual innuendo of all kinds would be prime banter for a group of witty teenagers. So the unwitting paraffin delivery man from East Molesey in Surrey was subjected to a barrage of camp innuendo from Quaife and the brothers – Mick was sure they were all "queer" – but when the group began to play, the chemistry was immediate and they all seemed to know that this was it.

Pete Quaife puts it into perspective. "The 'gay' banter was nothing more than a few young lads playing around," he told us. "Unfortunately, Mick walked right in on it. It must have been a shock to see three scruffy, pimple-faced boys acting like adolescent Liberaces – and asking him to join the band. Anyway, as always Mick's sense of humour pulled him through and he retaliated accordingly."

That retaliation took a while to come, though. After the audition the "gaiety" continued and Mick wasn't impressed; he was a no-nonsense lad with a steady girlfriend and would have none of it. But several days later he was confirmed as the fourth member and the line-up that would make some of the greatest pop music of the '60s was in place. The humour in the fact that Avory had had his long hair cut short – especially to look smart for this posh-sounding "go-ahead" band from London – was lost on no one.

Despite a still healthy flow of society dates and the occasional club gig, Collins and Wace's total lack of experience in the music business was getting The Ravens nowhere fast. Apart from a small publishing offer from Mills Music, nothing was forthcoming. Fortunately the duo were clued up enough to realise that a hard-hitting personality was required; one who knew the business and had all the right contacts. Everyone felt that the group was on the brink of something, and all it needed was a well-timed push in the right direction to take them on to the next stage. Larry Page ran a company in Denmark Street (London's so-called Tin Pan Alley) called Denmark Productions, which was in turn owned by music publisher Eddie Kassner. According to Hal Carter,

Page was always on the lookout for people who wanted to get into the business, especially if they had a good product behind them (eg a band that was soon to become The Kinks) and, in Carter's words, "Especially if they had a few bob."

Page had been a singer himself in the '50s. With blue-rinsed hair he had rampaged through the clubs as Larry Page The Teenage Rage. He came close to success but never broke through beyond supporting name acts of the day such as Cliff Richard And The Shadows. Leaving the sharp end of showbusiness Larry (real surname Davis) joined the lucrative Mecca circuit in Coventry, searching out and booking acts, before being lured to London by an offer from Eddie Kassner's publishing company. The deal was that Page signed the acts while Eddie secured the publishing rights. Grenville approached Kassner and through him was introduced to Page.

Robert and Grenville convinced Page to audition the band and, despite their obvious shortcomings – no proper equipment, no real singer, no original numbers and a stage act which consisted mainly of Dave's jerking movements – Page saw something. The deal that day gave Larry a ten per cent share in The Ravens and the rights for Kassner to place or publish Ray Davies' songs. With his limited creative output at the time and no guarantee of much to come in the future, it may well have seemed that Ray got the better end of the deal. But hindsight, as they say, is 20 / 20 vision, and while both Ray and Robert Wace have since rued the day they became involved with Kassner, Larry Page points out that without him things would have been very different. "Wace begged me to see the group," insisted Page, "and without that they would be nothing. You can say a lot of things about Eddie Kassner, but without that man they would still be The Ravens playing in a little pub."

Disputes also still exist as to who was the group's main manager. Wace and Collins say emphatically that it was them, with Larry Page playing only a side role, but many people involved with the business end of the band from that point on would insist that it was the reverse. But not only was Page a management asset, he also knew about pop music; what made a hit and what the public may or may not be ready for. And although The Ravens initially wanted a frontman and singer,

Page was astute enough to realise this was not necessary. Although Ray's voice and charisma were hardly the match for Presley, or even Lennon or McCartney, he enunciated a song in a certain way, could sing in tune – albeit with an adenoidal twang – and his taking on the vocal role kept the band down to a four-piece. Larry sat down with Ray and realised that here was a writer with potential; all he needed were the bones of some ideas and he would be off. One of Page's favourite bands was The Kingsmen, whose song 'Louie Louie' contained an insistent riff and a simple vocal melody. Together Larry and Ray knocked out 'Revenge', a fairly basic tune heavily reliant on Kingsmen ideas. But the thought of the pulsating riff had entered Ray's head and would surface again and again in some of his biggest hits of the decade.

Next the band made some demos. They went into Regent Sound Studios and put down several songs, included three originals: Ray's 'It's Alright' and two numbers from Dave, 'One Fine Day' and 'I Believed You'. The songs were naive but the music was raw and vital. Page used the demos to secure a deal with Pye Records and to link them up with the man who would oversee their early hits, the American producer Shel Talmy. Talmy had come to England from the States and, by his own admission, talked his way into production with no credentials whatsoever. Talmy: "Everybody here expected Americans to be brash and loud, and so that's exactly what I was. I walked into Decca and said, 'Here I am' and reeled off a list of hits I'd made, which of course I hadn't."

But Talmy did make a mark for himself by producing The Bachelors' hit 'Charmaine', which made the Top Ten in early 1963. This gave him a producer's contract with Pye and allowed him the discretion of bringing in acts of his own. Talmy told Pye he liked the demos Wace had given him and The Ravens had a record deal.

By early 1964, Grenville and Robert had also hooked up with The Beatles' promoter Arthur Howes – remember they had met at the Chinese restaurant gig on New Year's eve – and the Dave Clark tour was already proposed for the coming spring. This was a very powerful liaison and perhaps the single most important one in The Ravens' transformation into The Kinks and from playing local hops to topping the charts. But Howes was suspicious of Larry Page and, so Wace insists, wanted rid of him. Page in turn had little respect for Robert and Grenville and so the management team, already top-heavy, was even now beginning to crack at the seams.

But to a group of struggling musicians from Muswell Hill, everything was looking good. They could sense that success was just around the corner; after all, didn't they have all these important people looking after them? So it was an expectant time. But something still wasn't quite right. The name. The Ravens was okay but a little corny for the '60s, which were already coming into full "swing".

The choice of name is a source of great stress and contemplation for any band. Should it reflect the group's music? Or their style? Should it be humorous? Or suggestive? Then there's the potential embarrassment – nay, derision – which comes from suggesting something…well…crap. And so the memories of all those involved will often become hazy; no one accepts responsibility initially, but should fame occur everyone recalls their slice of input – "I suggested this" or "I thought of that". In the case of The Kinks, one word had consistently been used in describing this bunch of strangely clad, long haired louts: "kinky". Many people have suggested that the name stemmed from the cult TV show *The Avengers*, whose black-clad and cat-like leading lady Emma Peel (Honor Blackman) wore "kinky boots". But kinkiness was also a vogue; Christine Keeler was kinky, as were the exploits which every teenage boy imagined her getting up to at secret parties in Sloane Square or Chelsea. Kinkiness was in.

And so it was that Wace's old Etonian friend came up with the name; and Larry Page suggested it; and Ray decided on it after hearing Page mention it; and so on and so forth. Of course, the truth is to be found somewhere in the middle of all that. And the fact of who said what is much less important. What probably was crucial to the band's success is that someone did suggest it and the group adopted it. Notoriety was the name of the game – Larry Page spotted it immediately – and the band's weird clothes, way-out R&B music and outlandish stage antics were already garnering them a degree of it. So to call such a group The Kinks was indeed an inspiration.

The next stage in the band's evolution was to record a single. Arthur Howes had been in Paris where he had watched The Beatles wow the audience with Paul McCartney's lung-wrenching version of Little Richard's 'Long Tall Sally' (ironic, considering the song is apparently about a transvestite, a good seven years before 'Lola'). In the absence of anything forthcoming from Ray, Howes called Page informing him The Kinks must record this song; it was bound to be a smash. The group went into the studio that Friday night and put down four tracks, three written by Ray: 'You Still Want Me', 'I Took My Baby Home' and 'You Do Something To Me' – and of course 'Long Tall Sally'. "They didn't like any of my songs," remarked the singer, but it did give the band an opportunity to gauge the impact that their music might make. "It was the first time I'd really heard my voice," Ray says. "I came up the steps of the studio and Dave was there and he said, 'You know, you've got a really commercial voice.'" The prevalence of "you" and "me" in the titles of Ray's early songs was the direct influence of Page, who believed the use of these words lent an immediacy to the lyric and would more or less guarantee hits. It may not have been a coincidence that the first four Beatles' hits followed this same principle.

With a single on general release – 'I Took My Baby Home' was the B-side – Page was flogging The Kinks' kinkiness in order to gain any kind of media coverage, but especially a slot on the happening pop TV show of the time, *Ready Steady Go*. Although the record didn't manage to dent the charts it did gain them much needed exposure. Plus it gave them their three minutes on telly. A crowd of rented "fans" waited outside the Rediffusion studios and mobbed the band as they left. The second single, 'You Still Want Me' / 'You Do Something To Me', came and went as quickly as the first. But The Kinks had been on TV and had two singles released by a major label. Such exposure was enough to guarantee them second billing, over The Mojos, on the infamous Dave Clark tour.

4 IF HE CAN'T PLAY WITH YOUR SAND CASTLE, HE'LL KICK IT DOWN

Although still in their teens, the personality of each band member was well defined by the time of the Dave Clark tour. They'd been through more than most average English kids of college age; they'd played at late-night clubs, performed at society balls, rubbed shoulders with the rich and were now beginning to meet the famous. Tour troubleshooter Hal Carter got to know the group well during this time and here he gives his version of their characters: "There was Pete Quaife, who was always very bright and intelligent, but in a way almost superior, because I think his family had a few quid – certainly compared to the others they did. Pete always seemed a little bit above it all. And then you had Mick Avory, who was a darling man. Mick was a real working-class hero who would talk to anybody, help anybody. He had the biggest hands, like shovels, but he was basically a gentle guy and everybody liked him. Mick was funny. Sometimes we went on our own in the van to gigs, but other days we were on this big coach along with Dave Clark and The Hollies, etc. We'd often drive past a building site and Mick would go, 'Wow, look at that,' and everyone would look out of the window and say, 'What?' And he'd say, 'It's an XJ7-B digger,' or whatever. One day he got really excited because apparently there were only three of these particular diggers in the country. The other guys would get excited about Gretsch or Fender guitars, but old Mick knew every model of digger and steamroller there was.

"Dave was the flash bugger. He was an excellent guitar player for one so young and who was just coming into the business. But yes, he was a flash little git. He was always going to get a right-hander from somebody, one way or another." Dave was often in trouble, a reputation which tended to precede him. Tour manager Malcolm Cooke recalls one particular incident. "We were in Shrewsbury and I got a call from the receptionist at the hotel where the band were staying," he says. "She said, 'I've got a bit of a problem,' and I said, 'Oh yes? What kind of a problem?' And she said, 'I've got a battle-axe embedded in the reception desk.' And when something like that happened, you could almost guarantee it would be Dave."

The younger brother's campness was also legendary; although in truth the biggest womaniser of the band, many observers were convinced he was gay. Malcolm Cooke again: "One thing I remember vividly about Dave was when he walked up to the tour's compere, Brian Burdon, who was wearing slap, or stage make-up. Now just remember that at this point – and it's early 1964, mind you – Dave is wearing a pink hunting jacket, ruffs on both cuffs and down the front of his shirt, he's wearing skin-tight trousers and black suede thigh boots and hair down to his shoulders, parted in the middle. And he said to Brian, "'Ere, what's that you've got on yer face?' And Brian said, 'It's slap.' Dave said, 'What's slap?' and Brian said, 'It's make-up, stage make-up; why, don't you wear any?' And Dave looked straight at him and said, 'Nah, I think it's effeminate.' But he wasn't stupid, because very shortly after that, there he was wearing slap himself, because he realised it emphasised his features and made him look even more camp and even more attractive to the ladies."

"Ray was totally different again," continues Carter. "Whereas Dave would camp it up and you'd never quite know whether he was double-headed or not, or whether he was completely straight and just playing at it, Ray was very, very studious, always half in a dream, always deep in thought and mulling things over. He was always writing and always read a lot and was always interested in what was going on in the world around him. He was never so extrovert as Dave; he was conscious of his looks and he couldn't pull a bird to save his life. In fact I had to fix him up with a girl once. We met her in a shoe shop and I chatted her up for him."

One trait commonly attributed to The Kinks, or more particularly to the brothers Davies, is that of constant arguing, rowing and, not uncommonly, actual fist-fighting. The Dave Clark tour had its fair share of ructions. Hal: "Funnily enough, in the early days Ray would never want to get involved in any of the rows in the band. When we were in the van I'd often say to him, 'Ray, you're going to have to tell Dave before I throw him out of the door,' and Ray would never say anything. Even when Dave was being threatened, which was often, he'd never defend him. To Ray it was either, he's out of order, or he's going to have to defend himself.

"The most famous fight story happened in Cardiff. Mick and Dave had been rowing all afternoon, and that night they've gone on stage and they're still eyeballing each other. Anyway, what you have to realise is that Mick adored his drum kit; he used to polish it every night after the show and put everything carefully back in its cases. But that night Dave was swaggering around in his long Jesse James coat and camping it up, preening himself with his guitar and shouting stupid things at Mick, who wasn't really responding because he was getting on with the job of whacking the drums. Then Dave made the biggest mistake of his life, committed the cardinal sin; he was still jumping about and shouting at Mick, calling him a twat and everything and he went across and kicked his bass drum. Well, I've never seen anybody move so fast – and Mick's a big lad – but he jumped up, grabbed a cymbal and *pow!* He hit him right across the head with this cymbal and, I tell you, you've never seen so much blood; it was spurting everywhere. And Ray just kept on singing. Dave was rushed to hospital to have his head fixed, but you know, when he came back with it all bandaged up, they were still arguing. Dave could be a mouthy young twat then and he's just the same now."

Pete Quaife winces as he recalls the occasion, albeit slightly differently to Carter. "It started the night before, in Torquay," he says. "Dave got drunk and had a go at everyone. The last one he picked on was Mick who began to systematically rearrange Dave's face. We all jumped in and stopped the fighting and separated them and the next day we went to Cardiff separately, Ray with Dave and myself with Mick. Everything went fine in the show until I realised, with mounting dread, that the next number, 'Beautiful Delilah', called for Dave to turn and count Mick in. Dave counted 'one, two, three…', Mick started to play and Dave walked over and kicked his drums all over the place before returning to his mic to sing the number. That was when Mick picked up his cymbal and crowned Dave right across the head. End of show."

According to Hal, the personnel may have changed, but the story is the same. "Of course they keep breaking up," he says. "Ray will go off on his own and do a tour and Dave will go off to the States or something. Then Ray will write something new or set up a load of dates and they'll say, 'Oh, we've got to have Dave; it's not The Kinks without Dave.' So they hook up with Dave again and go out on tour, but within a couple of weeks they hate each other again.

"In the early days it wasn't at all like that," he elaborates; "well, at least I never saw them like it. You see, Ray had a very calm and demure attitude then and he just didn't get involved." Hal has a plausible theory as to why not: "I think it was because he didn't have anything to lose yet, because he didn't have anything at all. But once he'd succeeded, once he became important and recognisable as a writer, then he had to protect that and I think that's why he began fighting. Because Dave always had the potential to destroy what Ray had created. You see, Dave's one of those kids who, if he can't play with your sand castle, he'll kick it down. And Ray had to protect the castle because he was the one who had built it. But it does make life interesting."

The tour was also notable for big friction with the headlining act, The Dave Clark Five. Clark had recently invaded the high reaches of the charts with a couple of good-time stompers and was being touted as the southern band that could really topple The Beatles: London's "great white hope", in effect. Clark talked of it as his tour and made himself very unpopular with the other acts, who were made to feel, if not exactly second rate, then certainly second-class passengers on the Good Ship 'Glad All Over'. Although Hal Carter's charges – the new boys, the tearaways – could easily have been made the scapegoats for all the 'misfortunes' that all but capsized Clark's vessel, they escaped major blame. "None of us really got on with Dave Clark," exclaims Carter bluntly. "He was always paranoid about everything and I think he felt inferior because he was never really a performer, although he was a hell of a good businessman even then. There were a certain number of people on the show who caused a lot of trouble for him, and there was no need for that. So in that way he was right to be annoyed. But The Kinks weren't involved because they were young and new at it, and very much in awe of the whole thing. There were enough characters in the group to have all the fun they needed anyway, so they didn't need to involve anybody else." Malcolm Cooke is more specific: "Dave Clark was going to kill us all, including The Hollies and The Kinks. You see, in those days, the main act would have their equipment – amps and PA and everything – in place on the stage and all the support bands would use that gear throughout the evening. But Dave Clark had his own complete system, including piggy-back Vox guitar amps, and insisted on setting all this up and using it for his act only. And everything was miked up, including the drums, so that he could get that big sound the band was famed for. But his equipment kept being sabotaged and we always believed, rightly or wrongly, that it was Eric Haydock, The Hollies' bass player. Before The Dave Clark Five went on, someone used to pick up one of the amp heads, drop it on the floor so the valves inside would unseat themselves or some other damage would happen, and then put it back on top of the speaker cabinet; it still looked all right, but either didn't work at all or would pack up halfway through the set. One day Eric actually went out and bought a pair of boltcroppers and halfway through the set he chopped the multicore, which takes all the microphone signals from the stage to the sound engineer out front, in two, so all you could hear was Dave doing his famous 'boom boom boom boom' 'Bits And Pieces' beat acoustically. Everything else had gone completely dead."

"He bloody well asked for it," Pete Quaife reckons, "for trying to con everyone into believing he could play the drums! The sabotage was excellently devised by several of the other band members. It was funny and didn't harm anyone. Even Clarky saw the funny side of it."

Not before a big confrontation, however. "One day," says Hal Carter, taking up the story, "we were all in the coach and Dave told Sparksy the bus driver to pull the coach over. Clarky got up and told everybody that this was his tour and the only reason the rest were on it was because he deigned to have them. But it wasn't his tour. True, things were happening to his act every night and it must have been infuriating and frustrating – because at that time he didn't know who it was, although he probably suspected The Kinks. But he was an obnoxious twat and everybody just wanted to have a go at him. But he never forgave me, and I never did anything or said anything. A lot later, I was in Harold Waterman's accountants, doing The Troggs' tour expenses, and Dave Clark came in and saw me working. The next thing I know, the buzzer goes and I'm summoned in to see Mr Waterman who said, 'What have you done to Dave Clark?' I said, 'Nothing.' He said, 'Well, he's very angry and has told me that he doesn't want you anywhere near his account or he'll take his business elsewhere.' But I was only using the office to do The Troggs' tour expenses; I didn't even work there."

Ask anyone who knows them if a Davies brother ever bought them a drink in those days and the answer is likely to contain a string of references to their other claim to fame; their alleged meanness with money. Hal: "It's legendary. When we were on that first tour we'd be driving around in the van – I was doing the driving – and they'd always be asking me to stop for sweets. Like little kids they were. Dave always wanted cigarettes as well; macho man smoked too. And we had this running battle about getting to the gig or stopping for their sweets and ciggies. But every time we stopped, without fail Dave'd say, 'Lend us tuppence, lend us threepence' or whatever. This went on for weeks and then one day he said, 'Lend us tuppence' and I said, 'Dave, piss off. I'm sick to death of giving you tuppences, threepences and penny ha'pennies and you never giving them back.' And he said, 'Oh, go on,' and I said, 'No.' And he went, 'You bastard, I've got to break into a sixpence now because of you.' And that pretty much sums him up. Of course Ray would never ask to borrow anything, because that would mean he'd have to pay it back. But you could be dying of thirst before either of 'em would offer to buy you a drink."

Mal Cooke brings the story further up to date: "I was walking down Baker Street in London in about 1980, by which time Ray was definitely worth a few million, and there he was and he saw me and said, 'What are you doing?' and I said, 'Nothing really.' He said, 'Are you hungry?' and I said, 'Yeah, I am actually' and he said, 'Can I buy you dinner?' and I said, 'Yeah, that would be nice.' And so he took me into this little roadside cafe around the corner and bought me egg, sausage and chips." Carter was asked by The Kinks' office to say a few words about the band on a radio programme quite recently: "I said something like, 'They're a very tight band; you couldn't get a drink out of them if you tried.' That was only about four years ago." It seems Dave's wallet has remained firmly clamped shut too. Hal: "I went to a book launch some years back and he was there with this American girl, who I believe he got married to. As usual I was winding him up. I said, 'Free booze, free food; yeah, the Davies brothers'll be there.' And this American girl turned to him and said, 'He knows you well, doesn't he?'"

Although Carter became the butt of much criticism and derision from the band (in fact almost as much as they received from him), he stayed on for a while after the Clark tour to continue as general tour manager. Ray and Hal continued to discuss music and it's obvious that the two developed something of an understanding. Hal's own version of his artistic input into 'You Really Got Me' is more self-effacing than Ray's version. Hal: "The 'You Really Got Me' episode was all part of the stage presentation thing, because I thought the gap at the beginning of the song caused a pregnant pause and needed to be filled. So I suggested he put something in there, like 'Girl, you really got me going' instead of '...you really got me going'. But it was mainly because of the way he had reacted when I initially put the song down, that I came up with the suggestion; if he hadn't have reacted with such a long face I probably wouldn't have said anything. I suppose at the time I didn't realise how important the whole thing was; the fact that I was actually in the middle of something quite momentous."

Ray had originally come up with the basic idea for the song in his mother's front room, using the piano that so much of the Davies home life seemed to centre around. Ray has said that the song was structured from words that just sprang from somewhere, but that the insistent rhythm, the repetitive riff, was deliberate, due to his realisation that dance was instinctive; "tribal", as he put it. And as for the record's sound; that must be meaner and dirtier than even The Rolling Stones. The Stones' recent hits – covers of Chuck Berry's 'Come On' and The Beatles' 'I Wanna Be Your Man' – had been seen as rough and ready; but Ray had in his head a sound which, compared to this, would seem like it had emanated from Hades. The number had already been demoed by the band and trimmed down by Ray at the insistence of Carter, so when the band entered Pye Records' studio with Shel Talmy at the helm, the arrangement was more or less worked out.

Although drummer Mick Avory had now been with the band a while, it was decided by Talmy to enlist the help of studio drummer Bobby Graham; George Martin had done a similar thing on The Beatles' first session, due to the common difficulty of getting a good drum sound in the first place, and the worry that an inexperienced drummer might not keep a metronomic beat. Studio time was expensive. Poor Mick, probably with a great lump in his throat, played tambourine while Ray sang his new lyric.

Upon listening to the final mix on acetate, Ray was disconsolate; the sound was distorted – not aggressive distorted, but horrible distorted. And there was echo on everything, which made it sound swimmy and unnatural. Ray had wanted a live sound, but this was more like it had been done in front of one mic down at the local baths. He went to Larry Page to see what could be done; surely Talmy's ears were deceiving him. Larry said the record company would never hear of overruling the producer and re-recording the song. So he approached Grenville and Robert, neither of whom saw any problem with the sound. After a heart to heart with his ex-girlfriend Anita over coffee, she promised to speak to Larry Page and see if she could persuade him differently.

As it happened, Page saw a potential solution. An astute man, he realised Ray was probably right in his assessment that in this form the record would surely flop and that would be the end of The Kinks. He decided to help. Due to a convoluted contractual discrepancy between Kassner Music (the song's publishers) and Pye, which meant Pye actually had no licence to release the record just yet, Larry made some time available for another session. This was all strictly below board and, indeed, had the band not been broke already, would almost certainly have led to a court case from Pye for breach of contract.

Talmy, aware of Ray's dissatisfaction at the producer's first effort with his masterpiece, was determined not to repeat the process. He may also have wondered whether his cover had been blown by this young upstart and so did his best to surpass himself. His own description of the affair makes it seem far less fraught: "I worked with Ray to get that sound," he later insisted. "I was determined to get a good fat sound from the bass and drums. It was a team effort; that's the only way to work in the studio." Ray and the band, equally determined not to mess up themselves this time, went in and put down two takes in their three-hour session; Bobby Graham was still on drums (and Mick still on tambourine) and session piano player Arthur Gleenslade took up keyboard duties. In his own recollections of the recording, Ray is most descriptive about the many feelings that went through his mind as he opened his mouth to sing those unforgettable words; he was conscious about his pronunciation and made his delivery as clear as his adenoidal tone would allow. Despite a false drum fill at the start and an almost aborted guitar solo due to the brothers catching each other's eye at the crucial moment, at the end of take two they knew something special had occurred. Even the cynical session players felt it, Arthur Greenslade actually hanging around to listen to the playbacks.

A common myth that has sprung up over the years concerns Dave's solo. Jimmy Page, the top London session guitarist of the day who later joined The Yardbirds and thereafter formed the supergroup Led Zeppelin, was known to have sessioned on thousands of pop records. This was often due to the youth and inexperience of new bands, or simply because they couldn't actually play. Page is known to have worked on Kinks sessions and this has led to many people saying he took the solos on the early records. Ray's description of that session – "If Dave never plays another note, his performance on 'You Really Got Me' will always give him a special place among guitar players" – would seem to dispel such talk once and for all.

Of course, 'You Really Got Me' was a musical bolt out of the blue for the British pop charts of 1964, where it landed the Number One position in August of that year. Even though bands like The Rolling Stones from London, The Animals from Newcastle and Them from Dublin had given an R&B slant to the otherwise Mersey-dominated sound of The Beatles, The Searchers and Gerry And The Pacemakers, plus of course The Hollies and Freddie And The Dreamers from Manchester, this was different. This was aggressive. This was all the sound and the fury signifying...well, rather a lot, as it happens.

5 KEEP THE CROWD OCCUPIED UNTIL WE GO ON

Occasionally a sound comes along that is latched onto by the record-buying masses and aspiring musicians alike. Artists like Elvis Presley, Buddy Holly, The Beatles, Gary Glitter, The Sex Pistols, Queen and The Police have all reinvented the pop song in their different ways, and when 'You Really Got Me' zapped to the top of the UK charts it signalled a similar breakthrough. Not since Elvis' wriggling pelvis and The Beatles' disgustingly long hair ("you'll get nits if you let it grow like that" shouted intimidated parents) had a group created such a commotion. The name, the hair (even longer and therefore surely even more nit-infested), the clothes ("they're all fairies; a couple of years in the army'd do 'em good") and their behaviour all contributed to the outrage stirred up by The Kinks. But other bands were having a similar effect. The Rolling Stones offended the sensibilities of the adult generations with songs like 'It's All Over Now' and The Animals with 'Baby Let Me Take You Home'. Groups like The Yardbirds and The Pretty Things were playing irreverent R&B in the clubs and one or other band would have broken through sooner or later. The Beatles, whose initial explosion onto the scene had equally shocked the nation, were becoming establishment – mums and grandmas loved the mop-tops, who were now looked on as soft by the fans of the tougher and more street cred R&B.

As it happens, The Kinks had an early brush with the Fab Four. After the initial release of 'You Really Got Me' they were booked – using the influence of promoter Arthur Howes – to open the second half of two shows topped by The Beatles. This is the toughest spot on any bill, as the warm-ups will have done their bit, the audience had a drink or two in the intermission and come back to see the act they'd really paid their money for. Nobody could rout The Beatles and Ray, Dave, Pete and Mick were not relishing the thought of being put through the mill by hundreds of screaming Mersey Beat fans. Pye were already trying to market their new hit signing as all part of that same "beat group" wave and The Kinks didn't like that at all. They weren't Mersey Beat; they weren't R&B; they were The Kinks.

But start the second half they did. Ray tells how the first show was at Bournemouth Winter Gardens, where his first encounter with John Lennon set his teeth on edge. While The Kinks were tuning up behind closed stage curtains – and already delayed by photographers waiting to catch the Fabs entering the building – Lennon poked his head round the curtain and showed an interest in Ray's Fender Telecaster guitar; he even touched one of its controls, a violation rare between musicians, and questioned him intrusively about it. Ray said The Beatles would have their go soon enough, but now it was The Kinks' turn. Lennon peeked through the tabs to gauge his audience and, according to Ray, parted with the words, "With The Beatles, laddie, nobody gets a turn. You're just there to keep the crowd occupied until we go on."

As it happened, The Kinks made a big impression, despite the initial screams for the Liverpool lads and the intimidation of Lennon and Brian Epstein watching from the wings. The extent of their success that night was shown at the next gig. News had leaked out about the group that had given The Beatles a hard time at Bournemouth and accordingly Brian Epstein switched their slot from opening the second half to closing the first. A little known outfit from London took their place; they were called The High Numbers, soon to become the mighty Who.

On this show Ray's brush was with McCartney. Dave, Pete and Mick were already into the first few bars of the band's opening number and awaiting their lead singer to bound onto the stage. Instead, Ray was entrapped by Beatle Paul, who jibed the singer about his role as "star" of the band – a position Davies has always denied. After "confessing" to Paul that this was indeed the case, McCartney allowed him to begin his act, which was still reliant on the group's one self-penned hit for its own screams and cheers. Ray looked on this moment with relish. He thought John, Paul, George and Ringo looked like dummies in their crisp, collarless uniforms – a product of his hated establishment or "corporation" – and enjoyed the implicit admission by the world's toppermost poppermost songwriter that his little band represented something of a threat. Ray could not have known it then but McCartney would greatly enjoy Davies' own writing in years to come.

A hit single was one thing, but even in the '60s a band needed an album to consolidate their position. Although The Beatles had established themselves as the first true album band, every other act went straight into the studio to commit an LP's worth of material to tape. Usually this was their live act and so most first albums comprised mainly old rock 'n' roll and blues covers. Although Ray was now a published writer with a Number One hit under his belt, it was deemed by Shel Talmy that an LP full of new songs represented just too much of a risk. So The Kinks' eponymously titled debut aped first albums by the Stones, The Hollies and even The Beatles, whose *Please Please Me* had contained no fewer than six cover versions.

Dave has told how the record was made in just a week and how before the end of the sessions people were knocking at the door to get the musicians out. Ray also stated that Pye made it plain to him how privileged the group should feel at being allowed a studio to record in. He knew the time was short and so wanted the album to be like an early Beatles record; half originals and half good-time rock 'n' roll. Talmy recalls the making of the album as rather less frenetic: "It sounds terrible, like it only took a week; the way it sounds is that we rushed it. We didn't." Talmy also denies Dave's story about the studio's next client itching to get in, describing this as a "slight exaggeration".

The Kinks opens with Chuck Berry's 'Beautiful Delilah', played at breakneck speed with the high-pitched vocal sounding more like Dave than Ray. The rhythm section is as tight as any band of its time and the guitar break leaves one in no doubt that it was Dave who played all those contentious solos. This number was a staple of almost every UK village hall act in 1964. It's been pointed out that 'You Really Got Me' owes a good deal to 'Louie Louie' by The Kingsmen, but Ray's 'So

Mystifying' is the Stones' 'It's All Over Now' with different lyrics; or perhaps it's the other way around, since both songs were written and recorded at almost exactly the same time. It's an infectious tune of its type, nonetheless, with powerful bass and drums and a clever guitar lick from the 17-year-old Dave.

'Just Can't Go To Sleep' owes more to Liverpool than London, despite the band's aversion to being included in that genre. The guitar tones are pure Harrison and Lennon (both bands did use Vox AC30s) and the chord structure, harmony vocals and handclaps) possess the distinct stamp of The Beatles. Interestingly, several commentators have mentioned Jimmy Page being around on some of these sessions and a sound like Jimmy's trademark semi-wah-wah rhythm guitar (he used a DeArmond tone and volume pedal to obtain the same sound on Dave Berry's 'The Crying Game') can distinctly be heard in the slow middle section. 'Long Tall Shorty' is pure rhythm and blues, with Dave's raspy vocal redolent of Phil May of The Pretty Things, another London band making waves at around the same time. It's surprising how tight the group sounds here, considering their age and relative lack of experience. The harmonica intro to 'I Took My Baby Home' signals another Beatles-influenced track, but the song itself owes more to The Coasters' 'Poison Ivy'.

'I'm A Lover Not A Fighter' epitomises The Kinks' raw R&B sound at this time, but the vocals in the chorus and the guitar fills are pure Stones. Perhaps it's unfair to compare songs in this way (after all, everything is reminiscent of something), but young bands wear their influences on their sleeves and it does no harm to watch the evolution of a unique style through such experimentation.

Track six is the Number One hit, 'You Really Got Me'. This displays a polish that perhaps shows how speedily 'The Kinks' was in fact put together. Having already been recorded (twice) before the album and with rather less of a panic (it was due to the success of the single that the album was required anyway), the song sits head and shoulders above the rest of the collection, not only for recording quality but also because of its individuality – all references to The Kingsmen aside. And Ray is right; that guitar solo is a classic.

'Cadillac' is the obligatory Bo Diddley number; with its insistent rhythm and repetitive lyrics it was very much the order of the day. But it's hardly inspiring stuff, although Dave, who takes lead vocal, does it with unusual confidence for one so young. Quaife's bass playing is smooth and forceful (throughout the whole album, in fact); *de rigueur* for a kicking '60s R&B band. Stones / Yardbirds-style maracas to the fore, too.

Ever the astute self-promoter, Shel Talmy managed to wangle a couple of his own tracks onto the album. These songs were not self-penned, but rather traditional folky blues numbers which were out of copyright and which Talmy could rearrange and (quite legally) credit to himself. Nevertheless, 'Bald Headed Woman' is one of the weakest tracks on the record. 'Revenge' is the instrumental collaboration between Ray Davies and Larry Page (itself an admitted lift from 'Louie Louie') which is said to have spawned the riffing behind 'You Really Got Me' and eventually many Kinks hits. Ray's harmonica playing, while no better or worse than that of a Lennon or a Jagger, would not have left Larry Adler in fear for his session work. A second Chuck Berry number, the ubiquitous 'Too Much Monkey Business', was recorded by many bands, including The Hollies and The Yardbirds. The London lads do a commendable job on this, although Dave goes somewhat awry during his first guitar solo.

Talmy's second credit is 'I've Been Driving On Bald Mountain' and is by far the worst cut on the record; the band sound their least inspired here, as though they're going through the motions for their producer. 'Stop Your Sobbing' was and is a fine track. In his autobiography, Ray refers to his girlfriend Anita, who spent most of one night bemoaning her life and all it stood for (or didn't), all the while weeping uncontrollably. Ray's implication behind the story of his fruitless bid to arrest the poor girl's tears is that she was the inspiration for this track. Compositional maturity is beginning to creep in here; not only is the song more than just a trudgingly repeating motif, it also follows a lyrical theme and hints at the domestic thread that was to run through Davies' words from that point on.

The album closes much the way it came in, on a rumbustious and well-played evergreen stomper that all the groups were playing in early 1964. 'Got Love If You Want It' echoes all the enthusiasm of an era. Again, it could have been the Stones, Pretty Things or Yardbirds – and they probably all played it at one time or another – but this version stands up against any, with its verve and guts and basic youthful exuberance.

With hindsight and all the sophistication available to us in the 1990s it would be easy to pan The Kinks' first offering. But bearing in mind the speed with which it was recorded, the youthfulness of all involved and the quality of most of the competition, it's a worthy entree into the album business. Flashes of brilliance, such as 'Stop Your Sobbing' and 'You Really Got Me', should have been enough for any record reviewer to see exactly where The Kinks were headed.

The worst thing about the album by far was its liner notes. In the early '60s, music fans were patronised beyond belief – the record companies considered them almost as ignorant and uneducated as the groups themselves. So the idea was hatched – apparently over a drink by Robert Wace and Grenville Collins – to create a humorous sketch on the letter K. It went cringingly like this: "The Kinks, when they are knot making records or doing one-knight stands, are kampaigning to restore the K to its right and knoble place…" and continued even more embarrassingly: "First, the letter K should never be silent in words such as knee, know and knockout; secondly, where possible, K should be substituted for C in pronunciation; thirdly, money is reckoned in (K)rowns, ie 5/- is one K, 2/6 is half K and £1 is 4 K." It was awful stuff. The boys themselves – who were supposed to have invented and be living by this inane rule – must have gone as pink as their cerise hunting jackets. The silly kinky theme ran through the dreadfully written piece, which culminated in the suggestion that the band would never release anything unless they approved of it – these liner notes excepted, we sincerely hope.

All young bands crave their first chart success. But when it comes the pressure is on from all around; managers, record companies and agents all hear the ring of the cash register and want to get the most out of their charges before the bottom drops out of their particular market.

This manifests itself in a number of ways: first, a follow-up record is required; secondly, promotion is needed, in whatever medium is available – hence stupid record sleeves, endless interviews and TV and radio appearances – and the quest for stardom soon becomes the quest for peace and quiet.

The Kinks were hurriedly added to Billy J Kramer's UK tour and a new single to replace 'You Really Got Me' as it dropped out of the Hit Parade was recorded. Ray was informed by Eddie Kassner that a follow-up was needed; Kassner was no doubt aware that another Davies song would be a good idea (he was of course Ray's publisher and would make money from another hit) and so Davies sat down and bashed out a chord sequence. The song was routined in front of a Midlands audience and recorded in London the next day.

Casual listeners could be forgiven for thinking that 'All Day And All Of The Night' is 'You Really Got Me' in reverse; the jerky chord changes, the record's overall tone, the squealing vocal harmonies and that stuttering guitar solo sound so similar and yet the songs are completely different. Musically, the follow-up is cleverer, since the melody weaves in and out of the more complicated riff and the key changes are more subtle. The guitar solo is a killer too and it's this one that many of Jimmy Page's fans attribute to their idol. Again, Ray says otherwise.

Page was on the session, but he attended thousands during his many years as a studio pro. Apparently, when it came to the take, Jimmy and some of his cronies, who were dismissive of this group of cocky upstarts, watched as the track was put down and smirked as Dave improvised his guitar break on the spot. Page was probably the best all-round guitarist in England and he no doubt knew it; he probably could have supplied a far more musical solo than the outburst heard on the record from Dave, but the fact is he stood on the sidelines and watched history being made.

In describing the success of the band over the next year or two, which was not inconsiderable, it's easy to become lost in the belief that The Kinks were taking over the charts and the minds of the British people. This was not the case. The Beatles were still the kings of pop and their unrivalled success in 1964, with 'I Want To Hold Your Hand', 'Can't Buy Me Love', 'A Hard Day's Night' and 'I Feel Fine' proved it beyond any doubt. But it was The Rolling Stones that the Davies brothers wanted to whip; they were seen as the bad boys to The Beatles' goody-goody image (whereas in reality the Fabs were anything but that) and The Kinks felt that was their rightful position. But the Stones pipped them at every post; where they toured, the Stones had just been, where they charted, the Stones got higher or stayed for longer, where they made the news, the Stones grabbed the headlines. It was just too frustrating.

Where The Kinks made Jagger and the boys look like rank amateurs, though, was in their behaviour. Off stage as well as on. Jagger, Richards and Jones in particular had a reputation for womanising and drug abuse – at that time usually narcotics of the softer kind. But again, where they made the headlines with orgies and drug busts, The Kinks squabbled and fought like caged rats; the brothers were beginning to seriously dislike each other but at the same time began ganging up on their 'subordinates' in the band. Pete Quaife somehow remained aloof to it all, deciding that his best course of action was to keep quiet and get on with it. While this attitude saved him from the most violent verbal batterings, it didn't mean he liked it, and his pent-up feelings would eventually lead to him quitting the band for good, to Ray and Dave's apparent surprise.

So the quiet and unworldly Mick Avory took the brunt. Mick was the nice guy; the one everybody loved; the gentleman with hands like shovels who'd never choose to hurt a soul; the one whose drums and his life as a drummer meant everything. The insults levelled at Mick were of the most degrading kind and before long he and Dave in particular had bouts of black hatred between them. After a while the four could not travel in the same vehicle to engagements, and on those occasions where there was no alternative, Larry Page had to separate them; the brothers (probably still fighting between themselves) in the back and the "hired hands" as they were beginning to be treated, in the front.

'All Day And All Of The Night' had only made it to Number Two in October 1964, but the track was seen by many as superior to the band's previous chart-topper. It was at the same time more anarchic and more musical. By now The Kinks were a serious chart contender (the possibility of their being one hit wonders no longer a question) and the management needed to capitalise fast. Larry Page had already organised the recording of their 'Kinksize Session' EP which contained a version of the much-heralded inspiration for Ray's riffy style, 'Louie Louie'. The EP was another production line recording job and the results were similarly slapdash. Ray later admitted to singing his vocal while reading the *Record Mirror*. "That's how cocky I was," he confessed.

The stage act became more and more outrageous, with Dave in particular stealing as much of the limelight as he could. The 17-year-old was living the life of Riley, capitalising on his looks and position of fame and going through women like wildfire. He was also drinking to excess and taking drugs to keep him awake during his nights of clubbing. On stage his antics became wilder and wilder; playing solos lying on his back and reputedly even walking on stage with his testicles deliberately hanging out of his trousers. He would be pulled into the audience while still playing, leaving the security men to sort out the rioting teenagers later. The crowds loved it and such audience outbursts became a regular occurrence. Larry Page realised he must harness this energy, perhaps tame it a little and package it to where The Beatles and Stones were beginning to make the big bucks. In America. But first a trip was scheduled to Australia, where Arthur and sister Rose had emigrated and where The Kinks were avidly awaited.

One small task was required before the group left for their first serious overseas jaunt; they must nip in to the studio and put down a follow-up to their second hit. 'Tired Of Waiting' was an interesting piece of writing for Ray, as it maintained an element of the repetitive riff but in a much less frantic form; it also contained a traditional middle-eight (like most Beatles songs and Gershwin or Porter standards) and no manic guitar solo. Ray asserts that until he walked to the microphone to put down the vocal line to 'Tired Of Waiting For You' he had little idea of what he was going to sing. The band had done the backing track, oohs and aahs had been sung and a vague idea of the song's content suggested. "I told everybody I had finished the song," recalls Davies, "but all I had was the 'I'm so tired, tired of waiting' part." 'Tired Of Waiting' was another Number One, considered by many to be the group's best offering so far.

Ray had written the number partly about his new wife Rasa. Marriage had all happened very quickly – much too quickly for Ray, whose feelings ranged from utter contentment in the married state to total jealousy at his brother's promiscuity, which he, now in the constant gaze of the public, dared not emulate.

Rasa was of Lithuanian descent and was at convent school in Bradford. She also had a sister in London and would visit her regularly. Through a friend, Rasa had been to a Kinks show in Sheffield – she'd bunked off school, something she would be expelled for – and had arranged to meet the band since her friend happened to know Mick Avory. After the show, Rasa was given a lift back to the railway station; she and Ray swapped addresses and said they'd keep in touch. A week later they met in London and consummated their relationship. Ray described Rasa as a "five out of five"; he was in love, but as with everything else in his life at this time, it was to bring him into great conflict with himself.

Ray was already beginning to find his success limiting – confined to the house when not on tour, using secret codes and leaving home in disguise; hiding in dressing rooms, vans and cars and having none of the so-called good time that success was supposed to bring. It seemed as though they were not allowed to think any more; that was done by the management, whose now valuable charges found themselves wrapped in cotton wool and protected from everything – their fans, their friends and, it seemed, the knowledge of what was really going on behind the scenes. Apparently you were also supposed to become rich in this game – especially if you were the one writing the songs – but where was all the money?

6 A BUNCH OF COMMIE WIMPS

The tour to Australia was in fact preceded by a lightning visit to France, where The Kinks recorded a TV show in Paris, played a live gig at the Paris Olympia and were co-opted into another TV recording in Marseilles, on an American aircraft carrier. Ray took wife Rasa while the others took advantage of Marseilles' red-light district. After the official carrier show the band were blackmailed by the captain into playing a few numbers especially for his crew – it was either that or they didn't get off until Egypt. By this time Rasa was pregnant and Ray was green with jealousy at the US seamen's leering. He'd also hated the French television crews' rudeness and incompetence and wanted to get out of there sharpish.

Australia in 1965 was not the culturally buoyant, go-ahead place that it is today. It was more like a sprawling backwater to the UK, with total allegiance to the crown and a society largely dependent upon its massive sheep farming industry. Youngsters still felt they had to get away to where something was happening – usually England – while British families were still flocking to Oz on the Government's assisted passages scheme; £10 per adult. Rose and Arthur had moved there only a couple of years before, but to Ray it seemed like a lifetime and he enjoyed seeing his sister again and putting the world back to rights with Arthur. But it was Terry that Ray and Dave longed to see most; although their nephew, he was a special best mate, especially to Ray, who has often referred to him as more like a brother.

The tour was another package, as was the usual state of play in those days; this time they were matched with Manfred Mann, who were topping the bill, and The Honeycombs. The entourage disembarked from the plane in Bombay, Madras and Singapore, where rioting and police brutality against the waiting fans upset the groups a great deal. The recollections of Ray and Dave are that the Australian crowds loved the band. After their first show in Perth, Dave admits to being so overwhelmed by their warmth and generosity that it was difficult to hold back the emotion. The same went for the other members. But other sources reported a mutual dislike; The Kinks for Australia and Australia for The Kinks. The media certainly made the most of the band's controversial stage show and behind the scenes performances and made their puritanical displeasure felt with "Kinks Go Home"-style headlines. What certainly was true was that the Stones had beaten them to it in Australia and everywhere they went they were regaled with tales of how marvellous their rivals were. Fans generally believe that pop groups are all best buddies, drinking at pop star pubs, eating at pop star restaurants and generally being pop star pals. While The Kinks had their mates in the music world, The Beatles and Stones were unlikely to be invited to tea.

Whether the Australian tour was a success or not, 'Tired Of Waiting' smashed into the UK charts while they were there – Ray was actually handed a telegram from Arthur Howes at Singapore airport – confirming that The Kinks were now truly in the big league. And now at last America beckoned.

On the way home from Australia, The Kinks stopped off briefly in New York to capitalise on their two chart successes and promote their latest single. While there, Dave's Harmony Meteor was stolen and he had to replace it fast. It was then that he bought the only instrument that could possibly match his own outrageous stage persona; a Gibson Flying V. The Flying V was designed in 1958 and only a few were made; the instrument was deemed a flop by the company and it was withdrawn. In 1964, another run was produced, slightly different in design, but it is the original version – sometimes referred to as the Futurist – which Davies owns. Because of their scarcity these instruments are now worth tens of thousands of pounds. Dave got himself a bargain: "I bought mine in a thrift shop in America for about $200," he told *Guitarist* magazine in 1989. Anyone who can remember

The Kinks from the period will recall the visual effect of that guitar; one 14-year-old boy certainly does and the impact inspired him to take up the instrument. Thirty-five or so years on, he is editor of *Guitarist* and co-author of this book.

While in New York Ray was recovering from a severely swollen leg; he'd developed some kind of allergic reaction to an insect bite during the return stop-over in Singapore and could hardly walk. (He'd also developed an aversion to just about everything; flying was a terror and when he arrived at his Big Apple hotel he locked the door and stayed put.) The problem at hand was that the producer of the *Hullabaloo* show, on which they were booked to appear, wanted the band doing a dance routine. The programme's presenter was teen idol Frankie Avalon and Ray begged them to reconsider. No such luck. Then came the incident which, so Ray claims, was to herald the start of what can only be described as a vendetta by the American authorities to keep The Kinks out of the USA for good.

The group's obsession with homosexuality is common knowledge. They camped it up at every opportunity, either to shock the unexpecting or simply because they enjoyed it. Dave made a career out of effeminacy and had a large gay following in the early days, but Ray's apparent sexual ambiguity was more subtle, and so in many ways more plausible. Of course he was already married with a pregnant wife and Dave's reputation with women went unsurpassed. But, as has been mentioned elsewhere, these were awakening times; homosexuality was still illegal in many Western countries and yet the art movement and entertainment industries were populated by gays. It was almost the thing to be homosexual in certain circles and gays could easily get on if they knew the right people. This was just as true in America as it was in Britain, but whereas the UK was becoming more overt about such matters (and homosexual sex would soon become legal between consenting adults), in the USA a semi-Victorian mood still persisted. So when, on that fateful day in 1965, the *Hullabaloo* camera cut from the grinning Frankie Avalon to the dancing Kinks, it was actually Ray and Mick smooching cheek to cheek. Just too kinky for the land of the free and, of course, it was immediately banned.

On arrival back in England, the weary group were informed that the studio had been booked for the first session of their new album. Tomorrow. Ray was still in pain from his leg and the others jet-lagged and hung over from too much booze on the plane. The new record already had a title, too – *Kinda Kinks* – and the boys had all of two weeks in which to record it.

Since the early days, the band's listening habits had changed. No longer did blues or British-style R&B dominate their music; now it was Tamla Motown and American R&B, which was in fact more like soul. Dave's persistent clubbing had actually contributed greatly to the band's musical eclecticism, since he had subjected himself – subliminally or otherwise – to all the new music that was coming out. This made the selection of songs for the new record a difficult one. Whereas *The Kinks* had at least had a semblance of continuity running through it – raunchy, heads down rock – the follow-up would be a rambling, poorly executed jumble. Ray wrote all but three of the tracks; 'Got My Feet On The Ground' was a collaboration with his brother, while the bluesy 'Naggin' Woman' and an uncertain version of Martha And The Vandellas' 'Dancing In The Street' were the only covers. Again, the highlight of the record was their recent chart-topper, the evocative 'Tired Of Waiting', and while numbers such as 'Something Better Beginning' and 'Don't Ever Change' showed promise, they were at best derivative. *Kinda Kinks* nevertheless made the Top Five in the UK album charts and secured the band an even firmer foothold in the imaginations of record buyers on both sides of the Atlantic.

Ray blames the album's sloppy content firmly on the producer, record company and management, saying the band were railroaded into the studio ill prepared. Davies more than implies that it was all again to do with money; milking the golden cow before its reserves ran dry. He is also critical of the record's general production, describing it as "a slovenly, callous disregard for our music".

It was at this point that the band heard The Who's debut single, 'I Can't Explain', for the first time. They were shocked to hear how like themselves it sounded, initially accusing them of stealing The Kinks' sound. They soon discovered that The Who were in fact The High

Numbers, a band who had supported them on several occasions in the recent past – it was they who were switched by Brian Epstein to open the second half of The Beatles' show in Bournemouth. Pete Townshend of The Who has never denied his influence: "I always worshipped The Kinks and never let a bad word about them pass my lips," he said. Townshend also owned up to writing 'I Can't Explain' in order to attract the attention of Kinks producer Shel Talmy. (The Davies brothers, Quaife and Avory felt a sense of betrayal on discovering this connection.) "I had two songs," Pete told us. "'Talking Generation', which eventually became 'My Generation', and 'I Can't Explain'. We picked 'I Can't Explain' as the first song to play him and I re-recorded the original demo with staccato chords. Listening to it, it's a craftsman-like pop record and a lot of people's Who favourite. Shel Talmy was producing a particular kind of sound in the studio; a particular kind of arrangement."

It was single time again and most commentators agree that 'Ev'rybody's Gonna Be Happy' was not a great choice. Its lowly chart placing backs up this theory (it made Number 17 in the UK and fared even worse in the States). The song was full of vitality but lacked a real hook; the raw riffiness was gone and so record buyers ignored it in their droves. The song was inspired by Ray's fascination with The Earl Van Dyke Trio: "We wanted to copy them because we looked up to them," he said. Shel Talmy was never convinced of the song's potential and didn't want it released at all, but Ray had been right so far and who would gainsay him now. The B-side is without doubt a better song; it's Ray against the world in fine, cutting form, but even flipping the single over in America failed to significantly dent the *Billboard* chart.

Ray's behaviour was becoming stranger. His fears about money, while being completely rational in fact, were manifesting themselves in odd behaviour; he thought everyone was after his cash and refused to carry any on him. This resulted in him having to cadge pennies from road manager Sam Curtis for chewing gum, sweets or ciggies and reinforcing the "tight as arseholes" view taken of the singer by most who came in contact with him.

Meanwhile, management struggles were going on behind the scenes. One view is that Wace and Collins had taken a back seat and had allowed Larry Page to manage the band on a daily basis. Page was certainly there whenever there was a crisis – which was most of the time – and his knowledge of the business allowed him to sort things out as smoothly as anyone could, given the personnel involved and their various prima donna attitudes. But although they respected Page's workaday knowledge and got on with him on a basic personal level – he was in essence a working-class lad like them – both Davies brothers still looked up to Grenville and Robert. Ray remained impressed by their financially comfortable backgrounds and believed in their roles as 'gentlemen' and it would have been difficult for Larry to come between them at this time. He was also astute enough to realise it.

For their part, Wace and Collins believed Page was trying to usurp them; they had a 30 per cent stake in the band and he was after edging them out. For his part, Larry saw the pair as a couple of useless hooray Henrys who had smooth-talked their way into a third stake in one of the hottest pop properties around. There was no love lost between them.

By now live shows were the stuff of anarchy. If the brothers weren't feuding then Mick and Dave were at each other's throats. Pete still kept out of it as best he could. If all was quiet in the band then riots would break out in the auditorium, as in Copenhagen on the group's first tour as top of the bill. The beautiful Tivoli Concert Hall, a construction made largely of glass, was destroyed by fans who had completely lost control. In this case the band deny responsibility, citing over-zealous police as the real cause. But back at the hotel Dave still managed to throw a beer bottle at the huge mirror behind the bar. He was drunk, but he was often drunk and the Danish authorities showed little urge to be lenient, so Davies Junior landed a night in the slammer for his actions. Needless to say, the follow-up gig was cancelled. The day after the Danish debacle the band were due to play at the *New Musical Express* Poll Winners' party. Dave's face was cut – the police had taken revenge on him with their truncheons – and shortly before they were due to go on Grenville Collins informed Ray that The Kinks were closing the show, above both The Rolling Stones and The Beatles.

The band members were worried about not using their own gear – the event was live and they had to use The Beatles' equipment – and although their performance was understandably low key (bearing in mind what had gone on in the previous 24 hours) they went down a storm. Another storm erupted as their badges were presented. Ray and the band had been given to understand that they were receiving the *NME*'s coveted Best New Group award. Instead, as the first of the four badges was about to be pinned, the *NME*'s representative Maurice Kinn broke the news that theirs was the runners-up prize. Ray was livid; the Stones had taken the Best New Band last year – how could they win it again? It was a conspiracy; the establishment; the corporation against Ray Davies. He stormed off, refused to accept the offering and went home to get drunk with his dad.

It was three weeks later when the infamous Cardiff incident, as told by Hal Carter earlier, occurred. If anything, the fight was even more ghastly than Carter recalled it. Mick and Dave had been fighting since the previous day and Dave went on stage wearing sunglasses due to a pair of black eyes. Hal described the incident as Dave "kicking Mick's bass drum": he actually smashed it all over the stage; the audience, believing it to be all part of the show, went berserk. The "cymbal" which most onlookers describe as the implement of Dave's downfall, was in fact Mick's bass drum pedal: "A cymbal would have taken his head off," declared Mick. The unfortunate drummer was pursued by the police but Sam Curtis engineered a getaway – he made Avory board the first train out of Cardiff, no matter which way it was heading. After a pathetic cover-up story which revolved around a "new stage routine going wrong", the incident was allowed to rest as Dave refused to press charges. The rest of the tour was, to no one's real surprise by this time, cancelled. Most onlookers also felt that The Kinks could not survive this one. Indeed, they even routined a new drummer, should Avory fail to return; in the eventuality, Mitch Mitchell's services were not required and he went on to carve a career as one third of The Jimi Hendrix Experience.

Arthur Howes took the group out for a Chinese meal, to the same restaurant where he had first met them and gave Ray a pep talk. What the group needed was some new material, but more like the old material; that's what the fans really wanted and the relative failure of 'Ev'rybody's Gonna Be Happy' proved it. Davies' next offering was 'Set Me Free', a tune redolent of the standard riff formula but way above 'You Really Got Me' in sophistication; in fact it could be argued that this piece of writing marks the perfect seam between the initial, formulaic hits and later numbers such as 'Waterloo Sunset' and 'Autumn Almanac', with their cascading chords and introverted lyrics. Ray hated it, felt he'd sold out, but the record put the band back in the Top Ten in May of 1965 and assured them of yet another chance. If, of course, the frayed ties that were somehow still binding the group could be made to hold out.

In fact, by this time the band was having trouble playing anywhere in the UK, due to an almost total hotel ban around the country. Where The Kinks went, a wave of destruction followed. Hotel managers had had enough of fights, sleepless nights, damage and the unpaid bills of complaining guests and declared war on the band – and others, such as The Who, who were wreaking similar havoc. So it was that in a state of near panic, in real fear for the survival of the group, Larry Page called them individually into his office prior to their first proper tour of America. Their individual appointments, however, were all for the same time on the same day; four o'clock on a Friday afternoon.

Page himself actually believed this was the end; the friction – both within the band and between The Kinks and the rest of civilisation – seemed just too much for the weakened structure to withstand. Still, he valiantly delivered his pre-tour sermon and, despite Ray's childish refusal to sign the contract – he emptied Page's fountain pen over the floor and said, "But there's no ink in the pen" – they agreed to go.

It was the middle of 1965 and The Kinks looked on their way to conquer the biggest, most financially lucrative market in the world. Of course they blew it. In fairness it wasn't all their fault. As already mentioned, Popsville USA had become sanitarily safe and parentally sound. The rock 'n' roll virility of Presley had given way to the clean-cut, emasculated charm of Fabian and Bobby Vee; even the talented Ricky Nelson represented the acceptable side of teenage rebellion. The Beatles had arrived in their collarless matching suits the previous year, their hair tantalisingly tipping over their collars; Herman's Hermits and The Dave Clark Five had followed and the Americans expected more of the same. The Kinks were to prove a big surprise. But however rebellious this team of kids from London tried to be, they were no match for the American promoters and unions.

The local US promoters seemed intent on finding any reason not to pay Larry Page the agreed fee for the booking. So a minute late on stage, bad behaviour or any number of excuses was enough to warrant an argument. Many of the gigs were rather less auspicious than the band had been led to believe and so disagreements and tantrums were the norm (on their first date they were advertised in huge letters as THE KINGS). On several occasions, Ray extended 'You Really Got Me' – the group's biggest US hit so far – to many times its proper length; another reason for non-payment.

Eddie Kassner, Larry Page's boss and Ray Davies' music publisher turned up during the tour. Kassner followed the band from gig to gig, insisting to Ray that he was there to "look after my boy". This made Ray suspicious and he pondered whether, as well as his royalty share, Kassner had perhaps managed to cut himself in on the tour's proceeds. He felt uncomfortable in his presence and wished he weren't there. He and Dave were also nervous about America itself; the real people were very different from the Hollywood image that they had come to know and the prevalence of guns and the underlying feeling of potential danger in many towns unnerved them. Ray would often retire to his hotel room and phone Rasa, who had given birth to their daughter Louisa only a week before the start of the tour; he would just as often put the phone down even more depressed than before.

Ray missed his wife and had been badgering Larry Page – who for some reason had taken to wearing a three-cornered general's hat – to bring Rasa over. After witnessing Page being interviewed on television, apparently speaking as though The Kinks were a phenomenon that he'd conjured up out of thin air, Ray says how he stormed into his hotel room and demanded it. But this was not before the biggest Kinks-versus-Establishment flare-up of the tour and the incident which probably set the American unions against the band forever.

The scene was backstage at yet another Stateside TV show, hosted by Dick Clark, where various British bands, including Herman's Hermits, Peter And Gordon and The Zombies, had been packaged together in an attempt to capitalise on the so-called British Invasion. In fact Ray tells how it was his use of this very term that sparked the fight with someone from the TV company, who had come backstage to complain that the band was late. After a number of xenophobic comments including, as Ray tells it, references to The Kinks as "a bunch of Commie wimps" and Ray as "a talentless fuck who was in the right place at the right time", the trouble started. At the TV man's suggestion that The Kinks and all these other English groups were only there on the back of The Beatles' success, Ray argued that the American music scene was so awful that it needed such an "invasion". That was it. Messrs Davies and TV Person exploded, fists flew in both directions and Ray made his exit, but not before the promise had been made that the band would never work in the States again – "You're gonna find out just how powerful America is, you Limey bastard." Ray returned to his hotel room and barricaded the door. Of course he then began to fear for his safety. What about reprisals? They all carry guns, don't they? Kennedy had only recently been shot and Ray was already worried by the number of mob-style people that surrounded the band, from drivers to security men and various hangers-on. He also realised that he had almost certainly made a political blunder and that the American powers that be were indeed just that. The Kinks had found themselves up against an adversary bigger even than the Stones. The unions started closing in on the band, restricting where and how they could work, but all the while Larry "General's Hat" Page was doing his darnedest to keep the tour on some kind of track.

The climax of The Kinks' first American tour was to be a top-of-the-bill performance at the Hollywood Bowl. Page looked upon this show, quite rightly, as the band's moment; it was a fantastic opportunity for any young group, but they would be under close scrutiny and any tantrums or misdemeanours of *The Dick Clark Show* kind would not be tolerated. As it happened, according to Page it was Davies' own intransigence regarding Rasa that caused the bust-up that would signal

Page's departure from the inner sanctum and the reinstatement of Wace and Collins as full-time managers. Larry tells how, just hours before the band were due on stage after such great groups as The Byrds, The Beach Boys and The Righteous Brothers, plus a new boy-girl act called Sonny And Cher, that he was notified of Ray's refusal to perform.

"I'm not going on unless Rasa is flown out here" was the gist of it. But Larry had been trying to organise the trip for a while; the problem was her Eastern Bloc connection, which in the anti-communist America of the mid '60s spelt big problems. Nevertheless Page spent the whole day demeaning himself to Davies, pleading and cajoling him into a performance that almost any other musician in the world would have killed to do. Larry succeeded on both counts; the band duly went on and Rasa and Quaife's girlfriend Nicola arrived a few days later. The injection of female hormones into the testosterone-laden atmosphere would certainly be good for everyone; it would keep the band on better behaviour and render them easier to manage. The trouble was, they no longer had a manager – at least, they didn't have Page. Depending upon whose story one believes, Larry either saw the potential in Sonny And Cher and pounced upon them in a new management deal – about which the Davies brothers were terminally jealous – or he had simply had enough of Ray's never-ceasing whingeing and tantrums. He just couldn't take any more and so he left on 4 July.

It seems from most accounts that not much was made of Larry's departure at the time, although he informed all three Kinks except Ray. There were but a few dates left of the tour anyway and Sam Curtis was there to take care of them; even Eddie Kassner was around and so it could hardly be stated with any conviction that the group was left in the lurch. But when it all hit the fan and the court case was instigated to rid The Kinks and their managers, Wace and Collins, of what they considered to be a thorn in their side, it was just such a reason that was invoked.

As it was, the ructions created by the band in America, from Ray's brush with the unions – the guy he hit at *The Dick Clark Show* turned out to be an official – to their generally unacceptable behaviour on a daily basis, meant their US downfall, as Pete Quaife suggests: "It was complete and utter confusion. Everyone around us displayed the utmost incompetence. It was the start of Ray's drive to be the boss and we consequently had no idea of where we were supposed to go or what we were supposed to be playing. It was a total fiasco. It all ended with no one knowing what we had done or what we were supposed to do.

"By this time, however, I had become accustomed to the band breaking up and I took everything with a grain of salt. If we continued – good. If we never saw each other again – fine by me! History informs me that we still carried on after the American debacle. I don't think we will ever hear the truth about what went on over there, but I think a couple of members of The Kinks are not telling us everything."

And so, when The Beatles, the Stones and even relative lightweights such as Herman's Hermits and Freddie And The Dreamers were coining it in, milking the biggest gravy train in the world, The Kinks, who could have been the second or third most successful British band of all time, had messed on their own doorsteps again. They wouldn't work in America for more than four years.

7 POOFS, WHAT DO THEY KNOW?

The band's 1965 album *The Kink Kontroversy*, with titles such as 'Gotta Get The First Plane Home', 'When I See That Girl Of Mine', 'I'm On An Island' and 'Where Have All The Good Times Gone' seemed to spell out Ray's disillusionment with the "business" part of the music business, and his desire to get back to the arms – literally and figuratively – of home. But it's not all doom and despair. The record opens with a well-honed version of the John Estes R&B classic 'Milk Cow Blues', which demonstrates the band in fine form; Dave's searing lead licks and Pete Quaife's always underrated bass crescendoing into the finale. The acoustic 'Ring The Bells' is a pleasant but lightweight ode to love, while the sentiments in 'Gotta Get The First Plane Home' and 'When I See That Girl Of Mine' are couched in upbeat terms that belie the lyrical turmoil beneath. Musically, 'I Am Free' is hardly worthy of mention, whereas 'Till The End Of The Day', which would be the next single but one, is full of the true spirit of the early Kinks, with its riffy chord structure, time signature changes and Dave's guitar solo – which in this case is beset by out of tune string bends and the feeling that he only just made it. It's a standout track, nonetheless. Lyrically, 'The World Keeps Going Round' seems to say that there's not much the individual can do about events, so what do they matter; musically it says not a lot.

'I'm On An Island' is in fact a jaunty, almost comedic number, but displays little of the lyrical or musical inventiveness that Ray was capable of. 'Where Have All The Good Times Gone' was another tune redolent of older Kinks material; it's a reasonable effort, but there's a definite feeling – along with much of the material on this album – that Davies was going through the motions; fulfilling his obligation to come up with material for the record; or perhaps using the luxury of the LP format to see what worked and what didn't. Much of it didn't.

'It's Too Late' has a laboured acoustic rhythm guitar track and an almost nonexistent chorus. On 'What's In Store For Me', the sounds, the playing and indeed the chords of the classic Davies parody 'A Well Respected Man' can clearly be heard. The album closes in unremarkable style with 'You Can't Win', where the beaty rhythm and blues riffing barely covers up the weakness of the basic song. Ray Davies had much better in him, and it was soon to surface.

The next single was to prove monumental in its effect on the band's peers. Pete Townshend said how it made him prick his ears up and listen for the first time since 'You Really Got Me' and it's known that The Beatles were impressed enough to listen intently. 'See My Friends' contained both musical and lyrical innovations.

Ray tells of how, during a stop-over in India on the way to The Kinks' first Australian tour, he watched the fishermen hauling their nets in to the beach and was transfixed by the sounds of far-off chanting. Not until the fishermen came close did he realise it was them. Like American negro cotton pickers or Cornish trawlermen they were singing to lighten their work load. When the band arrived in Australia, Davies found himself in songwriting mood and among the many numbers which took shape there was 'See My Friends'. In the backing track of this 1965 song were sounds that would not become the vogue in British pop music for at least another year, and would then be credited to George Harrison for his sitar work on The Beatles' 'Norwegian Wood', from *Rubber Soul*. Ray wanted the droning sound of Indian instruments to create the haunting effect he heard in his head and so used feedback, generated by placing the guitar close to the amplifier so that the pick-ups "picked up" the amp's sound again and fed it back to the amp (hence feedback). This type of noise – usually anathema to sound engineers – when controlled, can be used to great effect, as it creates notes of infinite length – just like those Indian drones. It has been stated that Ray requested a sitar player but Shel

Talmy could find no one in London who could play one. So Ray used his Framus twelve-string guitar, the extra set of high strings reinforcing the drone effect. Talmy got Ray to tune down three semitones (in film footage he can be seen playing the Framus using G chord shapes, whereas the song is plainly in E); he then double tracked it and compressed the sound, squashing and flattening it, accentuating the drone even further. The melody makes use of what are called "modes" in music; the tune seems to change key over a static chord and it's really that which provides the unusual haunting effect. In fact these authors can hear none of the supposed sitar sounds on the record; just a clever musical device made to sound simple yet hypnotic. Ray explains: "'See My Friends' started from the sound of that guitar. I had all these memories; I was in India some time before that and I'd heard all these fishermen chanting – they weren't chanting, 'See my friends,' but.they were chanting a chant, all in unison. Unison is wonderful." Ray opines that the lyrical repetition in the verses makes the number more like a Chicago blues and that when it came to the third line, "she is gone", he deliberately thought of Dave singing the high harmony. "It was very easy," he admits; "very simple words."

Whether The Beatles heard the resulting sound and copied it, as has often been stated, who knows; they never pretended to be wholly original in thought but neither did they need to 'steal' one simple idea to boost, as must be the implication, a flagging career. It's safer to say that 'See My Friends' contributed to the fascinating pot pourri of sounds that was British pop music in that decade.

As for the controversy, in '60s parlance "friend" was a byword for homosexual partner, so those with the insight to see picked up on what were clear signals – clear as mud, that is. As usual, the gay issue was fudged, with Ray making it quite ambiguous as to his actual motives for writing the song. As has been stated several times already, the gay issue was at the forefront of '60s pop culture – and '60s culture was, by and large, pop culture. The very fact that homosexuality was broached at all in something so transient as a pop song makes 'See My Friends' special. Ray was mindful of the effect that the lyric would have and so sang both "See my friend" and "See my friends" during the song to heighten the confusion. In fact, try to find out whether the song is called 'See My Friend' or 'See My Friends'. And even that's not easy. On various Kinks albums it's listed in the singular, whereas in certain biographies – and indeed in Ray's own autobiography – the word is "friends". As for any homosexual intent, Ray's brother remains mystified: "It never actually occurred to me," states Dave, "because I always believed that the song was about loss, the loss of a great friend. But people said he was singing about a homosexual and perhaps, on one level, he was."

Whatever the answer – if indeed there is one or even needs to be – the single made the Top Ten. Although held up by many as the great Kinks song of the era, it was in fact no better musically than 'Set Me Free' and technically inferior to the songs Ray would write in the next year or two. The middle-eight's catchy change to a minor key gave it a melodic pop flavour and it was more likely that than the politically aware lyrics or pre-Beatles use of Eastern drones that made it a hit.

All but one Ray Davies composition on *The Kink Kontroversy* were credited to Belinda Publishing, part of the enormous Carlin group. This was all to do with moves that were going on between Boscobel – ie Wace and Collins – and Denmark Productions, meaning Eddie Kassner and, the brunt of almost everyone's ill feeling at that time, Larry Page. Page was in the throes of being ousted from the scene, even though at the time he didn't realise it. Having split his allegiance between his number one charges and the boy / girl duo Sonny And Cher, the whole band was upset, particularly the brothers, who felt personally snubbed – two-timed even. And when the duo, with Page, recorded one of Ray's songs, 'I Go To Sleep', Davies was enraged to the point that he burst into the studio and accused Larry of stealing his songs, or at least his ideas. Had the composer thought for a moment, he would have realised that any recording of his material by other artists could only be beneficial to him, not only financially but from a credibility point of view. To be fair on Page, he had always hawked Ray's songs at every opportunity, but the LP *Kinky Music*, a fairly putrid instrumental workover of some of Davies' best material to date, was perhaps taking things too far. The Beatles or the Stones would never have been so twee. What would have angered Ray most of all, though, was Larry's use of the hated Jimmy Page and his cronies (basically Led Zeppelin in disguise) to play the band's parts on the record. Page also recorded demos with the band in America, the impudence of which displeased Shel Talmy, although in truth he had no real say; the contract was with Pye records, not its producer.

And so the legal business started. Writs and notices flew back and forth between Boscobel, who were fighting for total control of The Kinks, and Denmark Productions, who had considerable publishing rights to protect. Of course the band was stuck in the middle of the furore, with injunctions placed on them releasing records by Denmark, while Boscobel simply wanted Page and Kassner out of the picture. So it was that in late 1965 The Kinks signed to the prestigious Belinda Music, who not only handled Elvis Presley's earnings but also administered the income from Tamla Motown. At the same time Ray's own music publishing company was formed. "Davray" (a portmanteau not of Dave and Ray, as is often assumed, but of the Dav in Davies with Ray prefixed to it) would receive royalties from the United Kingdom and the rest of the world and "Mondvies" (the other half of Davray in wordplay) would cater for the United States and Canada. Unfortunately for Ray, not only was the release of the pending single 'Till The End Of The Day' held up because of the Boscobel / Denmark battle but, due to Denmark Production's immediate serving of a writ for breach of contract, Carlin proceeded to put all financial dealings in escrow, to be administered by a firm of accountants until the matter was fully resolved. Davies would not receive any royalties until the end of the '60s, when the various appeals and counter-appeals had been through the courts. Due to his commercial naivete he also neglected to ask for an advance. It was not a happy time.

The single – one of the best tracks on the flawed *The Kink Kontroversy* – was eventually released in November 1965 and made the highest entry since 'Tired Of Waiting'. Ray had spoken to the great American songwriter Mort Shuman of a difficulty in finding inspiration (actually Shuman had been summoned by the management, who were gravely concerned that Davies' stream of hits was drying up for good).

Shuman, the seasoned professional, told him to simply find some chords he liked and write a song around them. This was not the Davies way, but according to Ray he sat down and drafted one of his favourite songs straight off. 'Till The End Of The Day' stayed in the chart – it reached Number Eight – over the 1965 Christmas period and kept The Kinks in the public's mind well into the new year. He didn't know it then but 'Till The End Of The Day' would herald the longest run of chart success the band would ever have and include some of the greatest pop singles of all time.

1966 would see The Kinks at Number One again. But it was a strange year for pop. The early innocence of the music that had caught the attention of the world was giving way to a cynicism in the lyrics of all the groups who wrote their own songs and were still around to sing them. Where The Beatles had cooed 'She Loves You', they were now crying out with 'Nowhere Man'; where the Stones had chirped 'Not Fade Away' they were similarly in the throes of their '19th Nervous Breakdown'. Pop music was becoming serious, and the '60s were beginning to grow up.

Meanwhile Ray had purchased, with an advance from his then publisher Kassner, a new house in Fortis Green, not far from the family home. The family – Ray and Rasa now had a daughter, Louisa – moved in and life perked up for Ray around this time. Domesticity has always figured large in his songs and it seemed, for the while at least, that domestic life was what the writer needed to settle him. Banned from visiting America, the band had continued touring Europe and the scenes of mayhem were no less fantastic there, but Europe seemed to take to the group and record sales were healthy.

Around this time too, the EP 'Kwyet Kinks' was released. For those who dip into his music lightly, 'Kwyet Kinks' contained one of Ray's best-loved songs; the humorous 'A Well Respected Man' was Davies against the establishment again. Having escaped to Devon to get away from it all with Rasa, he had been spotted by some of the hotel's well-heeled and snobby guests. It seemed to him that their requests to join them in a round of golf were not wholly altruistic; he felt as though they were celebrity hunting and resented being thought of as some quaint sort of side show, to be paraded in snapshots when the holidaymakers got home. These were the well-respected men that prompted the song, although it's commonly felt that Robert Wace, that upper crust city gent, was the true inspiration. Although never released in the UK as a single, the number received extensive airplay and would almost certainly have topped the charts had it been allowed the chance. It was put out on its own in the States, however – a market only denied to the band as performers – and the record's supreme Englishness caught the imagination of American record buyers and it made a respectable Number 13 in the *Billboard* Top 100.

The next single was another song which captured Ray's wry and satirical humour, although again its inspiration came originally from the singer's displeasure at an event. In fact it started with a punch-up. Davies tells of how he threw a party which was attended by many of Carnaby Street's elite; people in the fashion business and those who plied its trade. It seemed to Ray that several of the guests were mocking him and his refusal to pander to their trendiness. Eventually a fight started and he landed a punch on one of the designers. He decided right there and then to concoct a song about the sad army of fashion victims that surrounded the band.

The sound of 'Dedicated Follower' is interesting. Apart from Ray's squeezed and nasal vocals, the acoustic guitar sound is very shrill and thin. He used his trusty Framus twelve-string for the recording and Dave's heavy electric chords and lead fills were added later. This brought the song back towards the raunchy sound the group had become renowned for; indeed it's this juxtaposition of opposite tones that worked so well so often on Shel Talmy's recordings and which characterised much of the band's output from then on.

'A Well Respected Man' had used the word "fag" (English slang for cigarette but American for "queer"); although this ambiguity was not intentional, the success of the song in the States had brought the gay thing to the fore again. So when in 'Dedicated Follower' Ray sang about "pulling frilly nylon panties right up tight", the effect was to exacerbate the situation. Kinks songs, of course, were no more gay than anyone else's – The Beatles would later sing, "Desmond stays at home and does his pretty face," but no one batted an eyelid or castigated the group as gay; the Fabs would suffer their own examinations, not only through lyrical references to drugs but when it was rumoured McCartney had died; didn't everything from the *Sgt Pepper's...* cover to Paul's *Abbey Road* barefootedness confirm it? No, people wanted it and so they saw it. Ray is pragmatic as ever: "Poofs, what do they know?" he grins. "We had a gay following back in 1965, only you didn't have the *Gay News* then, and probably a lot of people following us were frightened to admit they were because they would be put in prison because there was a law. But we had a lot of gay people who were fans of ours."

The promotional film for the song was made by Ray's old art school pal and tutor Barry Fantoni. The film saw the group ducking in and out of Carnaby Street shop doorways, if anything allying The Kinks to the mod movement rather than distancing them, as Ray had intended. Barry Fantoni had become something of a pop personality by the mid '60s, with his own show, *There's A Whole Scene Going*. He also recorded one of Ray's songs, 'Little Man In A Box'. Another Davies cover version around this time was Leapy Lee's 'I'm The King Of The Whole Wide World'. Ray's abilities as a songwriter of some note were at last being picked up by the outside world. Later cover versions by artists as disparate as The Pretenders and Van Halen would signal a huge resurgence in the appreciation of Davies' genius. But it's an oft quoted saying that madness and genius occupy two sides of the same line. And it was at this point that Ray temporarily lost his grip on reality.

8 THE KINKS ARE NOT LIKE EVERYBODY ELSE

The rigours of constant touring and writing, plus the pressure of being in a band like The Kinks in the first place, all contributed to the spectacular breakdown which Ray Davies suffered during early March of 1966. Confined to bed for the week beginning the seventh, Ray was visited by doctors and psychiatrists and harangued by various members of the family; there were arguments and fights but Rasa remained by his side throughout. On the Wednesday the band were due to fly to Belgium and the singer was obviously not fit enough to go. So, just as The Beatles did their stint in Australia without Ringo while the drummer was having his tonsils removed (okay, this was a bit different), The Kinks went to Belgium sporting a new guitarist (The Cockneys' Mick Grace) and with Dave taking over the lead vocalist's spot. Since many have attributed the brothers' long-term feuding to Ray usurping Dave's position as bandleader, it's interesting to ponder on what the young guitarist was really feeling at this time. Later that same year Mick Avory would fall ill with Ringo-itis and Johnny Kidd And The Pirates / Tornados drummer Clem Cattini would step in. Shortly afterwards, Pete Quaife would take an even longer break.

Ray has said of his breakdown that he went to sleep and woke up five days later with a moustache and no band – he vaguely recalls Dave playing him audition tapes of his replacement for the tour. It was during this lost week that Ray flipped completely. For some reason, he stuffed all his money into his socks and ran all the way from East Finchley to the West End of London, where he proceeded to punch his publicist Brian Somerville on the nose, be chased down Denmark Street by the

Metropolitan Police's finest and finally whisked away by a psychiatrist. As he admitted in *X-Ray*, "Everything was centred on jealousy, greed, resentment, misunderstanding and a total lack of trust in everything and everybody." His actions – his rebellion against the establishment, his hated "Corporation", which for some reason poor Brian Somerville must have represented at that moment – proved cathartic, for the next day Ray was much improved. A trip to the country with Robert Wace and a decision to buy a house there was obviously settling his mind too (a song would soon emerge called 'House In The Country', covered by The Pretty Things in an attempt to make the band more commercial, the title would also resurface in the '90s as a Number One single from Kinks fanatics Blur).

But it had been a near thing. Ray: "Obviously, anyone can see that I'm quite a vulnerable sort of guy. You have to be vulnerable to write. I'm also very strong, strong willed, but that's not to say you don't crumble occasionally." Mick Avory is in no doubt that it was a simple case of workaholism, an addiction whose claws were already sunk into Davies' vulnerable psyche and which would inevitably lead to turmoil further down the line. Avory: "He just puts a lot of pressure on himself; I think he's a masochist in that way, but he's in earnest because he's tortured inside to get all that he feels out. When he's finally got it out he's all right, but it's during that process that he seems to go strange."

During Ray's recuperation he was not idle. Although he claims to have tried not to write, the stresses of the period proved inspirational, for during this short sabbatical he came up with some gems; most notably the self-explanatory 'I'm Not Like Everybody Else' and the wondrous 'Sunny Afternoon'. Whilst imbued with so many of the sentiments which would become synonymous with Ray's style and indeed his life – money worries, family strains and a general paranoia about life in general – the Number One smash of summer 1966 hit straight at the heart of Britain. 1966 was World Cup year and, as television repeatedly confirms – "they think it's all over; it is now" – England won the coveted Jules Rimet trophy. Sunny afternoons were the order of that year in the more literal sense too; 1966 was blessed with a beautiful summer, the '60s were in full swing, Carnaby Street fashions ruled the world and the most English of groups was at the top of the nation's pop chart.

Although notable as The Kinks' first chart-topper for 18 months (it knocked The Beatles' 'Paperback Writer' off the top spot after only one week, which pleased Ray immeasurably), 'Sunny Afternoon' also heralded a new Davies writing hook; the descending bass line. The song is in the key of D minor and the bass runs through the intro's two chords (D minor and A7) in almost funereal fashion. The lyrics, too, are morbid and even the upbeat middle-eight, which changes to a happier-sounding major key opens with the line "help me, help me, help me, help me please". It's a fascinating concoction of doom and despair and yet it leaves the listener feeling good about everything. One can feel the heat of those June, July and August days (the song remained in the charts for more than three months) and the listener is defied not to picture Mr Davies under a parasol at the side of his swimming pool, a glass of cold beer in one hand and that gappy grin belying his troubles, perceived or real. It's one of the most memorable singles of all time and a testimony to the insight of its composer.

'Sunny Afternoon''s B-side was 'I'm Not Like Everybody Else'. Dave takes the obvious parallel of his misfit brother a stage further, citing the band as a whole as not like any other. "It's very Kinks, because The Kinks are like no other band," he says. "We've managed to draw from so many different influences – sometimes it's worked and sometimes it hasn't – and tried to express ourselves in ways that nobody else has even touched on, and I think that's probably why we've never really had the great success of the Stones and The Who." Extending the parallel to the band's often strained relationships with its various record companies from the '60s on, he believes this breadth of musical output was the main problem: "A lot of the time I don't think the record companies really knew what to do with us; one song would be really light and folky and reflective and the next was aggressive and angry and hard edged. So yeah, I think The Kinks are not like everybody else."

The success of 'Sunny Afternoon' prompted Davies to seek a meeting with the management and iron out once and for all why he was still, after all these self-penned hits, living in a house paid for by borrowed money and on a wage of about £40 per week. Grenville conceded that it was all to do with the structure of the band's recording deal and that the only way was to renegotiate with Pye. The fact that all Ray's royalties were frozen until the outcome of the Boscobel feud with Denmark Productions wasn't helping Ray's finances, either.

Enter Allen Klein. Klein was rock music's famed contract troubleshooter; he'd recently negotiated a new deal for The Rolling Stones and would be at the centre of The Beatles' break-up some years hence. The Kinks were small fry to a top New York accountant – their success there had hardly been stellar – but Grenville, Robert and Ray were nevertheless accorded his hospitality. They flew to the Big Apple, accompanied by Dave and Mick (in their more lowly capacity as observers) and were given an audience by Klein and his lawyer, Marty, Machat. In simple terms, Klein's plan was to cite the band's youth and plain ignorance of business practices to get a better deal with Pye. Machat was also seconded to try to clear up the performance ban that the American authorities had slapped on The Kinks and Klein further enthused the Boscobel team by stating that Kassner and Denmark Productions stood no chance. Ray went home a happy if slightly brow-beaten boy.

After Ray's breakdown and Mick's bout of tonsillitis, the next Kink kasualty was Pete Quaife. While driving back from a gig in Morecambe in the north-west of England with road manager Peter Jones, their van was involved in a serious accident on the M6 motorway. Pete had stayed behind, according to Ray, to consolidate a relationship with a young lady he'd met there; he told the rest of the group that he'd go back in the van with "Jonah". Quaife tells it differently: "We were travelling in the van with the equipment and the only reason I went with him was so he could have someone to talk to and stay awake, because it was a pretty hectic tour. After a while I fell asleep and about 15 minutes later so did he, at 75 miles an hour." After the accident Jones was in quite a bad way, with severe head injuries, fractured pelvis and a broken nose; Pete was luckier, although his badly damaged foot and concussion were expected to keep him off work for some weeks. It was to be a good deal longer.

Pete had already voiced his disquiet at the unprofessionalism of the pop side of the music business, citing group quarrels, management disorganisation and the inanity of the pop press as reasons for wanting to get out – soon. Pete had been accepted on a scriptwriting course in California and was not backward in letting it be known where his ambitions lay. His temporary enforced retirement gave him more time to think. The doctors' initial prognosis of six weeks was to be an optimistic one, and although the band had played at least one TV show without their bassist (one of the rare benefits of miming), a stand-in was needed and quickly. John Dalton was suggested and the most interesting thing about him, according to Dave and Ray, was that he looked like a larger version of Paul McCartney – Pull McCockoff as they not so affectionately tagged him. Dalton: "The band were signed to the Arthur Howes agency and one of the bookers for that company used to work for one of the bands that I was in, The Mark Four, which turned into The Creation. The Kinks wanted a bass player just for a couple of weeks and so he phoned me up and asked if I'd be interested in doing it. I didn't really want to know at first, but he said I had nothing to lose and so he persuaded me to come along to the audition. I think I was the only one."

In assessing the group's initial antagonism towards their potential new member – which in itself is strange, considering they needed Dalton, or anyone, a good deal more than he needed them – it's easy to look back a couple of years to when a young Mick Avory received his baptism by fire. But Mick's audition, with its gay acting and high-spirited banter, was one thing; the band were now in the big time and had created a scenario for themselves where strife was an everyday occurrence and trouble, as they say, their middle name. True, Dalton was thrown straight in at the deep end, but he asserts that he never had problems with the band and indeed their attitude to one another during his tenure on bass was nothing short of harmonious. "It was all a long time ago but my recollection is that they all got on very well. There were only four of us in those days and we'd all travel around in one car and got on quite well. At that stage they were still really finding their feet and everybody was having a good laugh."

Having played in The Mark Four and The Creation (the latter mod band another inspiration for The Who), Dalton was a fine bassist, but his audition consisted of being asked to play the scale of D minor, which (more or less) constitutes the intro to 'Sunny Afternoon'. In a pair of jeans which, according to Ray made him look like he'd just come off a building site (in fact he had), John was offered the job on the spot. So how long was it before the new boy got to play with the band? "That night!" declared a bemused Dalton. "I just had to play through a few bits and pieces and they said how do you fancy doing *Top Of The Pops* – tonight? That was the Wednesday and the first proper gig was on the Saturday, where we did a double show in Birmingham."

Although a musician of some experience, John Dalton was not familiar with the band's notorious reputation; in fact he was not that familiar with them at all. "When I first went to the office to see the manager," he told us, "I looked at their picture on the wall and I couldn't tell which one was which. I knew some of their records – obviously 'You Really Got Me' and stuff like that – but I didn't know what they were like."

Dalton's first few gigs were the stuff of nightmares – even by The Kinks' standards. The band had been booked to do three nights at Madrid's Yulia club, but with Quaife's absence the promoter, whose ticket sales had been less than sensational, saw a chance to dock the band's wages. "The trouble on that gig," asserts Dalton, "was that the promoter hadn't sold enough tickets and the way to get out of paying the group was to say it's not the full line-up. We were booked to do a few gigs and we did the first one and that sold well – I've got pictures of it and it looks pretty full. But it was the next ones I think that caused the problem." Then the authorities discovered that John had been playing without a work permit and things became sticky. "I'd done the first show on Pete Quaife's permit," Dalton admits, "so when it all came out we didn't have a leg to stand on. We just had to get out of the country, really."

The next date was in Oslo, but because of the work permit situation and of course the general scandal factor, which the Scandinavians were well aware of by now, the band's management were worried that the Norwegian date would have to be scuppered. The ever resourceful Sam Curtis flew immediately to Madrid where he managed to calm the Latin nerves and ferry the band and their new recruit to Norway. But there was also a tone problem with the instrument that Dalton had inherited from Quaife. This was a Danelectro bass and Pete had heard John Entwistle of The Who using one – Entwistle's devastating solo on 'My Generation' used this instrument. The trouble was, the one characteristic of the Danelectro was its shrill, tinny sound and Kinks records were known for Quaife's big, thumping tone. So the first few shows with Dalton were, according to Ray, pretty disastrous from a sound point of view, although Davies was impressed enough with John's musical ability to offer him the full-time position when Quaife finally decided he was quitting. Dalton: "Pete had got this girlfriend in Denmark; that's where he went to stay and he decided he didn't want to come back. Of course, a few months later, he changed his mind and I was out."

Although only with the band a relatively short while, Dalton did record with The Kinks. "The first thing, which was more or less straight away, was 'Dead End Street'," the song which signalled the demise of Shel Talmy as The Kinks' producer. Dalton: "We'd already done it once with Shel Talmy, but Ray didn't like that version – it was slow and had the wrong feel – and so he waited until Talmy had gone and recorded it again." The following day, Ray played his producer the new version, which anyone could tell was completely different (deliberately more laboured and sinister, and with the French horn fade-out solo replaced by a trombonist who Grenville had found in the pub round the corner) and Shel did not recognise it as another arrangement. Still, although the re-recorded version was the one released by the record company, Shel was credited as producer. From that point on, rightly or wrongly, The Kinks' music would remain in the hands of its creator.

In later years, musicians would blame Ray's single-mindedness about his songs and how they should be recorded, for the hours of tedium and lack of creative input that they suffered. Dalton puts this into perspective. "Ray has always been the best producer for The

Kinks," he says, "because he's the only one who knows what's in his head. You can't argue with that. There were times when we put things down and thought they were great, but he said, 'No, let's do it again.' You've got to realise that he knows exactly how he wants it to come out." According to Dalton, Talmy was fine for the earlier stuff, but never would have made it with the more sophisticated material and arrangements that Ray was now beginning to write. "It was all right for 'You Really Got Me' and things like that," insists the bassist, "because they were just crash bash rock 'n' roll, but with the stuff that came after that Ray really needed to take control."

'Dead End Street' is another Davies classic. The song opens with a plodding march, the sombreness of which was reinforced by a plaintive horn motif. The lyrics mask any external influence (it has been suggested that Davies may have been partly inspired by the Aberfan tragedy of that year, where much of a Welsh village was engulfed by a mining slag heap; the death toll was horrendous, consisting mainly of children who were attending the village school at the time), pointing the listener in the direction of Ray's and their own domestic misery; a leaking sink in a two roomed apartment, with bread and honey for Sunday dinner. Of course, money raises its ugly head too, as the rent collector beats down the door for his 30 pieces of silver. In much the same way as the early singles capitalised on Ray's repetitive riff ideas, 'Dead End Street's chorus employed the descending bass line to clever effect. This sound now spelled Kinks, although Nancy Sinatra had shot to Number One in January of the same year with 'These Boots Are Made For Walking', which used a similar intro to 'Sunny Afternoon', except that it was played solo on double bass. In the case of 'Dead End Street' there are two bass parts on the record, one played by Dalton on the Danelectro and the other put down by Dave on the regular bass.

'Dead End Street' reached Number Five in the British chart at the end of November 1966, at the same time as Pete Quaife decided to return and the band's fourth official album *Face To Face* was released. Widely viewed as a musical triumph from Ray as a writer and the band as more finely-honed studio musicians, the record sold poorly. The production is much cleaner than on previous albums and the tidiness of the musicians' work wreaks of more time spent on arrangements, extra takes and overdubs. Dalton had played on a couple of tracks but when Quaife decided that life as a short story writer lacked something compared to his time as one quarter of a pop sensation, Dalton was summoned to the office. "The way they put it to me was that Pete wanted to come back, and as he was 25 per cent of the company, there wasn't a lot they could do about it." But Dalton left on good terms and in fact was working the very next day. "I got a job straight away. Before I joined the band, I was working on a building site, and when I left I got a job as a coalman. I got a bit of publicity out of it; there were a couple of articles in the papers – 'From A Kink To A Koalman'." But Dalton, just like Arnie's Terminator, would be back.

Face To Face opens with 'Party Line' and Dave on lead vocal. Before the days of digital telephone exchanges, phone lines were occasionally shared and eavesdropping on other parties' calls was common. Ray juxtaposes this use of party line with the same term in the political sense of "adopting the party line". Musically the song's rhythm is like an up-tempo 'Dedicated Follower', very '60s pop and a little Stonesy in sound. Ray even slips in some sexual ambiguity (no doubt with complete irony by this stage) with the words "Is she a she at all?". 'Rosy Won't You Please Come Home' is an overt plea to his sister in Australia, but what makes the song is the clever use of Dave's guitar, played in unison with the vocal melody – "Unison is a wonderful thing," Davies might reiterate.

'Dandy', another of Ray's "observation" songs, tips its hat musically to 'A Well Respected Man' and lyrically to 'Dedicated Follower'. The song was actually covered by Herman's Hermits, who were massive in America at this time. Ray's complicated mental state was spelled out in 'Too Much On My Mind' (the legal business had not yet been resolved and the idea had long been languishing in his mind that marriage and fatherhood may not have been his best move). The song is typically '60s, with its harpsichord-laden backing track. 'Session Man' is a sarcastic attack on the hired hands who are often called in to assist where band members need augmenting or simply can't cut it. There's universal antipathy between the two distinctly different breeds of musician, and Ray had obviously suffered at the hands of violinists who put their bows away on the dot of their three-hour session.

The stark production in 'Rainy Day In June' of drums, bass, piano, acoustic and electric guitars – plus thunder and hand claps – enforces the strength of this powerful and evocative number. Davies is rare among pop writers in his ability to summon the precise feeling of a moment – which of course he also does superbly on 'Sunny Afternoon', another inclusion on this LP. In 'House In The Country', Davies vents his rock 'n' roll spleen on the outwardly respectable, while 'Holiday In Waikiki' charts the disillusionment of an Englishman discovering the sad commercialisation of the beautiful American island of Hawaii. The imaginary tale behind an estate agent's sign board is played out in 'Most Exclusive Residence For Sale'; due to financial hard times (Ray even included a courtroom scene), the pecuniarily disadvantaged owner is forced to sell the property.

In 'Fancy', the same drone effect (musically, if not sonically) as used in 'See My Friends' appears, although this time a solitary twelve-string guitar picks out the chords while a single note, played bottleneck style on acoustic guitar, creates the hypnotic drone. Davies manages to see the blacker side of the lightest scenario – the most exclusive residence is sold due to bankruptcy; the prize of a holiday to Hawaii marred by exploitation and, in the case of 'Little Miss Queen Of Darkness', the tawdry reality behind the pretty face of a disco beauty. Dave sings the rather uninspired 'You're Looking Fine', which features the tinkling talents of Nicky Hopkins, the legendary session pianist who graced the recordings of so many artists from the '60s and '70s. 'Session Man' would not, surely, have been aimed at him. Guitarist Jimmy Page perhaps? With its middle-eight reminiscent of 'Set Me Free', the record closes with 'I'll Remember'. Not the strongest track on *Face To Face*, 'I'll Remember' falls back on the Ray-plays-acoustic-while-Dave-hits-the-backbeat-on-electric formula, which many of Shel Talmy's productions featured. Whether this was simply the way the band played in the studio and Talmy captured it, or whether it was a deliberate stylisation of the group at that time, in hindsight it's clear that The Kinks needed more on their albums if they were to compete on the same level as The Beatles and even The Rolling Stones. Listening to this album and comparing it with *Rubber Soul* (1965) and *Revolver* (1966) by The Beatles – a stark contrast is seen. The Liverpool lads had become embroiled in the intricacies of studiocraft; and their songs, while each one an obvious Beatle production, were quite different to one another in both form and arrangement. Davies, on the other hand and for all his brilliant social commentary and skill with words and music, wrote and recorded within certain boundaries. An unkind critic might say that he had only three song types; the 'You Really Got Me' song, the 'Dedicated Follower Of Fashion' song and the 'Sunny Afternoon' song. While that view is both untrue and unfair, that it can be said at all shows that The Kinks were in need of an injection of something into their recordings. And perhaps John Dalton hit the nail on the head when he said that Shel Talmy's time was nigh; the producer had worked magic with the minimum of materials (and had one final brilliant stroke to play), but 1967 would see the dawn of a new Kinks era.

9 IT REALLY IS A DIRTY OLD RIVER

1967 was the year of the nonsense lyric; the year of Procol Harum, of Traffic and of course those damned Beatles. "The room was humming harder as the ceiling blew away," sang Procol's otherwise sensible Gary Brooker; "I looked in the sky where an elephant's eye was looking at me from a bubble-gum tree," cooed Traffic's Steve Winwood, not altogether convincingly; but of course Lennon said it most eloquently in 'Strawberry Fields Forever' – "No one I think is in my tree; I mean it must be high or low..." Yes, John, we know what you mean, mate. And of course there was Jimi Hendrix chomping at his upside down Fender Stratocaster through a permanent purple haze; Cream with their psychedelic painted guitars and silly Afro hairdos; and just about anybody else who could scrawl an acid-induced lyric onto some expensive hotel stationery or napkin. That's what set Ray Davies and his Kinks apart from everyone else – except perhaps Tom Jones and Engelbert Humperdinck – in that year of Haight Ashbury and flower-power. "It was a fad and a fashion and I wanted nothing to do with it at all," asserts Pete Quaife. "We all conformed for a few seconds by wearing multi-coloured gear, but we knew we didn't fit into all this, especially Mick Avory – just think of it, Mick Avory as a flower-power child."

Perhaps a good lawsuit helps keep a level head on your shoulders (when it's not inducing a mental breakdown, that is); or maybe Ray was just so English, just so working class and down to earth that he'd die before putting his name to such a load of old cobblers. Whatever the answer, The Kinks did not drown in this all-encompassing tide of lyrical hogwash and indeed their next single, which would not come about until May of this year, was to be their most straightforwardly poetic yet. In the interim, the legal problems between The Kinks and Kassner would be partially resolved and an empty tour diary (courtesy of bans from much of the group's traditional stomping ground, Europe) allowed Ray, Dave, Mick and the re-recruited Pete to take a break from the rigours of the road and studio. Of course, Ray could never really shut down and he used at least some of the time to write new material.

Meanwhile, Larry Page was back on the scene, trying to make legally sure that he kept his ten per cent management share in The Kinks. The band had hoped Larry might be out of the picture by now; after all, he'd had hits with Sonny And Cher and was now in the throes of massive success with Reg Presley's Troggs. The group already had four Top Ten hits under their belts, including the chart-topping 'With A Girl Like You'. This year would also see the release of 'Love Is All Around', later the theme from the film *Four Weddings And A Funeral* and which in 1994 gave Wet Wet Wet one of the longest running Number Ones in British history. No, Larry wanted what he felt was rightfully his, and so the case went to the High Court.

The upshot of it all was that Page lost his claim, the judge (Justice Widgery, who went on to become Lord Chief Justice) decreeing that, due to the breakdown in trust between the parties, his situation had become untenable. Ray left the court ecstatic – it had been his own vitriolic statement against Page, detailing his abandonment of the group in America, that sealed his fate – and it might have been supposed that he'd think, "Okay, let's write some great tunes, get the band back on the road, sort ourselves out and the new Kinks can take on the world." But no. As almost everyone we've spoken to close to the band has told us, whenever things were going great, Ray appeared hell bent on doing something to wreck it. So he announced that from now on he would be taking a back-seat role, like Brian Wilson of The Beach Boys, still writing and producing Kinks material but not performing it; that could be handled by Dave on vocals and a stand-in guitarist.

Of course, the press jumped on the rumours of a split – which was in truth far more than a rumour because it had come from the horse's mouth – and so the management went into damage-limitation mode.

Wace denied everything; Davies was forced to see the error of his ways and took back everything he had said. Larry Page's announcement of a House of Lords appeal contrived to put Ray back in the position he'd just come from; with everything hanging over his head and actually nothing resolved. In fact, Page did get his appeal the following year, but after a closely fought battle a compromise was reached – Ray called it a draw. It was accepted by the three eminent Justices that Page had indeed forfeited his management rights by quitting the 1965 American tour without informing Ray (even though he'd told every other band member). In turn, Denmark Productions (Kassner and Page) were to retain the publishing on everything up to and including 'See My Friends'. So what had started out as a simple matter of who would manage the band finished, somewhat inevitably, in a scrabble for the rights to Davies' songs. Here was the money go round in full swing.

They say that from adversity comes strength and Ray, in true Battle of Britain style, came back with the song that for many sums up not only The Kinks but the '60s themselves. Any pop fan worthy of his salt would put 'Waterloo Sunset' on a shortlist of the best singles of all time. This was to be Shel Talmy's final outing as The Kinks' producer, but in fact the final version owes little to his talents; as with 'Dead End Street' the band went in and recorded their own version of the song with Davies calling the production tune. Shel had originally drafted Nicky Hopkins in to play piano on the track but Ray felt the basic instrumentation was enough. He was right, and the result shows a four-piece pop-rock band at the peak of its powers. When Talmy's contract came up for renewal shortly after the completion of 'Waterloo...'. all parties agreed to an amicable split. The partnership had created eleven Top 20 singles and three credible albums, but after an amazingly fruitful three years it was time for a change.

Ray has said that of all his compositions 'Waterloo Sunset' was always going to be right; from the moment he first played the chords to Dave until the day he recorded the vocal track – he was unsure as to how the others would take such a romantic view of Waterloo Bridge and the filthy River Thames so he kept it back until the final moment. Needless to say, they loved it. From its original inception until the final version the track changed a great deal. In the early days it was the Stones who seemed to get everywhere first and bigger and better, but this time it was The Beatles. Ray had originally called the song Liverpool Sunset, but the Fabs' double A-side ode to their home town ('Penny Lane' / 'Strawberry Fields Forever') was released in February, scuppering any thoughts of a Liverpool theme. As to the characters of Terry and Julie, it is implied in *X-Ray* that this could be Ray's nephew Terry and the mystical (mythical?) girl of his dreams, Julie Finkle. But Terence Stamp, in talking of the film *Far From The Madding Crowd*, in which he starred with Julie Christie, is in no doubt that the inspiration for the characters was them. Ray has said much the same himself at other times.

Musically, 'Waterloo Sunset's unmistakable intro uses the descending bass line theme again. This time it's a B major scale with a flattened seventh note; but as Quaife's bass cascades down from the B, Dave's guitar persists in playing the note, creating musical tension which is only released when everything resolves to the waiting E chord of the verse. The electric guitar is treated with old fashioned slap-back echo, the kind used on Elvis Presley's vocals on early hits like 'Heartbreak Hotel'. Ray's wistful delivery and gentle strumming are complemented in the strangest way by Dave's raunchy guitar fills and crashing middle-eight chords.

Sat on Waterloo Bridge talking of the song for a 1995 BBC documentary, Ray said, "Today it really is a dirty old river. But I imagined it. It's so much better when it comes from how you imagine it, rather than how you report it. I think they call it poetry." In commenting on how he manages to still perform the number 30 years on, he had this to say: "I do it as if it's a new song. I can't recreate what was then; I can only do the song based around what I feel about it now. But I still get that emotional feeling, that thing tugging you. I don't want to be immodest, but it's like an actor doing Hamlet every night. The great thing is that I wrote it as well."

Surprisingly, 'Waterloo Sunset' just missed the top slot. But it had some tough competition: Sandie Shaw's Eurovision winner 'Puppet On A String', The Tremeloes' big ballad 'Silence Is Golden' and The Beatles' *One World* broadcast, 'All You Need Is Love', held the Number One positions consecutively for the three months 'Waterloo' was in the charts.

To follow such a song was going to be difficult, if not impossible, and in what can only be seen as a bizarre turn of events the situation was salvaged by none other than the singing, guitar playing Kink himself – no not Ray, but Dave Davies. A year earlier, Dave had gone to Ray with a line for a song, "death of a clown", and Ray had persuaded his brother to go away and come up with some more lyrics. Together they finished off the number, recorded and released it and it made an astonishing Number Three in July of 1967. The hit had a two-fold effect on the guitarist. First, it boosted a flagging ego – Dave often felt belittled by fellow musicians as the hanger-on to the talented one. The secondary but probably more beneficial side to Dave's success was that he realised he didn't really want it; he felt uncomfortable taking centre spotlight although his antics in the band had always led others to believe that was exactly what he craved. In his own mind the younger brother had proved his worth – to himself, to Ray and to his many critics. There would be future solo projects – like the flop single 'Lincoln County' the following year – but for now that was to be the end of it. He didn't even want to record a follow-up, although 'Susannah's Still Alive' was released later in the year and scraped into the Top 20 in December. Altogether, a successful and happy interlude and one which diffused the problem of what to do after 'Waterloo'.

As it happened, no one need have worried, because the next Kinks single proper was to be one of their very best. Both lyrically and musically, 'Autumn Almanac' is graced with pure pop genius, from the opening line to its poignant middle-eight which touches the heart strings of every Brit who lived through the post-war years of coal-fired chimneys, black and white television and the days before the break-up of the nuclear family. The song was too clever to reach Number One but 'Autumn Almanac' made a more than respectable third position during October.

Of all the Davies compositions so far, perhaps 'Autumn Almanac' showed Ray's most brilliant description of everyday themes. As he explained recently: "One of the things I do that grates on other musicians is to put ordinary words in; un-rock words, un-blues words. But then I think that words are just like pieces of plasticine that you mould. But it's only words and there are no rules."

The song starts with a strong acoustic guitar motif, probably played on Ray's recently acquired Fender. Dave doubled on his own acoustic, a Vox twelve-string while he and Rasa (Ray's wife had appeared on many, if not most of the band's singles thus far) sang falsetto harmonies. As with many of Davies' minor key songs, he shifted to major for the middle section and in this case included his trademark bass lines to pump the tempo along. This was Ray's first solo production and the results were more than promising.

With three Top Five Kinks hits so far in 1967 it might have seemed inconceivable that their new album *Something Else By The Kinks* would flop. But flop it did, managing a paltry Number 35 in the UK album chart of October 1967. There is no rational reason for this, other than perhaps Pye's lack of dynamic marketing – but then, in the '60s, records were not marketed as ferociously as they are today; even Beatles and Stones LPs seemed to just "come out". One explanation, however unsatisfactory it may seem, is that the group just wasn't seen by the public as an album act. It certainly wasn't a unique phenomenon, as a similar parallel can be seen with The Hollies, whose catalogue of singles hits includes no fewer than 17 Top Tenners, but whose album sales, like those of The Kinks, were relatively abysmal. The fact that two budget compilation albums, *Well Respected Kinks* and *Sunny Afternoon* (both released by Pye on the Marble Arch label) dented the LP charts with significantly more clout than many of the band's regular releases could prove the point. Of course, it could be argued (and has been) that these budget releases were the very reason the market was not there for new Kinks product.

If *Something Else By The Kinks* deserved not to be bought it was for the album's appalling liner notes. Embarrassingly and badly written, they hark back to the K-obsessed mumbo-jumbo of the first album, treating the record's content like transient bubble-gum for 13-year-olds, not intelligent and grown-up music designed to put people's minds to work. Perhaps it was just the '60s.

Ten of the LP's 13 tracks were Ray Davies compositions. The other three were 'Death Of A Clown' (a Ray and Dave collaboration), 'Love Me Till The Sun Shines' and 'Funny Face', both written solely by

Davies Junior. The opener, the very Troggs-like 'David Watts', seems to be based around an amalgam of two characters in Ray's life: a school friend and a rampantly gay gentleman who later took a shine to Dave. That The Jam would record the number over a decade later in more or less the same form sets it as a timeless piece of writing from Ray. 'Two Sisters' is quite plainly Ray and Dave, with Ray exposing his envy for his younger brother's life of freedom from the drudgery of marriage and fatherhood to which he was tied. For 'No Return', Ray dips into his jazz repertoire to produce a smooth, Jobimesque bossa nova which predates McCartney's 'Step Inside Love', written for Cilla Black's TV show, by nearly a year.

Using cockney rhyming slang for fag (the English "cigarette" meaning), 'Harry Rag' is an inconsequential and only semi-humorous ditty about addiction to the evil weed. 'Tin Soldier Man' and 'Situation Vacant' are vignettes in the manner of 'A Well Respected Man' and 'Dedicated Follower Of Fashion', although not as clever or funny as either. It seems through this album that Ray's ability to knock out a song from any given situation, theme or idea was used as an excuse to make up the track numbers, and although hailed as something of a masterpiece by true Kinks fans the record really doesn't stand up to comparison with *Sgt Pepper's* or indeed that other 1966 classic, *Pet Sounds* by The Beach Boys. Again, the arrangements – although more courageous than those of Talmy – were nowhere near what George Martin was doing with The Beatles or Brian Wilson with The Beach Boys. With a few exceptions – 'David Watts', 'Waterloo Sunset', of course; 'Lazy Old Sun', which showed more depth in its arrangement than many of the tracks; 'No Return'; and indeed Dave's inclusions, which showed spirit and a surprising maturity – it was all a bit superficial.

The failure of *Something Else By The Kinks* (let's be frank; the title was a put-off, too) to make an impression on the album charts was nevertheless surprising. But at least The Kinks saw 1967 out with some success, in the shape of Dave's Top 20 single 'Susannah's Still Alive', a stomping, riffy number; the kind of stuff Pete Quaife thought the band should be doing more of. "Some of the records were really good," he told the band's fan club magazine *Now & Then*, "like 'Dedicated Follower Of Fashion', 'Sunny Afternoon' and 'Dead End Street', but there were songs I didn't like. I think we should have done some really heavy numbers in between."

1968 began with the release of *The Kinks Live At Kelvin Hall*. The record, a musical snapshot of the band in action, shows just how scrappy their shows could be. Although largely drowned out by audience screams – almost certainly pushed up in the mix, either to mask the indifferent performances or to show just what an effect the boys had on the youth of the day – the out of tuneness of the band and Ray's poor vocal delivery are self-evident. The track selection included mainly the early hits – 'You Really Got Me', 'All Day And All Of The Night', 'Tired Of Waiting' (in an odd but enjoyable medley which incorporated 'Milk Cow Blues' and the *Batman* theme), 'Sunny Afternoon'; plus 'A Well Respected Man', 'Dandy', 'I'm On An Island', 'You're Looking Fine' and 'Come On Now'. Although it would be difficult to recommend the album as anything but a Kinks curio, it does highlight the problem that the band would face on their UK tour of that year; their live incompetence would be in stark contrast to the slick performances of the other acts on the show, most notably The Herd and The Tremeloes.

Peter Frampton of The Herd was heralded in *Beat Instrumental* magazine as "The Face Of '68" and The Tremeloes were in the middle of a string of massive hits. The bill also included Gary Walker (of the teen idol trio The Walker Brothers), as well as newcomers The Rain and Ola And The Janglers. By comparison The Kinks' show was tired and unprofessional; many of the fans had seen it in its heyday (just a couple of years before) and had probably come to watch the lighter weight but altogether more trendy support acts anyway.

In order to capitalise on the tour Pye, in its wisdom, decided to release two singles; one from Dave and one from The Kinks proper. Ray and Dave fought against this and in the end only the band's 'Wonderboy' surfaced, a song Ray had desperately tried to restrain, due to its overt uncommerciality. As he suspected, the track lacked the instant appeal of 'Waterloo Sunset' or the lyrical melancholy of

'Autumn Almanac', and so 'Wonderboy' provided the group with their first chart failure (36 was not a hit by their standards) since 'You Still Want Me' in early 1964. For all its joy and wit, the song sounded like a children's ditty and its effete "la-la-la, la-la-las" clashed with Ray's lead vocal, making the tune cluttered and uncomfortable to the casual listener. Tour reviews slated the band and cited their recent album and single failures as evidence that this was the beginning of the end for the self-destructing madmen. With their tails tucked uncomfortably between their legs the wounded group left the country for a stadium tour of Europe, while 'Days' was hurriedly released to restore chart credibility. The B-side, 'She's Got Everything', was an old recording, very much in the style of the early hits, which Pye rescued from the vaults and included at the last minute.

In hindsight, 'Days' is one of the band's best-loved tunes. Successfully covered by Kirsty MacColl and used in a prestigious TV advertising campaign in the '90s, the record was a medium-sized but tenacious hit for the band – it reached Number Twelve in July 1968 but hung around the charts for most of the summer. In 'Days', Ray bares his soul for all to see; it's an unashamed and touching love song which needs no explanation.

Also in July the brothers announced their latest idea; a production company that would nurture new artists rather than suck them in and spit them out the way Ray felt that record companies did. Although it never really got off the ground (the required financial backing proved impossible to secure), this Davies idea pre-dated The Beatles' Apple Corps (set up for the same idealistic reasons) by a full two years. If Ray and Dave's production company and the so-called "raga rock" of 'See My Friends' and 'Fancy' (*Face To Face*) had been pop innovations that beat The Beatles, The Kinks were all set to gazump Pete Townshend's rock opera *Tommy* with perhaps their best LP, *The Kinks Are The Village Green Preservation Society*. But, as so often happened with this group, best was not to be confused with best-selling. Believe it or not, The Kinks would never record another hit album.

10 I KNOW WHAT I AM AND I'M GLAD I'M A MAN

The Kinks Are The Village Green Preservation Society finally hit the streets towards the end of September 1968, but not before it had undergone several changes. Initially contrived as a concept album taking the rise out of old English life and customs, the record was originally to be called "Four More Respected Gentlemen". However, for reasons unknown this album never materialised (although labels and a running order did); instead, many of the scheduled tracks were incorporated onto a record based on Dylan Thomas' *Under Milk Wood*. This version was quickly withdrawn and an updated selection of tracks replaced it. *The Kinks Are The Village Green Preservation Society* set the group as guardians of all that was good about England. Ray had long been known as an Anglocentric; singles such as 'Waterloo Sunset' and 'Autumn Almanac' had celebrated the Englishness that he so loved, and the new album consolidated the theme.

While Ray was inventing parochial pop, Ned Sherrin was at the vanguard of the '60s satire movement in London. Commenting on Davies in 1995, he said, "Almost all popular singers and songwriters have been influenced by America, and many of them sing in an American fashion. Ray shone out as someone who was not doing that and was in a way celebrating the Englishness, which in the first place has an appeal and a reality for the people in his native country. But it's so vivid that it's been able to leap across the Atlantic – mostly, I suppose, in that album *The Kinks Are The Village Green Preservation Society*."

There's no doubt in many people's minds that this was indeed Davies' best work to date. Pete Quaife concurs, but states that it was due, in part at least, to the involvement from the other band members. "Ray relaxed for a while and allowed everybody to have some input," affirms the bassist, "so what you got out of *Village Green* was a combination of everybody's ideas." He goes on to confirm *Village Green* as his own favourite Kinks album and the track 'Animal Farm' his favourite Ray Davies song. Quaife: "He was saying, 'Imagine what it was like in an English village.' When he explained it to us we all understood and we went into the studio and had a thoroughly good time. 'Animal Farm'; that really appealed to me. I remember having the shivers when I first heard Ray banging it out on the piano."

Maturely produced by Davies and employing several additional musicians (including the uncredited Nicky Hopkins on harpsichord), the sounds on *Village Green* were better defined than on Talmy's recordings, with obviously much more time allotted to the sessions. 'The Village Green Preservation Society' sets the theme for the rest of the album in an upbeat ditty singing the praises of, among other things, china cups, strawberry jam and virginity (and, curiously, those American institutions Donald Duck and vaudeville). 'Village Green' continues the theme, while the other tracks see the characters – such as Ray's 'Johnny Thunder', the local witch and the village's lady of pleasure, 'Wicked Annabella' and 'Monica'; even the 'Phenomenal Cat' – acting out their daily lives. The Electric Light Orchestra would ape the piano / drums intro to the evocative 'Do You Remember Walter?' a decade later with their hit 'Mr Blue Sky'. Hal Carter had castigated the band in '64 for their poor attempts at R&B classics such as Howlin' Wolf's 'Smokestack Lightnin''. Hal gets his come-uppance on 'The Last Of The Steam Powered Trains', where Dave's intro mimics 'Smokestack's opening lick closely. 'Picture Book' and 'People Take Pictures Of Each Other' contrast the comfortable nostalgia created by a browse through a photo album with Ray's confessed dislike of the camera. The powerful 'Big Sky' alludes, not too cryptically, to the God of the village, who sees it all, good and bad, but seems somehow too occupied with other things to get involved. Among the most memorable songs on *Village Green* are the title track; 'Do You Remember Walter?'; 'Sitting By The Riverside', where Davies' voice is at its languid best; 'Wicked Annabella' (which boasts the best guitar sound on the album); and Quaife's favourite, 'Animal Farm' – "I still love listening to it," he commented in 1994.

Tragically, Pye seemed disinterested in promoting the record and it failed dismally as a commercial project. Pragmatic as ever, Davies is thankful of the respect as a writer that he gained from creating *The Village Green Preservation Society*, an album which has done much to sustain generations of fascination with The Kinks. "The things that have given us most longevity are the things that have not been successful," said Davies at the end of 1995. "If we're talking about *The Village Green Preservation Society*, worldwide we'd be lucky if it did 100,000. I mean, even the people who talk about it, haven't heard it." A wry view, certainly, but one which is probably quite true.

Following the recording of *Village Green*, in October 1968 The Kinks undertook what can only be described as a bizarre series of gigs. The northern British cabaret circuit was traditionally the stomping ground for comedians, dinner music crooners or chart acts from the '50s and early '60s who had fallen on hard times (courtesy of groups just like The Kinks). Stockton's Fiesta club and the famous Variety club at Batley were hardly suitable venues for the UK's rowdiest, noisiest band but it was proving difficult to find work elsewhere in their own country – the tour with The Herd had just demonstrated the point. So it proved an unworkable situation for several reasons: first, it really did suggest the death rattle of a once successful act; secondly, The Kinks' repertoire was hardly dinner music; and finally, the band were simply too loud. One night, Dave's opening chords to 'You Really Got Me' almost blew one unsuspecting punter's scampi and chips right off the table.

But there was good news. As 1968 turned into '69, America's four-year performance ban was lifted and the US record company, Reprise, mounted a campaign to bring attention to the group and to get The Kinks back on American soil. Before that, though, it was single time again and in a desperate attempt to win back public approval for his group, Ray really dredged the bucket.

'Plastic Man' was another poor pastiche of 'A Well Respected Man' and 'Dedicated Follower Of Fashion'. Although it had always been stated that the band never followed topical whims – least of all flower power and its ensuing "underground" movement – 'Plastic Man' nevertheless reiterated tired hippy values. He was Mr Normal, at a time when it was cool to be a drop-out; he lived his plastic life without realising the rut he was in (the hippies, of course, would all be chartered accountants themselves soon enough).

Although Ray both despised the song and defended it to the press, he was pleased when 'Plastic Man' looked like it was entering the charts. It had received reasonable airplay and so a spot on *Top Of The Pops* was scheduled. But Auntie BBC, that bastion of British morality, deemed the word "bum" (English slang for buttocks) unsuitable for *TOTP*'s early evening slot and suggested Ray change the line "he's got plastic legs that reach up to his plastic bum" to the far more innuendo-laden rhyme "plastic thumb". This little bit of notoriety helped the single to its uninspiring chart position of 31 but 'Plastic Man' can hardly be deemed a fabulous success.

Good news followed bad and bad followed good. At least that's how it seemed when, after the luke warm reaction received by his last offering, Ray was asked by Granada Television to produce a pop opera for proposed screening later in the year. Ray would call the project *Arthur* and the central characters, Arthur and Rose, a couple who emigrated to Australia, would bear a striking resemblance to his long lost sister and brother-in-law. Davies was immediately enthused and began writing songs straight away. But no sooner was the project under full steam than Pete Quaife, the prodigal bass player, announced that he was finally quitting the band. Ray was distraught; he believed Pete had come back for good and was mortified that the original line-up was no more. As for Quaife, it was the same old problem; he was bored with the music and felt the lure of pastures new. But many observers of the band feel that a resentment for Ray was at the core of his decision. Dave tells of a photo finish in a school race, where Ray can clearly be seen pipping Pete to the post. Had such childhood rivalries festered for all these years? "I think there was a lack of communication," confessed Pete. "There was nothing to say and I was simply a person playing bass."

The press pounced on the story and much was made of the band's musical differences. "What I would have preferred was to make a nice, quiet, clean break," admitted Quaife, "but I remember the press jumping onto it and making it out to be something absolutely ridiculous."

Recalling the events to Martin Kalin in 1998, Pete explained why his exit the second time had to be final. "The first time I was recuperating from a car accident so I couldn't have been there even if I'd wanted to," he said. "Inadvertently it was a good break for me. The band was fighting all the time and I was getting sick of it. When I did quit altogether, I wanted to run as fast as I could in the other direction. I just couldn't take the constant brawling amongst everybody any more."

Pete formed a group called Maple Oak with some Canadian friends and although some recordings were made, the band had no success.

"I was the only Brit in the group," he says. "We were into different stuff and the whole project was short-lived. After that, I moved to Denmark and returned to art as a profession and lifestyle." 2000 would see a Maple Oak album, featuring Quaife on a couple of tracks, released for the first time.

Pete moved to Copenhagen with his Danish wife Annette (whose cousin Lisbet had married Dave two years earlier). They had a daughter in 1968 who lives in Denmark while Pete now lives in Canada, with his second wife, Hanne. "Hanne was from Canada," he explains. "She was living in Denmark when I met her. We moved to London for a while before settling here."

So yet again The Kinks needed a new bass player and who better to fill the void than John "Nobby" Dalton. If Ray felt that the loss of Quaife damaged the group's wholeness, then at least Nobby was a known quantity; he was a decent, likable guy and his musical abilities were beyond question. Nobby was not surprised at Quaife's decision to finally depart. "I think it was a case of the grass being greener with Pete," he says. "Once he'd been away for a few months he'd forgotten about the hard times and wanted to rejoin. Then once he was back he thought, 'I dunno, I think was better off out of it.' But he was always unsettled, I think." So Dalton was asked back and of course there was no question of an audition. "Mick Avory just phoned me up one night and said why didn't I come back. There wasn't much new stuff to learn and so it was really a question of stepping back in. The first new thing I did was *Arthur*."

During this period Ray was involved in a variety of extra-curricular activities. These included producing the album *Turtle Soup* for the American west coast band The Turtles (hits 'Happy Together', 'She'd Rather Be With Me' and 'Elenore') and writing the theme for the feature film version of the TV show *Till Death Us Do Part*, written by Johnny Speight and starring Warren Mitchell as Alf Garnet (a kind of bigoted Arthur). He was also conscripted by Ned Sherrin to come up with six songs for his weekly show, *Where Was Spring*. On top of this he supplied several numbers for the soundtrack of Leslie Thomas' hit film *The Virgin Soldiers*. Dave, too, was trying out new solo material and tracks were even recorded for a new album which never saw the light of day.

In mid 1969, The Kinks lost the Arthur Howes agency. They were taken on by Barry Dickens, who found the act a difficult one to market. A theme park tour of Sweden was undertaken and an aborted gig for a Lebanese chocolate magnate in Beirut's Hotel Finosia almost left their recently recruited road manager, Ken Jones, detained as a hostage due to a disagreement with the authorities.

Meanwhile, the TV programme of *Arthur* was going well. Ray had discussed his ideas with screen writer Julian Mitchell and the idea of using his uncle Arthur as a loose basis for the hero appealed. But Arthur's character was to be older, and it was he who was struggling with the thought of his children emigrating; being left behind in a country that had changed beyond recognition during his lifetime. Ray's writing was not only prodigious but good – Wace even referred to it as poetry – and before long the album, which was to released alongside the TV film, was completed. Then, at the eleventh hour, Granada called a halt; production had run over budget and no persuasion or cajoling from Ray or Robert Wace – including the threat to sue for breach of contract – would dissuade them from their action. Ray was beside himself, and to cap it all The Who's *Tommy* was released at that precise moment, hailing Pete Townshend as the great innovator and simultaneously consigning *Arthur* to the "also-ran" bin.

Despite the different success levels, similarities between The Who and The Kinks were apparent. Shel Talmy had produced both 'You Really Got Me' and 'I Can't Explain', so the feel of the groups was the same, something Ray recognised.

"Obviously I focused on Townshend's work," he revealed to *Guitar World* in 1998. "It didn't surprise me when they came out with *Tommy* because I'd met them briefly at gigs and they were a bit more – I hate to say the word 'intelligent' – focused than a lot of the other bands back then. Most of the bands The Kinks toured with were just in it for the fun, to make money and buy a nice car. But with The Who, you got the feeling that they were out to rewrite the rules, which attracted me, because I was trying to do the same thing."

Despite one or two truly brilliant songs – most notably the flop singles-to-be 'Victoria' and the wonderful 'Shangri-La' – *Arthur* was a predictable sales disaster. Its full title, *Arthur, Or The Decline And Fall Of The British Empire*, did not endear it to the average record buyer, who was looking for entertainment rather than an intellectual battle. The first single to be culled from the album was 'Drivin'", which came out in June and failed to chart at all; 'Victoria' scraped into the lower reaches of the Top 40 early the following year, but 'Shangri-La', perhaps Davies' all-round best composition, failed completely in a travesty that saw both Edison Lighthouse's 'Love Grows Where My Rosemary Goes' and 'Wand'rin' Star' by Lee Marvin at Number One.

'Mr Churchill Says', which has Ray embarrassingly reciting some of Winston's best-known speeches and a second half redolent of The Everly Brothers' 'Wake Up Little Susie', is typical, in that its existence seems only justified by its context. 'Yes Sir, No Sir' deals with the mindless acquiescence of the general soldier while 'Some Mother's Son' extends the theme to its logical conclusion; with typical bluntness, Ray was expressing Lennon's 'Give Peace A Chance' ethic of the late '60s. With the luxury of hindsight it's all a little obvious. 'Drivin'" recalls those carefree motoring days when an outing in the car was a pleasure – leave the taxman and rent collector behind. 'Brain Washed' features a fabulous distorted guitar sound from Dave – had he brought the "fart box" out of hiding?

Just as Arthur and Rosie had capitalised on the British government's relocation package to the Antipodes, so Ray's 'Australia' sells the idea of emigration to his main character's children, Derek and Liz. One of the album's saddest and most endearing tracks is 'She Bought A Hat Like Princess Marina', which highlights the futility of the downtrodden classes emulating those who kept them so squarely in their place. 'Young And Innocent Days' and 'Nothing To Say' deal transparently with nostalgia for better times, while 'Arthur' simply describes the life of our hapless hero.

The real Arthur was touched by Ray's characterisation of him and his family and the band seemed to enjoy making the album. Whether or not the content of *Arthur* missed the point of pop music in 1969 is missing the point itself; Davies was producing the music he wanted to produce, just like he'd always done, with little or no mind towards external trends or forces. And for that he must be fully applauded, rather than pitied for the record's lack of success. Ray's failure in the face of Pete Townshend's highly acclaimed *Tommy* obviously hurt the writer, but Davies, as ever, understood the fundamentals: "It's got words like lavatory in it," explained Ray, "but lavatory isn't a good rock 'n' roll word – it's not like 'pinball', which is much more rock 'n' roll."

Musically and production-wise, the album represents a pinnacle for The Kinks; the band is loose but tight and John Dalton's bass playing is conspicuous in its inventiveness, although Ray would later say that the recording lacked Quaife. It's still one of Dalton's favourite records and Nobby recalls how the composer seemed to know exactly what he wanted. "I liked *Arthur* and thought it had some great tracks," he told us. "They're still playing 'Victoria' and 'Shangri-La' today. We did the record at Pye's studio at Marble Arch and we were there all hours of the day and night, really working hard to get it out. Ray was totally in control; of course, he'd written all the songs and was producing it, and the general feeling of the band was, 'Let's do it and get it right.'" Dave goes further, stating how *Arthur* represented a new height for The Kinks which, although completely ignored by its own countrypeople, was somehow understood and latched onto in America. "I remember feeling at the time, 'Now we're doing something really good,'" says Dave. "We'd had all the hits and the singles every couple of months and Ray was driving himself into breakdown after breakdown trying to come up with ideas for songs, and all of a sudden I felt that we were doing something original, developing our art. And it did absolutely nothing. I was a little bit confused. It's really strange, because when we went to America, the Americans got it straight away."

In fact America was now ready to open its arms to The Kinks. Reprise spoke of organising a massive publicity campaign to hype the band's return, with crowds at the airport to greet them and false arrests for drugs and tax evasion. Fortunately, these ideas were vetoed by Ray, but news had leaked to the press and the effects of this double hype were almost as good. But America had changed since the group were last there and so had The Kinks' pecking order. Supporting acts such as Randy California's Spirit at Bill Graham's Fillmore East and their rivals The Who in Chicago, the band were made aware of their shoddy equipment and stage show, which paled under the onslaught of Daltrey, Townshend, Entwistle and Moon. It was a paradoxical tour; depressing and at the same time highly great to be back. The Kinks learnt a lot on that short visit and by the time the tour closed at the Whisky A Go Go in Hollywood, with at least two members of the band on less than top form, the reputation of The Kinks as a cool English band playing groovy new music was assured.

It had been a long tour, though, and they were relieved to see it end. More than 30 years later, Dave would appear as a solo artist at the Hollywood club, grateful of the chance to make up for the band's last appearance. "The last time I played there in 1969," he told *Guitarist's* Roger Newell, "I was so out of it I couldn't play, so I kind of owed them a gig. We were supposed to be promoting *Arthur*, but nobody wanted to be there. I'd been on acid for a week and Ray was drunk because he wanted to go home. He was hiding in the background, singing songs like 'Tired Of Waiting' and 'You're Looking Fine' and I was like the front man. Then, in the middle of the show, I was so out of it I just unplugged my guitar, put it in the case and walked back to the hotel. So I owed them a gig."

1970 would mark a strange moment for The Kinks; it would provide them with their two biggest hits (on both sides of the Atlantic) since 'Waterloo Sunset' and herald the dawn of a new era for the band as a touring concern. The lessons of the past would be fully learnt and, although there would still be feuding and fighting between the brothers and abuse of the hired hands on the road, The Kinks would claw their way back as one of the leading acts on the US rock circuit.

Early in the year, Ray helped Pye in compiling an album that chronicled The Kinks' output so far. Originally, a book dealing with the life of the band up to this point was also envisaged by Davies but, as so often seemed to happen with these projects, it never materialised. 1970's big thing, though, was 'Lola'. But before recording was complete a new face would take its place in The Kinks' line-up. Enter John Gosling.

For a long time, Ray had been playing simple piano on the band's records, while on those occasions where something more demanding was required, session players such as Nicky Hopkins would be called in. It was finally decided that a professional keyboard player was needed if The Kinks were to consolidate their position as a top touring rock act on the US circuit – most bands, even The Rolling Stones, augmented themselves in this way. Thus it was that John Gosling answered a magazine ad and found himself in front of The Kinks in Morgan Studios. Gosling's audition consisted of playing various keyboard parts from pieces of paper put in front of him by Ray. As John explained to us, he would later find his "audition" surfacing on a hit record. Gosling: "What happened was that Pete Frame, who ran *ZigZag* magazine, used to be my school prefect. I very rarely met him after school, but he knew I was getting cheesed off with music college and so he called me and said there was this job about to go in the magazine's classifieds, looking for someone to do an American tour with quite a big band. We didn't know who the band were, but he gave me the number before the magazine went to press to give me a chance. And so I phoned it. This well-spoken guy answered and told me the tour was with a group called The Kings. I thought, Christ, that sounds like some awful showband. 'The Kings?' I said. He said, 'No, The Kinks.' Oh, God – I went cold when he said that.

"But I went along to Morgan Studios, where they were rehearsing for an album and we did a few tracks, one of which turned out to be 'Lola' the single. As far as I knew they were just demo tapes, but a lot of those sessions went on the album. It's quite unusual for your audition to be on a Number One single. I had no idea how the songs went; they were just chord sequences with a bit of words thrown in. 'Follow these chords, do a few little fills,' he said, and I did. I didn't hear anything for a while after that and then I got a call to say I was in."

Nicky Hopkins was the only other keyboardist who had gone for the job, but the busy sessionist was committed to too many other things. Gosling had to leave the Royal Academy for his nine-week American tour which, in the beginning, had him just augmenting the line-up. After the tour all went silent, while John waited to hear if he'd got the job full time – they'd all gone on holiday. "I finally got the call to go into the studio again," recalls Gosling. "I never actually got told I was a member of the band, but over the next six months I gradually integrated and became one."

Grenville came up with a nickname for the long-haired and bearded keyboard player. Gosling: "We had two managers at the time – they were like the Thompson Twins out of *Tintin*; Robert was the original Kinks singer but he was so bad that Ray stepped in, thank goodness – but it was Grenville who dubbed me John the Baptist, because of the way I looked, and also because I was still a church organist when I joined."

Gosling's nine-week induction into life as a Kink surpassed all expectations. "It got a bit wild," admits John, "but once I got into my stride I joined in and a few hotels suffered. There was an incident where I nearly drowned in San Francisco – I got thrown in the swimming pool by one of the band members. During those nine weeks we got worse and worse; things got silly and we got very drunk. But at the same time we were having to do sessions and TV shows because 'Lola' was just taking off. That was their first trip to America for years because they'd been banned by the Musicians' Union, or something. I never did understand what that was all about."

One of Ray Davies' most memorable hits, 'Lola' is remarkable for a host of reasons. First, and most obviously, it's a great track; from Ray's own Dobro intro to Dave's classy guitar fills and the song's many key and time signature changes, it has "classic" written all over it. Then there are the lyrics. As is quite well known, the song tells the story of an encounter between two people in a nightclub; he, a sexual naive taking his first tentative steps and "she", a big girl with a dark brown voice, who walked like a woman and talked like a man. The upshot of the story is that the young man – sung in the first person by Ray – consummates his relationship with the worldly-wise Lola and the song ends with the gloriously ambiguous line, "I know what I am and I'm glad I'm a man and so's Lola." Now the question is, is Lola glad he's a man or is he glad Lola's really a man?

Ray: "Of course, you had the Andy Warhol set in New York, with people like [transvestite] Candy Darling – who I dated, thinking it was…Candy Darling; I forget his real name." But in the early hours in the club, something came up that made Ray realise he'd made a mistake: "It was the stubble that gave it away," states Davies wryly. The 'Lola' issue can be debated until the cows come home. Suffice to say Ray is keeping quiet, instead enjoying the speculation that seems to consume the superficial Kinks fan – the one who knows all about *Village Green* but has yet to hear it.

Due to the legalities involved in using trademarks (the song's original version used the name Coca-Cola, but as a non-profit-making organisation the BBC were not allowed to mention product names and so the song was unlikely to receive UK airplay), Ray went into Morgan to overdub the words "cherry cola". It was this version that made Number Two in July 1970. ('Lola' also became a Top Ten hit in America, assisting in no small way the band's successful return. However, in true Kinks style there was a two-week delay, as the master tapes were mislaid in transit.)

Ray tells how, due to the song's particularly demanding vocal, he almost hoped 'Lola' would follow his last few releases into oblivion. "I knew I'd have a problem," he explained, "because it starts off in my low register and then when the chorus goes, 'I'm not the world's most…' I've either got to sing it falsetto or take it like a man and sing it out. So in some ways I hoped it wasn't a hit, because I'm going to have to sing this every night for the rest of my life. I'd get varicose veins in my neck and all sorts of problems."

'Lola' was part of another Davies concept compilation, *Lola Versus Powerman And The Moneygoround, Part One* – another catchy little title. The track listing for "Part One" (the mysterious "Part Two" never surfaced) ran as follows: 'The Contenders', 'Strangers', 'Denmark Street', 'Get Back In Line', 'Lola', 'Top Of The Pops', 'The Money-Go-Round', 'This Time Tomorrow', 'A Long Way From Home', 'Rats', 'Apeman', 'Powerman' and 'Got To Be Free'. This set of largely vitriolic jibes against the business side of music – Wace and Collins were not impressed – was unleashed on the British public in late 1970; it didn't chart in its home territory but made the *Billboard* Top 40 early in the new year. Another single culled from the LP was the satirical but self-explanatory 'Apeman', which for some reason Ray sang in a mock West Indian accent. Like 'Lola', it crashed into the UK singles chart of December 1970, where it peaked at Number Five, although somehow the number failed to capitalise of the success of 'Lola' in America.

The activity brought about by The Kinks' new-found UK singles hits and their acceptance in America – including minor invasions of the *Billboard* charts – prepared the band to take on the rest of the '70s. True, the raggle-taggle pop group of the last decade was no more, but Ray, Dave, Mick, Nobby and now John, were about to embark on a whole new era of success.

11 I'LL DO IT MYSELF

In his autobiography, Ray Davies recalls a day at school where he had to take part in an important inter-school relay race. Amid the myriad sports references throughout, this occasion appears remarkable for the insight it gives into the character of Ray. Despite a painful spine problem which meant he started all races, even sprints, from an upright stance, the young Davies was put in at the prestigious yet crucial final leg. The logic of the gym instructor was impeccable: Ray may not have been the fastest on the team, but he was the one who could be relied upon not to let himself be beaten.

On the day, the game plan proved successful and Ray apparently pulled off a stunning victory. Tenacious, resilient and prepared to win at all costs – his working-class roots would not permit the acknowledgment of failure then and they do not now. Several decades after the race in question, that memory serves as a useful metaphor for Davies' life – at least through his own eyes. With the power of supreme authorship and with no hint of a sequel, the autobiography of Ray Davies has The Kinks' history ending in 1973, despite the fact that fewer than half of the group's studio albums had been recorded by then. It is arguably the closest he has come to admitting what has emerged as an all-too-common yet horribly accurate synopsis: The Kinks really were largely finished as a thriving concern by the end of the '60s. A lot since has been little more than keeping the body alive artificially long after the vital organs have died.

Ray in truth denies this version of the facts. "That's a constant problem with The Kinks," he told us. "But I think people are beginning to realise that we have this big catalogue of work other than those early hits. It's the recent work that has sustained us over the years. I like my songs and I like to treat them with the respect they deserve but at the same time not let them overrun the concert."

That's not to say that with hindsight he doesn't know when he's batting on a slippery wicket. Since 1970 he has produced some remarkable work, but the harsh facts cannot be ignored: chart-wise and sales-wise, The Kinks are a commercial spent force and all the unbought brilliant albums in the world cannot alter that. But Ray is without doubt a winner of redoubtable steel and rare ego. In his own mind, the creative merits of the latter work make them worthwhile but even he cannot argue with statistics; in fact he won't even try, although other members of the band admit the truth. "Of course it bothered him when the singles stopped selling," John Dalton concedes. "You're obviously dying for it to be a hit, and when it's not you hurt. But he didn't really show it; he just kept going with the next thing." And so, in his autobiography, he'd rather kill himself off in text than be seen to lose the race. His gym teacher would have been proud.

Of course the group did continue, albeit within different parameters. With the end of The Kinks as the world knew them then and perhaps most people remember them now, changes came about, changes that, in retrospect, may or may not have contributed to the subsequent slide in success, but changes nonetheless. Most significantly for the group, they ended their long-term relationship with Pye. It was 1971 and relationships between the company and the band had become increasingly strained. It might have looked to the casual music observer that the company humoured some of Ray's more esoteric projects with uncharacteristic patience, but there was a price. While concept projects like *The Village Green Preservation Society* and *Arthur* didn't exactly rake in millions, they did keep the band's name in the public's awareness, propelling many nostalgic fans to return to the illustrious back catalogue, courtesy of the record company's budget-priced re-release programme. For a band that still considered itself a vibrant and far from spent force, it seemed unnecessary. Embarrassed to be seen to consign themselves to the Woolworth's bargain bins, they refused to support the re-packaging efforts.

Then there was money. Ray was far from satisfied with the band's slice from the back catalogue sales. He felt the royalty rate an insult to his efforts, adding further impetus to his decision not to support the mid-priced rehashes.

Another project not meeting with his full approval was the band's next full price album. Released in March, *Percy* was the soundtrack to the comedy film of the same name, an obligation that Ray lost considerable interest in as time passed, although it had been his choice to commit to it in the first place: "Like everything else," recalls John Gosling, "if Ray said yes to something, we did it. Except the two brothers always disagreed, so we'd have Dave kicking up and away we'd go for two weeks of arguments. But we'd usually end up doing what Ray wanted."

But the project wasn't a total chore. "No, it was actually quite interesting," John Dalton insists. "Knowing you're doing something for a film that people will watch instead of just a record they'll hear was very odd and quite a challenge."

Despite being in the film, the music was released separately anyway to be their first album of the year. To judge it against their earlier – or indeed later – catalogue is to miss the point of its inception. A pot pourri of differing standards, it shouldn't be made to stand with the proper albums since soundtracks as a genre demand a category of their own. Indeed, as soundtracks go, the band's music for the humourful rompflick was actually not that bad – certainly warranting better treatment than it got at the hands of the film's injudicious editor who butchered the tunes to plug the quieter gaps in the movie rather than use them to add to the mood. "The music might as well have not been there," says Gosling. "It was in the background all the time and you couldn't hear it."

Like, say, Queen's *Flash Gordon* or later versions of The Beatles' *Magical Mystery Tour*, the album fares better in hindsight than it did on release. Today it seems an occasionally delightful curio; then, no doubt, it was a frustratingly inchoate hotch potch and a disappointment to fans.

Among the album's critics was Ray, less happy with the project the longer it dragged on. Keeping as far away from the film's genital obsession as possible ("percy" is slang for penis in England), he somehow managed to salvage some respect from the assignment with a batch of above average numbers, much to the delight of at least one of his band. "The film was just awful," recalls John Gosling, "but the album was really good. Some of the songs off that album are my favourite Kinks songs. 'God's Children' and 'Moments' are brilliant songs and should have gone on a legitimate album."

The opening cut, 'God's Children' certainly is the pick of the pack, a touching call for a return to innocence sung against a fittingly emotive backdrop of strings, courtesy of Stanley Myers. 'Just Friends', too, begins with a child's music box before being replaced by a harpsichord as Ray's lullaby vocal, again against smooth orchestrations, enters. The effect is neat rather than naff, a surprising success in the vein of Ringo Starr's heartfelt vocal on 'Goodnight'; and one not totally lost as a mock Cowardian second voice is introduced.

'Moments' unwittingly continues the slight Beatles theme with Dave's playing owing an obvious debt to George Harrison. Similar in both finesse and style (the descending chord sequence in the solo is pure George), this is just one aspect of a very fine song. Yet again the strings complement Ray's poignant vocal and romantic lyric. Denuded of its film origins, this quite beautiful piece, with Ray declaring that the world isn't going to get him down, matches any of his other ballads.

'The Way Love Used To Be' comes close as well, this time with an acoustic guitar leading the rentastrings. It's another fine song, orchestrated to sound like 'Ruby Tuesday' and, in fact, similar in delivery to Mick Jagger on 'Angie'. The similarities to other songs don't end there, although the earlier roots of 'Dreams' are less controversial, sounding as it does like an alternative arrangement of the band's own 'Apeman'. Taking the self-tribute one stage further, the album's first instrumental is actually a version of 'Lola', played with guts and verve by the electric Dave who turns in a good tribute to Eric Clapton's style of the time, before the track ends 'Day In The Life' style.

Such underrated efforts aside – things can easily be underrated in a 30-album career – *Percy* did have its failings, each one symptomatic of the soundtrack genre. Firstly, of course, via its instrumentals. The awkward blues of 'Completely' appears at odds with the smooth feel of the rest of the record. 'Whip Lady' offers almost no entertainment without the accompanying pictures, and 'Helga', although titularly reminiscent of the film's scantily clad stars, Elke Sommer and Britt Ekland, is empty as a song. Secondly, many such albums descend into pastiche sooner or later and this one is no exception. 'Willesden Green' sees John Dalton singing as a country-style Elvis about the London suburb; amusing on first listen, especially the obligatory sincere talking section, niggling thereafter although never intended as more than a bit of fun. "There are a few silly songs on the album, but none more so than this one," the bemused Dalton admits. "I got to sing so it's probably the worst Kinks track of all time. It was going to be a laugh so Ray said, 'Right, you're doing that one,' and that was that."

Needless to say the film wasn't a stunning success, although that didn't prevent its sequel being commissioned (*Percy's Progress*, featuring a cameo role from a young Barry Humphries, aka Dame Edna Everage, possible star of the 'Lola' lyric). The album suffered more by association than merit, with little made of it by the record company and just one disappointingly under-bought EP, led by 'God's Children', to flag it to the increasingly indifferent singles market.

While the singles and album charts began to flex their disapproving muscles, little could be done to dampen the band's pulling power as a live act. As *Percy* slipped anonymously into and out of record shops, The Kinks embarked on a successful world tour. Kicking off in the UK, it stretched itself to include Europe, America and even a fairly intensive trip around Australia. Nobody emerged unscathed from the experience, and the sprawling flights, poor organisation and unsatisfactory equipment took their toll on everyone.

"Looking back at the gig list for the early years I can't believe we managed it," recalls Gosling. "The first tour was nine weeks, then we had a European tour, but after that they tended to last about three weeks; we'd have enough by then, tempers flaring and everything. There'd be spitting on stage, drums being thrown, stacks getting knocked over, keyboards suffering – generally the equipment taking the punishment and not the people."

John Dalton, relatively unscathed by his years with the band, puts the brothers' relationship squarely at the core of the troubles. "The arguments had set in between Ray and Dave by *Lola*," he explains. "It had been brotherly hate since the early days. The fact that it used to be Dave's group and now it isn't is probably the whole reason for everything. But people's talents will always come out. I know Dave's very talented himself, but Ray's got this special gift. Some of the songs he's written are just amazing; he's got a unique talent."

Whatever their origins, after a while, the on-stage activities became something of a draw in themselves. "It could be a bit hairy, but people actually started to come along just to see the fights," says Gosling. "Even though it was all done away from the PA the audience still managed to pick up on it. It had been going on for years of course, between Mick and Dave, and Dave and Ray."

Tantrums aside, with the band still doing the business on stage, real business affairs were being examined away from it. After a particularly drawn-out legal embroilment, it was finally announced that Pye's claim on the band had expired and that RCA were providing a new home for The Kinks. The failure of recent releases in general, and 'God's Children' in particular, didn't stop the new company's UK bigwig Ken Glancy calling it "a triumphant day for RCA" and "the biggest deal the company has become involved in since becoming independent five years ago". Enthusiastic words, no doubt, but ones that were soon backed up by action as The Kinks were treated to a remarkable launch party at an exclusive New York restaurant. No expense spared on the invited celebrity guests, the final bill clocked in at a little under 5,000 dollars – at last Ray had found someone willing to match his tastes.

At least that's what he thought at first. But despite their obvious delight at snaring the group, good marketing sense restrained RCA's total acquiescence to Davies' every whim and his long desired double concept album was vetoed by the second record company in as many years. Not put off, his next project was to be one of his most celebrated yet. *Muswell Hillbillies*, the punningly titled precursor to groups like The Notting Hillbillies, saw Ray leaving the fantasy world of *Percy* to deal with safer fare: namely himself. Penis jokes and country pastiches left firmly behind, the album saw the results of his examination of his past and the area where he grew up.

In *The Hitch-Hiker's Guide To The Galaxy*, Douglas Adams wrote of a torture so horrendous that no man could survive it with his sanity intact. Essentially, the device caused the victim to appreciate only too well his absolute insignificance in the universe. Although perhaps extreme, there is a case for suspecting that this machine exists and that Ray Davies has survived it somehow. On *Muswell Hillbillies*, he takes his renowned working-class ideals, enforces them with his working-class background and comes up with a sense of class division that is so strong as to impinge on paranoia. The album explores the social divide with powerful skill; throughout, the little man is against the overwhelming control figure, desperate to win, destined to fail. The omniscient "Corporation" prevalent in his autobiography is hinted at here for the first time in the band's career; it would not be the last.

The album's title may have had its roots in the American sit-com *The Beverly Hillbillies*, but it was London that provided the focus. With his songwriter's guard down, more than one heartfelt message was lain before the listeners as Ray explored the post-war cattle-herding approach to inner city housing. Hidden behind the suggestively gloomy sleeve picture of the Archway Tavern, songs of real resentment festered: 'Have A Cuppa Tea' recalls the shame of his 90-year-old grandmother at being moved from her home into an approved flat. The song's title exploits the English belief that any problem, however bad, can be solved by one hot beverage. "She was like a fairy godmother," Ray recalls. "It was a real privilege being with her."

The relocation theme continues in the title track, with the heroes kept within "identical little boxes" and dreaming of American climes. A touching, moody work, Ray sings with the clarity of self-belief and the musicality of the truth, focusing on a real character from his past called Rosie Rooke. 'Oklahoma USA' claims to provide a solution that perhaps tea cannot achieve; anguished yet aspirant. 'Alcohol', on the other hand, offers a more sinister way out.

'Acute Schizophrenia Paranoid Blues' looks at another member of the Davies family, namely the father. Applying a rock 'n' roll treatment to his dad's partying habits, Ray conjures up the sort of clannish resilience seen rarely outside of *EastEnders* and Mafia films. 'Uncle Son' strengthens these claims, with the remnants of a remembered relative taking centre stage in a tale of hard luck ill earned. The world, it is made clear, is not fair. Indeed, one song, 'Complicated Life', says more of Ray's frustration in its title than many songs say in their entire lyric.

Calling the album a hit would perhaps be an exaggeration (it made no impact chart-wise), but a success, yes. Both in the minds of its author and its audience, the work struck nerves and memories to the extent that, 23 years later, the title track was plucked for inclusion on the band's "live in a studio" album *To The Bone*, with a touching intro from Ray. "I think it's definitely one of our better albums," John Dalton avers. "There are a lot of good songs on there; some different ones and some good ones. And it's probably the best album cover of them all. We took ages to get that picture of us in the pub right."

With the landmark honesty of *Muswell Hillbillies*, Ray looked inward into himself as a person. As a consequence, though its stars were Dave Davies' family as much as Ray's, the album showed the cracks in group sovereignty appearing for the first time. Like individuals in the British government are compelled to be ruled by the cabinet's decisions, the rest of the band found themselves having to adopt Ray's personal grievances in song as their own, although in truth they were no closer to the subject matter than the audience.

More so than ever before, Ray was emerging as the solo star of what used to be a band. He'd always written the songs, of course, but now he had virtually written out the rest of the group. Even Dave was a musician for hire, although the younger brother was loath to admit it: "It's by no means a dictatorship," he told the *NME*. "He can get upset, but he will compromise. Otherwise, there would be no working relationship at all."

In December 1971, a distinct lack of compromise saw The Kinks part company with Robert Wace after eight extremely lucrative years. Like the band itself, this "working relationship", although once fruitful, had eventually failed to respond to the elastic demands of those within it. With The Kinks changing as an act on every recent record, and those records pivoting on Ray's caprice, Wace couldn't have expected to keep up indefinitely.

His exit, following that of Collins earlier, meant that, in terms of sheer numbers, The Kinks were a holed ship. Whatever Ray might have felt about his own powers, it couldn't be ignored that they had lost one of the players batting for their own team. Wace, in fact, pictured himself as Ray's partner, opening the innings against any opposition. With the rest of the band largely unconsulted, it was left to him, he claims, to steer Ray: "He's with a bunch of musicians who are not enthusiastic about what he does. You need somebody there who's an enthusiast, who'll say, 'That's terrific,' so that he's almost making a record for you. I was able to make reasonable criticisms that he would accept."

Wace's egress was all the more surprising for his integral role in the decision-making, but, as John Gosling recalls, there was blame – and a price to pay – on both sides: "Ray was desperate to get a lot of things done that just didn't seem to be getting done when Robert and Grenville were around, and he thought, 'Right, I'll do it myself.' I can understand his attitude at the time, but I think it damaged us."

The damage would not become apparent immediately, and so it was with the liberating sense of a load lightened that Ray alone led the group into the new year. But like a coiled spring released from its box, he soon expanded to fill every possible area – and not always with the best results. Proof of this came with the band's February tour of America. It began traditionally enough, with stage japes attracting as much attention as the songs, but Davies soon instigated a change that was to dominate their gigs for the rest of the decade: he added a brass section. Guessing at Wace's probable reaction were he still involved provides a diverting pastime today, but ultimately it's a redundant activity. The fact of the matter stands that Ray had autonomously altered the very core of The Kinks – from one of the hardest, rockingest acts around to jazzed-up showband in a stroke – and on little more than a whim. Before the end of the decade, he would do much worse.

12 TRYING TO DO THE DECENT THING

Hindsight is both a gift and a curse, potentially the greatest ally but often our keenest foe. Who can say whether The Kinks' slide away from chart success could be attributed to one factor? Certainly the band lost more than their audience: their direction seemed to evaporate with every passing year. Comparisons with other groups offer the slightest help. In 1970, as The Kinks waved goodbye to the Hit Parade in the UK, The Beatles split up, thus being spared the despair of a dwindling fan base. While they were together, the Fab Four set standards unmatched in music, adroitly transforming themselves from mop-topped live wires into cultured studio craftsmen early on in their short career. Orchestras and extra instrument augmentation were nothing the group hadn't tried, perfected and rejected by 1970 – still months before The Kinks even began to experiment with the brass section on *Muswell Hillbillies*. Consequently, when Davies did attempt the change in style, arguably his guitar-based market niche was already too well established and no amount of persuasion was going to alter that.

And so it was that, in his first days of control, Ray brought in the brass section. To his liberated mind, the success of The Mike Cotton Sound on *Muswell Hillbillies* suggested greater things: "When we perform live without the brass, the songs lose a lot of their character," was his reading of the situation. John Gosling disagrees: "I didn't think the brass was right," he remembers. "I liked soul brass sections, things like Tamla Motown; but not old music hall brass. Mike and the other two were just great; but the sound of a three-piece brass section playing 'You Really Got Me' just sounded awful. And then the girl backing singers came along and that just put the tin hat on it. I didn't enjoy that period at all, and all along there were promises that they'd drop them; and then after I left they did."

Even the placid John Dalton wasn't impressed by the move. "It's all right doing the records with them, and on tour we had a laugh with Mike Cotton," he explains, "but we added more and more people and we got away from the real band. It wasn't just 'You Really Got Me' they played on, though; there were lots like that. I guess if you're paying them to be there, they might as well do something. But it just didn't fit." In the end Ray was the only one of the core band satisfied. "Yeah, nobody liked it, but I don't suppose we really let him know because that's what he wanted."

In the final analysis, of course, one man paid the wages and the others received them. Ray won the day, and the next and the one after that. With Wace gone, there was no one to question his movements, whether it be a live brass ensemble or that long hoped for double album. Given that Wace claims to have salvaged 'Lola' after two less successful attempts, it may be supposed that the things he and Collins were delaying on were hardly worthy of the attention Ray accorded them. As if to test the point or even prove it, The Kinks' next album was the high-reaching *Everybody's In Show-Biz, Everybody's A Star*, an ambitious project comprising basically two separate halves: a live set and a complete new studio collection. At last it was the double album Ray had so long been denied.

For all its luxury, however, the actual LP was the tip of Ray's creative iceberg. He'd originally envisaged a film made to accompany it, met with opposition at RCA and eventually funded the project himself. Essentially plotless, the film took the theme explored on the album, namely that of star excess and life on the road. A constant swirl of parties and partiers mingled with action shots of the band filled the screen – at least they would have done, were it actually shown anywhere. With both Ray and even RCA unable to find a commercial outlet for the film, it disappeared as yet another project that never was.

More than ever before, Ray was ahead of his time with the film idea. The Beatles and other groups had successfully diversified into this area over the years, but no one had taken on the medium of film so specifically with the intention of exploiting it, of making it sell the music. Ten years later, the video age would welcome the band's advances with open arms, providing the perfect aperture for Ray's cinematic aspirations to fill; the band's '80s return to the UK Top Ten would later come, after all, with the video success of 'Come Dancing'.

But in 1972, the time for commercial video, most notably pioneered via Queen's 1975 promo film 'Bohemian Rhapsody', was several years off and The Kinks' project failed. And yet as one idea sank, another seemingly audacious venture took off as *Everybody's In Show-Biz, Everybody's A Star* made its way from planning stage and into the record shops. Cream's double album *Wheels Of Fire* had suggested the format a few years earlier, and so the split live and studio concept wasn't unheard of. And yet, despite RCA's hopes, The Kinks were not the unit-shifting certainty they had once been and an expensive exercise of this nature seems surprising in hindsight. Of course, the record company may have seen the live album as more likely to attract the band's vast numbers of lost fans. Just as Sony in 1995 issued the commercially challenged Michael Jackson's new studio album *HIStory* alongside a Greatest Hits disc, RCA undoubtedly saw The Kinks' live use of tried and tested hits as a surefire way of attracting disillusioned buyers to the band's new material. Sadly – from the marketing division's point of view, at least – even this certainty wasn't to be.

Introducing The Mike Cotton Sound to the tour of 1972 was not Ray's token attempt to alter the live essence of a Kinks show. As if the brass ensemble didn't dilute the pure rock experience enough, the eclectic singer took to delivering bursts of way-out show tunes to further cabaret-ise the band. For the purposes of the tour, classics like 'You Really Got Me' were present and accounted for as ever, but so were things like 'You Are My Sunshine'. The rockers of only the year before had become the all-singing, all-dancing Kinks revue, and consequently, when it came for the album to be put together, the selection of live songs showed further signs of a band out of sync with its original fan base. In the end, no sign of 'You Really Got Me'; in fact, no major hits at all bar a rousing audience-heavy rendition of 'Lola'. Instead, cabaret ditties like

'Baby Face', 'Mr Wonderful' and 'Banana Boat Song' take up a quarter
of the tracks, with the remainder heavily drawing on *Muswell Hillbillies*
– as if people had forgotten it already. In short, not the album RCA had
perhaps hoped for, as Gosling recalls.

"I don't know if Ray was trying to make a statement," he says, "but
he put the worst tracks on the live side; they were rubbish. Old music
hall songs, all the camp stuff at the expense of the decent hits. At the
time you wonder what the hell he's doing, but in hindsight he was
obviously making a statement about the band. It wasn't just about hits
for him. But of course it didn't sell very well so I don't know if anyone
got the point." John Dalton: "Oh yeah, we put all the silly ones on. It
was a strange choice."

Ray's vision of The Kinks can be pointed at and, if necessary, blamed
for the group's direction with the live side of the album. But, as Dave
has said, Ray only led where no one did. In fact, more than 20 years
later, the elder brother is as unsure of himself as ever: "I was thinking
the other day," he told *Mojo*, "I'm the lead singer and I always stand on
the right on stage. It's very odd. It's because psychologically I don't think
I'm the lead singer. It hasn't sunk in yet." False modesty aside, Dave has
this to say on the talents of his brother as a singer: "He's a very good
communicator," he told us. "Over the years, he's evolved the art of
communication, although sometimes it's happened due to necessity,
when things weren't going very well."

As tracks like 'Lola' on *Show-Biz* testify, record sales may have
slowed, but in front of an audience the band still commanded respect.
Ray plays the crowd like marionettes in the hands of a master puppeteer
and the result is as successful a finale as you could imagine. The
camped-up fun songs sound like good ideas at the time, but as an eternal
recorded memento they don't stand up, like a joke on its second telling.
From the *Muswell Hillbillies* selection, the best songs are the title track
and the portentous 'Alcohol'. The band whip up the right degree of
sleazy charm and the increasingly theatrical Ray hams up his vocal with
inebriated glee (and obvious real experience) while the audience throw
themselves into the role of pub scene extras with boozy abandon. "It
was surprising, but that song, 'Alcohol', was one of the biggest stage

hits," Dalton reminisces. "Although it wasn't a chart hit, everybody knew it and it was part of the act; it was expected for us to play it, along with 'You Really Got Me' and 'Waterloo Sunset' and that. It went down well because Ray got into it, although he wasn't that great a drinker. A few of the lads liked a drink – and lots of it – but he kept pretty much away from that, until it came to that song."

But, the occasional highlight aside, the live content of *Show-Biz* never looked like anything more than a bloated liberty committed to tape. With its focus on cabaret numbers and too-recent albums, it failed to win back the meandering listeners. Quite unexpectedly, it was the studio side which came closest in this respect. The first track released from the sessions in May was 'Supersonic Rocket Ship', a finely played calypso pastiche. The song went Top 20 in the UK and the band were invited to appear on *Top Of The Pops* once again to promote it. That appearance remains memorable for several reasons, not least because it marks the group's last major hit for more than a decade, but largely because Ray celebrated the occasion by allegedly pouring beer over glam rockers Slade, who were also appearing on the show.

Undoubtedly a decent pop number, 'Supersonic' was outshone on the album's later release by at least one other track – the staggering 'Celluloid Heroes'. Record historian and broadcaster Paul Gambaccini is among its fans: "'Celluloid Heroes' was one of the most perfectly realised pieces of pop to come out in 1972," he notes in his 1985 essay on The Kinks, and he is not wrong. For once turning his attentions away from his beloved England, Ray took the American fascination with celebrity to task in this abrasive yet moving number. Manufacturing a kind of modern-day Gloria Swanson from *Sunset Boulevard* character, it celebrates the pros and cons of the business of being famous. Gambaccini: "It poignantly placed the private person behind the Hollywood star alongside the fantasy figure created by the myth-making machine, and contrasted both with the inadequate narrator who felt the need in himself to yearn for the cinematic immortality even he knew was illusory."

The tone of 'Celluloid Heroes' was nothing new. Ray looked at the fantasy existence of the fading star with the same ironic eye he'd focused with in 'Apeman'. And yet the subtext was Hollywood and not London – the well-travelled writer had finally thrown the doors of his mind open to new resources and was flourishing with the result. Bela Lugosi, Bette Davis, Marilyn, Rooney and Garbo are all used as lyrical fodder by the wistful narrator. Like the band's own movie-that-wasn't, he looks at the film star with a jealous gaze. Whatever ills befall them on screen, the actors walk away unlike those of us cursed by living real lives. To Ray, the stars have the advantage because "celluloid heroes never really die".

Hidden beneath these wistful longings is a similarity to Ray's own position usually overlooked. It's not just movie stars who hang around, as he would have us believe. Consider the "girl" of 'You Really Got Me', the heroine of 'Lola' or even the character in 'Dedicated Follower Of Fashion': each one as famous as its creator, and destined to remain so long after Ray has gone. Despite his multimedia yearnings, the elder Davies brother is as responsible for some immortal slices of cultural work as any cameraman – if he'd only believe it himself.

John Gosling, for all his harsh words on the live selection, is a firm fan of the studio half. "I couldn't believe the live stuff when it came out," he sighs, "but some of the new songs were excellent. 'Celluloid Heroes' was just a fantastic song. We did that at Morgan Studios at about three o'clock in the morning, just laid down the backing track and piano parts and everything. For some reason, because we were so tired the mood was just right and it became the highlight of the album. Even now, I think it's one of the best songs he's written." During the session there was even one of those moments which made a lot of the bad times worthwhile: "When it came to recording the vocal track, I was amazed. You have to stand in awe of someone who can write lyrics like that, that good. The sad thing was, lyrics didn't really matter back in the '70s. No one was listening, and he was like a fish out of water. But I always liked them, and that was a great moment for me. It was a shame he never found a niche like Bob Dylan or Paul Simon so it didn't matter what we did."

The remainder of the studio selection on *Show-Biz* is a mixed bag as far as both quality and styles are concerned. 'Sitting In My Hotel' follows closely from 'Heroes' in majesty and in subject matter. From movies back to music, the song exposes with cynical precision the sheer emptiness of the rock 'n' roller's private life. Away from the audiences' love, the roadies' attentions and the follow-spot's glare, pop stars have to exist in the real world beginning with the lonely, at times soul-destroying hotel lifestyle – not at all like they show it in the movies. Very often the lure of alcohol – itself a song on the live side – provided the only comfort during the months on the road. And for once, Ray spoke for all the band with this lyric: "It doesn't matter how luxurious your surroundings are," Dave confirms, "you go back to your hotel room and it's like a prison. We used to do eleven-, twelve-, 13-month tours of America and leave our families at home because we couldn't afford to bring them over. It was hell."

The album's travelogue feel continues through tracks like 'Motorway', 'You Don't Know My Name' and 'Unreal Reality', each offering itself as a diary entry for the band on the road with differing tones and mostly average success, apart from the occasional fan: "'Sitting In My Hotel' was really good, and the one about motorway food I really liked as well," Gosling recalls. But where each half is essentially unremarkable, as a joint package there is the presentation of both the live experience and, via the studio portion of *Show-Biz*, a fair look behind the scenes of a rock tour.

While *Everybody's In Show-Biz* marked the band's return to the record scene with its portrayal of the road life, the real thing was still in full swing as usual. The year had begun with excursions into foreign climes but, as winter approached, the band were pleasing audiences closer to home. Among the London venues were two gigs renowned more for their name than their size, each places where audiences mattered. Fittingly, both the Imperial College and the Rainbow Theatre saw The Kinks on top form with no hint of a band on the wane, whatever record sales were suggesting, and so another year closed to the screams of adoring fans.

Venue-wise, 1973 would itself become remarkable for the band's choice of London locations. None of them particularly significant at the time of booking, each serves as a pertinent bookmark in retrospect. The first, the historic Theatre Royal at Drury Lane, saw The Kinks' most extravagant performances to date. Appearing quite fittingly in the heart of the West End's Theatreland in January, the band set about presenting their own history in music; a sort of self-addressed *This Is Your Life* with Ray as Michael Aspel or Ralph Edwards. But instead of wheeling on hordes of back-slapping B-teamers from yesteryear, The Kinks' show featured themselves and some very special guests – their music. Drawing largely on the *Village Green* album for the core of the performance, since this was the project closest to Ray's heart, the evening also aired some of the more memorable 45s from the band's illustrious and popular past. 'Waterloo Sunset', 'Sunny Afternoon' and 'A Well Respected Man' were all included, much to the audience's enjoyment, although perhaps not Ray's, as John Gosling reveals: "I always felt for him when he used to go out and all they wanted was 'Sunny Afternoon' and he was trying to get the new stuff across. A lot of the songs were really good but audiences – in England especially; America was more receptive – just didn't want to know. That had its own effect, of course, because he'd work so hard at getting a 'hit' sound that he lost his way musically and what decent stuff he did get after a while he over-produced away."

On paper, Drury Lane might not seem the obvious place to host a rock show, but then The Kinks were no longer ordinary rockers and by 1973 they'd left the notion of a rock show some way behind. With the vaudevillian dabblings of the previous year encapsulated for all to hear on the *Show-Biz* album, Ray and co now took things further. The brass section that had escorted the *Muswell Hillbillies* tour was adjudged to have worked, despite Gosling's misgivings, and so a six-piece ensemble augmented the London gig. Not only that, but the group also added half a dozen backing singers to create that authentic chorus line effect.

The extended cast wasn't the only change planned for the evening's performance on 14 January. Still infatuated by the medium of film, as pined for in 'Celluloid Heroes' and as proven by the accompanying movie made for *Everybody's In Show-Biz*, Ray introduced a slide projector designated to imbue the sounds of the songs with images of the age. For the purposes of history, it doesn't matter that on the night the machinery let him down and the filmic backdrop never appeared; what does matter is that his growing fascination with another vehicle for his art was seen to be evolving at the expense of the music.

The show in the end went ahead with Ray enjoying the more theatrical aspects of the occasion and the audience getting their kicks most obviously from the unleashed rock moments – Dave's flash-started fiery rendition of 'You Really Got Me' would have melted the most stern of listeners' hearts. But overall, as was becoming the tendency, there was confusion: the dichotomy that placed the "greatest hits" credentials of the band up against Ray's desire to go forward and upward, never looking back. "I don't think I could do tours just to feed people's memories," Ray told us. "The great thing about live concerts is you had to be there. It's a theatrical moment."

The step from theatrical moments to momentous theatrics is not large, and flushed with the concept – although frustrated by the delivery – Ray was eager to push onwards with his meisterplan. The rock show was finished. The band would take a proper show on the road to little theatres and play in a variety hall style, blending film with music, history with the future. Enraptured with the idea, Ray pursued its outcome with undaunting passion, seemingly possessed with the need to prove himself right. By March, he had the soundtrack to the shows ready, produced at a punishingly efficient rate. But it was not enough – the project was postponed while more songs were tried, more hours were put in and more nights passed without proper sleep for Davies.

The second significant venue for the band in 1973 was the Royal Festival Hall. Before a largish audience and several home press, The Kinks turned in a not-unimpressive show. The promises of something spectacularly different hadn't been upheld – yet – but Ray was working on it. He was working on it very hard indeed, so hard that he failed to spot the danger signs appearing in his marriage. Or, if he did detect them, rather than confront the problem, he threw himself further into his work – which is how the trouble started in the first place, and which is why, in June 1973, Rasa Davies left her husband, taking their two daughters away with her.

Whether or not Ray loved Rasa with any real feeling is debatable because, like so many before and since, he allowed his work to dominate their lives. But certainly he had invested a hell of a lot emotionally in their relationship. Despite Dave's camera-ready looks and extrovert personality, Ray had been the media's focus and the groupies' target. Unfortunately, with a pregnant wife forced on him by circumstance (admittedly, he played a part in that circumstance), he found himself living the single pop star's life vicariously through the dirty deeds of young, immature Davies Jr. While the others relished the sex-on-tap touring lifestyle, Ray – the one without whom none of it would have been possible, of course – was obliged to behave, or at least be seen to behave. No great sacrifice for a man in love, but a task for a young man just trying to do the decent thing.

Whatever the intricacies of their relationship, the compounded effect of Rasa's departure – and at her own insistence; she was the one thing that Ray hadn't fully seized control of yet – on his own work-addled brain was disastrous. He was hospitalised after taking an overdose of drugs and when, barely a week later, he went ahead and appeared at the White City Stadium dishevelled and drawn yet seemingly buoyant, it came as a shock to most spectators. As the show wore on, his chirpy stage banter assuaged most doubts about his welfare – which made it all the more stunning when he kissed Dave, took hold of the microphone and announced to a nonplussed stadium that he had had enough. Ray Davies was retiring from music. For good.

13 PRETEND LIKE NOTHING HAD HAPPENED

"What made me realise I could do this was when I saw The Beatles on *Top Of The Pops* and noticed that they didn't have a real singer, just singing guitarists. I thought then that we could go on and do it because they were just ordinary guys like us" – Ray Davies in conversation with the authors in 1993.

The idea that stars are born is a notion often tossed around the pop ether but, a couple of notable exceptions aside, the role of cultural icon is often bestowed on the unlikeliest shoulders. When Raymond Douglas Davies first saw The Beatles, he had little idea that he would soon be appearing on the same shows as them, hustling for the same Number One chart position as them and, sadly, be suffering the same tribulations of mass success. Who would have imagined in 1963 when the four cherubic-faced lads from Liverpool first appeared with 'Love Me Do' that they would go on to have affairs, indulge in drugs and – worst of all, as far as many parents in the '60s were concerned – grow their hair long. Paul McCartney ended that group, of course, in 1970 after seven short years at the toppermost of the poppermost. Notably during that time, he'd assumed the role of dominant while the others – happy-go-lucky Ringo Starr, eager-to-please George Harrison and even the giant personality of John Lennon – were either content to be led or too distracted to prevent it. And so it was, when he felt like it, when he'd prepared his own solo project, that he called it a day on behalf of the others.

The parallels barely need articulation. For what had been Lennon's group, read Dave Davies'. Where the latterly superior songwriter McCartney had unilaterally decided on splitting the group, replace with

Ray. "The Beatles made it possible for a lot of people," Ray told us, little guessing the significance of those words.

Unlike Paul McCartney, however, Ray didn't have a complex masterplan in his head, he wasn't following any solo career plan or goal list. In truth, it still remains a mystery as to whether he meant to say what he did that summer's night. Certainly his own office had not been primed, and in fact Marion Rainford, the band's press secretary, was quick off the mark delivering a sanitised explanation of events. "One has to understand that Ray is in a very emotional, confused state," she explained, laying the problem at the door of Rasa's departure. "But I must say that neither The Kinks nor I believe for one moment that Ray really will quit the business. He's a grieving man and he made an emotional statement."

John Gosling for one wasn't convinced that Ray would be back. Nobody in the band had seen it coming and the future looked bleak. "He was a real mess at the time," he remembers with pity. "Nobody knew that he was going to announce his retirement on stage; certainly nobody knew he was going to do it with a can of beer balanced on his head. He used to put across this persona of being a bit of a lad and a drinker but really he wasn't like that. But at White City I think he was really out of it for once, and shortly after that he tried to commit suicide."

"I think Ray was going through a nervous breakdown by that stage," Dalton admits. "He was so emotionally upset. We knew he wasn't right, so we didn't really know what to believe when he said he was finishing. It was a total shock and it didn't settle for months."

With the confusion abounding, plans were even discussed whereby Dave would continue as frontman in a worst-case scenario. A waiting game ensued, during which time Ray convalesced with his brother's help. "I thought we'd really split up because I didn't hear anything," says Gosling. "I called Dave and he didn't know anything either. But then Dave went to visit Ray in the hospital, Ray came home to recuperate and before you know it we were all back in the studio again." Dalton: "It was all quiet for ages, people kept phoning up and we didn't know what was going on. Then he just decided he wanted to work again. To be honest, even then I don't think he was totally better, and he's been a different person ever since." The whole problem had arisen, of course, when his wife had left him and for once he had no control over the situation. "A couple of other people have left him since then," the bass player quips, "so he's got used to it by now."

For Dave Davies, the horrors of White City were compounded by the fact that, for all their rows, Ray was his brother.

"God, that was horrible," Dave told us. "That was when Ray tried to top himself. I thought he looked a bit weird after the show – I didn't know he'd taken a whole bloody bottle of weird-looking psychiatric drugs. It was a bad time. Ray suddenly announced he was going to end it all – it was around the time his first wife left him. It was a terribly tragic time. She'd left him and taken the kids on his birthday, just to twist the blade a bit more. I went round Ray's house and I saw him through the window, sitting there like a sad old man staring at the phone – it was fucking awful. He came close to death.

"I think he took the pills before the show. I said to him towards the end that he was getting a bit crazy. I didn't know what happened – I suddenly got a phone call saying he was in hospital. I remember going to the hospital after they'd pumped his stomach and it was bad. We looked at each other and we looked around, and some guy had died a bed or two up. They'd taken all his stuff but they'd left his boots and me and Ray just burst out laughing. I mean, it's not a thing to laugh about, but the thing that's kind of kept me and Ray together in a lot of ways is this kind of special sense of humour. It kind of makes everything okay. It's one of those things that people who are very close have. You can impart a lot of information and communicate a lot between each other without really saying anything. To anybody else, they'd think this pair of boots was really sad, but we thought it was hilarious.

"Then he spent some time with me, and we started digging out some old Chuck Berry records and realised why we started doing it all in the first place. And somehow he dragged himself out of that horrible place – I know what it's like because I've been there: I visited that horrible place a few years later. It was a particularly horrible period."

The first the public knew of the outcome of the months of rumour and inactivity came in September, when Ray issued the following statement: "Several weeks ago, I wrote a letter to the world. It turned out to be a letter to me. But I do feel that I made a decision, whether emotionally motivated or not, to change the format of the band. The White City was not a good place to say goodbye. The sun wasn't shining, my shirt was not clean, and anyway rock festivals have never held many happy memories for me personally. The Kinks are close enough now to work as a team in whatever they do, and anyone who believes they are only my back-up band is very mistaken. There are still things to extract from The Kinks on an artistic level – whether or not it turns out to be commercial remains to be seen."

Two things leap out from Ray's defence, and seemingly both opposing stances. The refutation that he is a solo act backed by hired hands is to be applauded but questioned – especially given his desire to experiment when the rest of the group would have been happier continuing down the rock trail that they had arrived along. Sentiment aside, just about the truest line expresses Ray's doubts about the commercial viability of some of his products – at last the coming to terms with slipping success.

The press release had the effect of showing to the world a man back at the helm, but in truth matters were a little different. "We all had to pretend like nothing had happened," Gosling remembers, "so there was this strange atmosphere in the studio all the time. Ray was doing weird things like walking around with glasses with no lenses in and nobody was supposed to say anything. No one did until one of our roadies went up to Ray and said, 'What are those glasses for – reading or long distance?' and we all fell about. He'd said what everyone had been thinking but daren't say."

Whatever his outward appearance, having removed the cumbersome management level from the organisation, an obviously on-the-ball Ray now turned his attentions towards grasping as much control for himself – and the others, of course – from other areas. One project that he was not alone in wanting to succeed was the setting up of a studio for the band. Here, at their surprisingly well-equipped facility in Tottenham Lane, Hornsey, they would be free to pursue all manner of recording experiments without the all-seeing eye of the record company worrying as costs escalate. In the coming months, the studio would take the name "Konk", which it would also share with the group's fledgling record label. Now if Ray could only control album sales.

But all that was yet to come. Still in the last months of 1973, the band remained employed by RCA, through whom they finally released the album that had been recorded way back in March. Called *Preservation Act I*, it contained several of the new songs premiered during the Drury Lane extravaganza. Given the fact that it was completed before the recent "retirement", it's little surprise that the album takes a strongly narrative approach and holds nothing back in its theatrical ambitions – hardly supportive of Ray's claim for them all to be a real band again, but 100 per cent confirmation that new artistic challenges were going to be tackled.

Sadly, the result was not the bumper Christmas success the band hoped for. The very title seemed off-putting, with *Act I* suggesting something quite incomplete. In truth it was only half of the story, although the same marketing ruse was employed by George Michael in the '80s on his as-yet-unsequelled *Listen Without Prejudice Volume One* to no detrimental effect.

Extraneous reasons aside, the real cause of the limited sales was, it has to be said, the weakness of the material. The camped up troubadour of *Everybody's In Show-Biz* makes a more formal return, but in this complicated concept work its influence is more a distraction than anything else. Taking the album as a single piece is actually quite difficult, since there is something of a linear plot running throughout and several main characters recurring to tell their separate tales. Slightly adjusting the thinking behind *Muswell Hillbillies* and mapping it onto the milieu created on *Village Green*, Ray conjures up a sociological landscape defined by the rapacious advances of capitalism in one corner and the poor, innocent country dweller overrun by modernisation in the other. For his players, he presents the Arthur Daley-meets-Alan B'stard character of Flash, the maverick Cliff Richard-in-*Summer-Holiday*-type rebel of Johnny Thunder and the all-seeing but downtrodden Tramp, and Ray laps up the challenge of each characterisation. Arguably, he has always played a role, whatever the song; but the obvious stage designation of *Act I* meant he took each song more like a virtuoso audition piece than as a pop song aimed at an established market.

The main victims of the recent *Good Old Days* music-hall approach were several half-decent songs, namely 'Demolition' and 'Money And Corruption', both actually tolerable efforts beneath the "cor blimey" stage school delivery. Backed by the increasingly ferocious brass arsenal and the Drury Lane chorus line, such tracks pinned their colours firmly to the rock musical mast erected by Lloyd Webber and Rice – except that even by this stage Lloyd Webber and Rice were known for their strong tunes, of which there is an audible dearth on *Preservation*.

'Cricket' sets itself up nicely as the perfect topic for Ray Davies, Professional Englishman, and to a certain extent it succeeds. But again the tune is unworthy of the elaborate and incisive lyrics, and the less said about the affected delivery the better. On a happier note, the guise of Johnny Thunder gets to rumble to raucous effect on 'One Of The Survivors', showing that Ray can still cut it live if he wants to and that Dave leads a hell of a tight rock 'n' roll band with some of the most emotive guitar work on the album. Moodier numbers are attributed to the Tramp persona, which Davies seems to fit as comfortably as a real mendicant's shabby old coat. 'Where Are They Now?' looks back to when the sun was hotter, the sea was wetter and The Kinks were successful. It works because Ray is still visible behind the mask and not obliterated by some grotesque visage.

And so it goes on. Years of listening to *Preservation Act I* haven't made it distinctly any more palatable: 'Morning Song' perhaps grows as an opener and 'Sweet Lady Genevieve' tugs closer to the heart strings, but 'Sitting In The Midday Sun' still seems like a joint rewrite of 'Sunny Afternoon' and 'Sitting By The Riverside' – and that was never necessary. Yet again the band had produced with some effort a work of almost universal insignificance. It went largely unbought and boded ill for its anticipated sequel and, more drastically, the concomitant stage play based on the songs.

Perhaps the pressure of earlier events in the year surrounding his impending marriage break-up had drained him, but the songwriting evident on *Preservation* lacked most of the trademark hooks and twists and soaraway melodies on which Ray had set his store. As a singer, he was better than anyone else in the band; as a guitarist, he was competent enough to accompany Dave on electrics and pick his way on an acoustic; but as a songwriter, Ray Davies, in his day, had few peers and that is why overblown escapades like *Act I* seem so shallow. The problem was not in its diffusion; after all, Ray has always liked to blend styles. "I draw my influences from all sorts of music," he told us. "From country music, from classical music and from blues. I felt close to blues players like Big Bill Broonzy but also to the classic songwriters like Cole Porter. I love great tunes; I love construction."

Ray's structuralist influences are certainly in evidence on the production and concept sides of *Preservation*, and perhaps Cole Porter's wit is somewhere in 'Cricket', but the passion for tunes seems somewhat over-emphasised, given the end result. Lucky then, perhaps, that he has his reputation as a wordsmith to fall back on. Ray: "Lyrics are very important to me, but I try to keep them out of my psyche. I think about them a lot and write lots of them down and my mind goes through a kind of process of elimination." Regardless of quality, he still believes in the good old-fashioned "tune before words" approach. "Yes, I write lyrics to fit a tune because otherwise they get carried away."

Being a songwriter has its downside as well as its up, of course. In an interview on Radio 1 in the mid '80s, the young pop star Kim Wilde was asked how she was coping now that her hits were beginning to dry up. Her reply was pragmatic and pertinent to the story of Ray Davies and many like him. "It doesn't really affect me that much," she responded. "But it's my brother and dad who really suffer because they write my songs. It's them I feel for when a record doesn't chart."

And so it was with The Kinks. He'd publicly denied it was a one-act show, but at the same time Ray was openly steering the ship and it fell entirely to him to fuel the engines. The rest of the band, Dave included, were relatively happy just to be working; anything else was a bonus. And yet for Ray, each successive failure smacked of public humiliation which on a good day he shrugged off, but on a bad day wounded him deeply. "I'm basically remembered as the man who wrote 'Waterloo Sunset' and all those other Pye singles," he admits, "and that's great, in a way but, every time I do new work, it's a barrier."

When it came for the annual tour of America, Ray admitted the truth, albeit in an exhausting fashion. As well as mounting the full *Preservation* show, replete with costumes and stage sets, The Kinks also provided a full rock 'n' roll warm-up show. John Gosling: "We had a big crew that swallowed up all the money with projections and costumes, but it was a laugh. We dressed up and all played these various characters and that was fun. But in America, we'd go out first as ourselves and do about an hour-and-a-half warm-up show, then come off, change and go back and do the full two-hour show. In LA, I think we actually broke the record when we did two double shows; we went in at four in the afternoon and finished at two in the morning."

"We had this cult following in America and they just wanted the early stuff," John Dalton admits wryly. "They wanted the hits, and in the *Preservation* set, we weren't delivering. That aside, it was a long show, but it was interesting doing it. It's all changed now with these videos, but then we were working with slides and it was like an old orchestra doing a film score – we had to watch the slides and come in at the right bit. All the films went along with what we were playing, so there was one for 'Demolition' and another for the others.

"The actual show went like a play, but even today I don't know where it came from. I look at the album now and it's a strange mixture of characters; I don't know where Ray got them from. I was supposed to be Che Guevara, I think, Mick was one of the Krays and John Gosling was a vicar – I just don't know where they came from. Dave was Mr Black, but that was out of the plot, and of course Ray was Mr Flash. We just stood there and played, but Ray was doing his big acting part; all the costume changes, leaping about the stage."

The attempts at theatre tried out originally on *Village Green* had finally been realised. "We had the lot," recalls Gosling. "The sets, the backdrops, costumes and costume changes for Ray and the girls. It was just like a travelling circus, really, but without the fun. Everybody got on everyone's nerves and nobody liked all the extra people; there were so many to rehearse that soundchecks took four hours. It was chaos. The projectionist used to get the slides in upside down and Ray would go mad, but that would cheer the rest of us up."

The next barrier went up in the spring of 1974 with the release of a brand new single, the return to form, jugband-sounding 'Mirror Of Love'. Cynics of the band's proffered solidarity were proved correct when it emerged that the track was actually Ray's original demo featuring him playing every instrument apart from mandolin and brass contributions (which were left to Dave). It wasn't a surreptitious manoeuvre by Ray to sideline the group; rather, morale was apparently so poor that recording sessions for the track had been aborted before the song was finished.

As was becoming the norm, 'Mirror Of Love' was put out and left to fend for itself as the band set off for foreign parts when they should have been at home on the promotion trail. The level of Kinks worship Stateside meant that things went relatively well, but soon the band were back home to prepare for the June release of their next project, the adventurously titled *Preservation Act II*.

Before that could happen, however, there was the small matter of Ray's solo career to be accounted for. (Dave's plans for a solo record had been shelved the previous Christmas, otherwise he would have been the first to step away from the group.) At last a personal dream had come true because Granada Television – makers over the years of the award-winning shows *Coronation Street, Brideshead Revisited* and *Jeeves & Wooster* – had asked Ray to write a TV play that had as its theme the idea of songwriting. Accepting with little notion of how to fit in the time, Ray somehow pulled it off. Building on the thoughts behind the road album *Everybody's In Show-Biz*, he crafted a half-hour show starring himself as the "Starmaker", a non-entity who believes himself a successful composer. An artistic success, the project undoubtedly served some psychological advantage, also: Ray's character was forced to come to terms with the fact that his superb work was ignored by an ignorant world.

That task completed, there remained the matter of the new album. Critics and fans hoping for the unanswered questions of the first half to be explained were largely disappointed as the new, bulkier double album seemed to offer a different slant to the plot idea. With Johnny Thunder now missing from the action, the emphasis is altered, as the sleeve notes explain: "A world-travelled Tramp returns to his village green and finds a corrupt and dictatorial regime run by Flash and his gang of spivs. But the people have had enough and a military coup brings Flash tumbling down. Face to face with his own conscience, he eventually repents his evil ways and is conditioned to take his place in the new society."

With the fall of Flash comes the twist: the oppression of the tyrant is gone, but in its place comes the oppression of the pure – and in the end, is there any distinction to be made? Yet again, the Orwellian nightmare that dominates his autobiography is pre-empted here, with the little guy still a victim no matter who the big guy is.

Song-wise, the album fails to clarify the confusions of its predecessor. With the plot-change, the consistency – which might have justified the existence of both albums – is lost; the unexplained loss of major players doesn't help matters, either. And even more so than the first album, this collection of tracks is so tightly woven together that hearing them outside of a theatrical presentation seems terribly incomplete; like watching television without the sound. Even playing them in the wrong order affects enjoyment: 'Flash's Dream' precedes 'Flash's Confession' because that's the way it should be, not because they sound nice together.

Enjoyment as an album is also denied by the intermittent "announcements" which attempt to jolly along the plot but have only the effect of tiring the casual listener on the look-out for nice tunes. Overall, the effect is the same as on the first half. But there are a few good songs: the single, of course, as well as the tuneful 'When A Solution Comes' and the carping 'Artificial Man', both of them tastefully performed without the over-the-top caricatures. But from such an excessive selection, the pick of the crop is poor. As John Gosling says of the band's feeling at the time, "By the time *Preservation II* came along, we'd all had quite enough of part one." Even the mild-mannered Dalton agrees: "The stage show didn't really change much between *Preservation I* and *Preservation II*; it just got longer. I really just wanted to get back on stage as a five-piece and play without the entourage and the wardrobe people, because everything was just so big and took so long."

It should be the case that a man of Raymond Douglas' prodigious talent should have been able to come up with better melodies than he did – but yet again other factors played a contributing role in the sound of the album. For a start, Ray's uncanny knack for booking away every moment of his life for one project or another meant that he had hardly any time to compose freely and not under pressure. Touring the States, filming and writing *Starmaker* and setting up the Konk studio and label were not any of them easy jobs. And then there was the free studio time at their own facility. According to John Gosling, every spark of originality was re-recorded and remixed until it was lost. "Having that amount of time to try things out was destructive rather than constructive," he admits. "In many ways, having our own studio was the worst thing for us."

Where the records failed, it was commonly agreed, was on the lack of supportive media for the full experience. Winter saw The Kinks return to the States to put things right, taking a slightly abridged *Preservation* tour complete with costumes for the various characters on stage, slides and even films to complement the performances and help the songs exist. At last, something like the intended majesty of the whole piece could be sampled; it wasn't great, but it sure made sense of the records. That continent done, it was back to England for the usual Kinky end-of-year celebrations, this time culminating in three nights at London's Royalty Theatre, where the show won its first ecstatic reviews, most notably in *The Guardian*. At last a glimmer of light at the end of the tunnel. Suddenly, Salvation Road beckoned where once Scrapheap City called.

14 MUCH TOO DUMB TO EDUCATE

The Ray Davies exposing his soul to the world in his comeback manifesto believed The Kinks to be a group of equals; the group had other ideas. But then Ray has believed many things over the years which, to those around him, or even those reading about him or buying his records, were rarely short of surprising. The band's slide from riff-orientated pop construction to grandiose cod-theatrical presentations had caught most people unawares. If record sales are anything to go by (and bearing in mind the band were rarely an albums act, even in their mass-marketed heyday), the directional deviation had not been successful. Where once a concert audience could visit a gig and be treated to a couple of hours of hits, as the decade wore on, more and more shows began to resemble album premieres since the majority of the crowd had yet to buy the latest daring release.

Ray, at least, seemed not to notice. "I might be wrong," he told us, "but I think I can pick up on the emotion every night. I don't blandly go on and play song after song just because that's what's written down." But when it's a choice of one song hardly anybody knows or another equally obscure recent track, the decision becomes Hobsonian. Ray disagrees. "I think it's important to hear the music and experience the event with a little bit of theatre as well," he avers. "That's more what my music is about."

For the fan of The Kinks in the '60s, what the music was about was fun, pure and simple. Good, old-fashioned, English fun, perhaps with a dash of lyrical erudition and a slice of rebellion thrown in for good measure, but fun nonetheless. The Rolling Stones were darker, more blues-based, and The Beatles too clean. Marty Wilde and Cliff Richard were the teen choice that the parents approved of, while The Dave Clark Five and Manfred Mann went all out courting the lover of throwaway pop. Ray Davies' songs, on the other hand, even if they were poppy, were like little aural gems to be treasured and remembered; fun you could go back to again and again, the joke that still made you laugh the fifth time around.

So far, the '70s had seen a different spin on that earlier ethos. What enjoyment there was to be had from the various albums released in the first half of the decade came after a certain amount of intellectual investment on the listener's part, as the different themic concepts had to be unravelled. And most recently, the returns on that investment were becoming less and less enticing.

The obligatory tour of North America in the spring of 1975 saw the *Preservation* idea put on hold – but only so a new, equally audacious project could be unveiled in the shape of *Soap Opera*. Elaborate costumes this time included bizarre Afro wigs. "We wore these hideous frightwigs and coloured satin suits; again it was fun for a while," remembers John Gosling. "We all got these silly suits and silly hair things," John Dalton winces, "but I didn't really enjoy it." As well as the costumes, huge ducks were employed to illustrate the Hilda Ogden-inspired 'Ducks On The Wall' (Dalton: "These huge plaster things just stared out from behind us!"). The *Coronation Street*-type allusions didn't end there, with Ray reinvoking his gritty television play of the previous year, *Starmaker*, to provide the show's core. No longer Mr Flash (and Dave spared the roles of Mr Twitch and Mr Black, Avory no longer Big Ron and John Dalton unencumbered by the soubriquet Big Knob), Ray presented himself as…Norman. While the audience tried to amend his assertion by heckling his real name, Ray plodded on through the script, living the mundane life of the fame-seeking non-entity. Finally he could bear it no longer and admitted to the audience – and perhaps himself – who he really was, before settling down to steal the show with a few long-awaited classics from his bulging attic. One minute he's singing 'Ordinary People' to the polite appreciation of the loyal few; the next, entire arenas are erupting into heaving masses as 'A Well Respected Man', 'Dedicated Follower Of Fashion' and 'Sunny Afternoon' are unleashed.

Following that particular trio would have been hard on a good day. On a tour day, they didn't even try. The props-aided 'Ducks', 'Face In The Crowd' and 'You Can't Stop The Music' wrapped up the American shows with something of a bathetic resolution. Strong songs all, they still failed to give the people what they wanted on a nightly basis. As adored as 'Lola' and 'You Really Got Me' were when sneaked into the set early on, who wouldn't have preferred to have the shows end on such a high? "We didn't do too many of our old standards," Gosling admits, "because they didn't fit into the play we were performing. But people still wanted to hear tnem and so I don't think the whole thing went down very well." "As an album, I didn't like *Soap Opera*," Dalton admits. "For me, it was just a TV piece and I can't recall too many songs off it that I actually like. 'Ducks On The Wall' is all right, I suppose, but not much else. Strange album, that one."

Proof that the finale numbers were actually a return to form came with two of them, 'Ducks On The Wall' and 'You Can't Stop The Music', being released as singles. Chart action for both plus another 45 release, 'Holiday Romance', was again negligible, but critics found all three indicative of a band tiring of its theatrical dabblings. Guitars were once again dominant where trombones might have been expected. The same could be said of the singles' parent album, released in May. *Soap Opera*, the album formerly known as "Starmaker", appeared stronger on all counts than a lot of what had gone before. Musically there were moments of excellence, as the singles testified, and conceptually there was a return to the more tangible ideas that people could relate to: working-class ills, suburban woes with the odd touch of light relief thrown in for good measure. The road half of *Show-Biz* had returned to its homestead, and where that led with anecdotes of a suitcase existence, *Soap Opera* concentrates on real people's problems; like the rat race in 'Nine To Five' (quite a different song to Dolly Parton's '80s smash) and gridlock in 'Rush Hour Blues'. The Ogdens' ornithological wall ornamentation takes centre stage of course on 'Ducks', and even their dinner (or at least the meals of millions of people like them) stars in 'You Make It All Worthwhile'.

Something else that makes living tolerable is romance, and a 'Holiday Romance' in particular. On that song, Ray leaves London behind for a while and meets the girl of his dreams. Lavinia is her name and, while she's the shyest lass the elder brother claims to have encountered, she dances a mean foxtrot, samba and waltz. The effect of the whole song is one of half smiles and tender hearts; quite a return to form for the old softie songwriter even as recently as on *Percy*. And yet its saccharine mood doesn't totally gel with the album as a whole. More in keeping with the type of families described elsewhere would be something like Blur's '90s hit 'Girls And Boys'. Holiday love is displayed in bucket loads there, but emotion doesn't enter into it. Rather the whole lyric centres on a raucous 18-30s rompathon where physical attraction is the name of the game and physical reaction is its swiftly pursuing sequel, aided and abetted by large dollops of alcohol.

If a two-week love tryst away from your spouse doesn't cure the tedium of the humdrum existences of the wannabes in *Soap Opera*, then there's always the star of an earlier song, the dreaded liquor. 'When Work Is Over' sees the advocation of liquid solutions to all those suburban problems. Encouraged not to think, but to have another drink, the listener is sent on a tour of desperation, where the only way out is to black out. It's a theme laboured further in 'Have Another Drink'. Here the camaraderie of ordinary people, erected in *Muswell Hillbillies* and lost ever since, returns to the fore. A decent dose of alcohol can alleviate some of the world's harshest pressures: not just dead-end jobs, but fascism and terrorist bombers are all no match for the mollifying powers of pub fare. Again, Ray insists we have another drink for the second song in a row. It's obviously a palliative measure when life is really harsh, but it does provide a momentary escape route for millions – and not just ordinary folk; rock stars as well.

"We were in America and near the end of the tour," a sheepish Dave recalls, "and I'd been drinking nearly all day. It was a great crowd that night but I was so pissed I had to sit on a chair behind my amplifier and play – I couldn't stand. Ray slipped over on some beer – he'd been throwing it at the audience and insulting them – and hit his head. I eventually managed to get up from behind my amp, went over to the microphone, dragged Ray off and then started to take over. We just started doing this jam thing which was probably terrible, and I remember thinking, 'This is so ridiculous. What am I doing here?' But the audience seemed to like it."

For Ray, the road to inebriety was a short trip, since he could feel drunk after just one pint, hence the often exaggerated stage drunkenness. But that didn't stop him trying, and even today beer is a common prop on stage. "Prop" just about sums it up, since even now he tends to spill more than he consumes. Dave: "We used to get frustrated when audiences were too out of it to listen to us, so once in Canada Ray just got these cans and threw beer over them. Soon the audiences were demanding that Ray throw beer over them."

And so one type of stage theatrics was augmented by another. For all the intellectual posturing of the albums' concepts, when it came down to actually communicating with the crowd, the slightest thing could become part of the show's ongoing mythology. Mighty stage props are one thing, but a spontaneous peccadillo one evening could have the same effect, as Dave confirms: "It's just silly things you pick up that become part of your act."

In the mid '70s, those "silly things" could have been a lot worse. At a time when *Top Of The Pops* was populated by characters wearing ten-inch-heeled silver boots, tartan shirts or facial make-up that resembled a lightning storm in space, The Kinks were actually being quite conservative. Hair lengths obviously reflected the fashions of the time – Dave wasn't about to let his keen eye for the sartorial statement rest for a moment – but pretty much concert gear began and ended with the theme of the show. While Gary Glitter's performances resembled Christmas at the Tin Man's family home just for the sake of it, The Kinks' garb was an extension of their songs, and had been for some time.

The conceptual clotheshorse approach to the band's work stretched onto their next musical project. Released just six months after *Soap Opera*, November's *Schoolboys In Disgrace* saw the lads totally kitted out in school uniform (a style a certain Angus Young from Aussie rockers AC/DC was later to claim as his own). The juvenile delights of that photo session were not to be seen on the front of the album, sadly; that spot was taken by a cartoon of a, quite literally, cheeky schoolboy baring his backside for the headmaster's cane.

The theme of *Schoolboys In Disgrace* is pretty much summed up by the title, but if there is any doubt, the sleeve notes reveal the tale: "Once upon a time, there was a naughty little schoolboy," it begins, going on to explain how he and his gang were always playing tricks on the teachers and bullying other children in the school. Following an overly productive carnal encounter with a schoolgirl (she gets pregnant) the lad is sent to the headmaster, who decides to disgrace the naughty boy and his gang in front of the whole school.

The plot, such as it is, is not world shattering. Boy meets girl, boy screws girl, girl gets pregnant, boy gets seven bells caned out of him. What appeals to readers of lyrics is the similarity between the lad and Ray. His culpability for Rasa's maternal condition wore him down during the band's days of crazy living and wild excess. He had to do the decent thing – he was, after all, a decent man – and he paid for it with his restricted pleasures and the insidious frustration that that was not how he'd planned it. Society had offered him a way out through an acceptably speedy marriage and he had taken it. Society had claimed another couple of souls for its homogenised collection.

The comparisons continue with the sleeve notes' revelation that "after this punishment the boy turned into a hard and bitter character". Pop psychology at this level isn't the most creditable pastime, but wilder accusations have been levelled and this one seems supported at least in part by fact. For the schoolboy – and Ray – the punishment is epiphanous, opening his eyes to the socio-political strata within society. The theme of the haves and the have nots returns, and the idea of the Corporation from *X-Ray* is again invoked as the kid realises that "people in authority would always be there to kick him down and the establishment would always put him in his place". Ray's answer in the character of the mischievous boy is to swear selfish revenge on the world, vowing in future to always get what he wants. It is an idea that few would argue seems extraneous to the persona of

Raymond Douglas Davies the control seeker, and further evidence is submitted as the boy grows up into...Mr Flash.

Even after the acknowledged return to form with *Soap Opera*'s concentration on little things that matter to lots of little folk, the project hadn't been an unqualified success and so it was time for something new, as Gosling sums up: "At the end of *Soap Opera*, Ray realised it was time to try something new, and so we did *Schoolboys In Disgrace*, which was still a show but a bit more fun." Ray couldn't leave his creative favourite alone, however, and like Hollywood producer George Lucas filming three new movies for the *Star Wars* series and setting them all before the original movie, he took a step backwards to examine the formative years of his own role from the *Preservation* shows. Where the life-weary anecdotes from *Soap Opera* struck chords with all who heard it, *Schoolboys*, like *Preservation*, offered a world that was not immediately accessible for everyone. The school scenario was not the problem – everyone has been to school. The drawback was the insularity of the narrative; the railings against the establishment, the underage sex, the gang warfare; none of them as commonplace as getting drunk or having a holiday fling.

That said, the album as a collection of tunes was not as retro-looking as the concept behind it and, in fact, the rockier road experimented with on the year's earlier album was continued, most notably on the second side. There Dave's mighty Gibson Flying V is unleashed for what feels like the first time in ages, really flying on 'The Hard Way', a riffy exposé on the non-achievers. Accompanying Dave's sharp chops, Ray cries he's "much too dumb to educate", as both brothers hit the target at once. 'Headmaster' is another guitar-based rant, this time taking the form of a confession from the boy to his principal, full of venom and matched by Dave's electric squeals. Ladies and gentlemen – The Kinks.

Although failing to make an impression in Britain, the album reached the low 40s in the American charts and won friends even among the band. "Apart from making us dress up like schoolboys, that was a good one," Dalton recalls. "There were a couple of good tracks on that album. Ray got more into the raunchier stuff then, the rock 'n' roll stuff that we all used to like." In many ways, the heavier tracks succeed despite themselves, since neither is the most comprehensible to those not following the plot, but the mood on each is right, and the playing superb. Other songs pivot less strongly within the narrative framework so tightly suggested by numbers like 'Education'. 'I'm In Disgrace' actually hits a few lyrical highs in its tale of high-school adoration. Ray is charming, honest and resigned to his fate, and sympathetically backed by the band. 'The Last Assembly', while nominally a reference to one of the most detestable educational facets, is actually a *crie de corps*, a paean to the power of brotherhood that must stand firm against the mighty outside world. 'Schooldays' provides a moment of balladic reverie, with Dave restrained and Ray seduced by emotional memories. But all shackles are discarded for 'Jack The Idiot Dunce', a foot-tapping rock 'n' roll workout of the first order. Gangly, awkward and with teeth that look like they're back to front, 'Jack' emerges as another of Ray's classic caricatures, up there in detail with 'Plastic Man' and 'Dedicated Follower Of Fashion.' Performed as a well-paced slice of rock 'n' roll '50s-style, the song rattles through its hilarious lyric before you know it's on. Wonderful.

Despite getting back to the band's rock roots, once on stage the album took up a whole show just as the earlier concept pieces had done. "We'd run through the whole thing," Dalton remembers, "and throw in a few hits at the end. But at least we weren't doing two shows, like with *Preservation*, where we'd come out and do a 'hits' set before we got on with the new record."

The current new record's notion of returning to further examine the character of Mr Flash from two albums that hadn't exactly set the record-buying world on fire was a strange one, and perhaps not one that any other person alive would have come up with; certainly not John Gosling: "The idea of Flash is good. This unscrupulous guy making a killing from property development and everything, that was a good, relevant idea then, and it still is in the '90s. I feel as strongly about the rehousing policies as anyone, but he'd said it all brilliantly in *Muswell Hillbillies*; there was no need to do the *Preservation* albums; you can only bang on about something for so long. It seems to be something very close to Ray's heart but he just can't get it out of his system."

Far from showing any signs of purging Mr Flash from his work, Ray actually toyed with the idea of writing the sequel to *Schoolboys*. Only agitation with RCA sidetracked him from the project. Lackadaisical PR campaigns and ineffective promotions had failed the band, Ray was inclined to think. A new year was approaching; Ray wanted to start that year with a new label to call home.

15 THE STORIES, HOWEVER BIZARRE, ARE TRUE

If the audiences were disappointed with The Kinks' treatment of their rock roots, the label that had plucked them away from Pye's regressive marketing felt equally let down. For all his craving of success, critics maintain that Ray hadn't even tried to achieve it during his time with RCA. He'd worked hard, without question, but the very real doubts remained about his commitment to being a major hit. Did he honestly believe that his obsession with one concept project after another was what the audiences wanted? Had this been what had propelled the band to rival The Beatles and The Rolling Stones sales-wise a decade earlier? Far from it.

The enthusiasm shown by both sides at the band's signing had clearly been lost by 1976 and Ray was actively seen courting other labels. As their final shot, RCA took a leaf from Pye's book and released a "best of" compilation called *Celluloid Heroes – The Kinks' Greatest*. The veracity of the title was questionable, since the package omitted 'Supersonic Rocket Ship', the band's only single success gained on the label. In the end, sales were poor in the UK and in America it failed to make the Top 100.

Summer arrived and eventually a decision was made. This year's lucky candidates were Arista Records, home over the years to acts as diverse as Meat Loaf and Whitney Houston, Aretha Franklin and The Thompson Twins. Yet again a record label's president, Arista's Clive Davis, was heard celebrating the deal. "I couldn't be happier that they've chosen Arista as their new home," he announced, "and am confident that the future of The Kinks lies very much in front of them."

Champagne bottles uncorked, emptied and thrown away, it was back to business in the studio. The studio in question was the band's own, Konk, which after something of a hiatus was once again operational. There was now also a second strand to the business; a record label set up to cultivate new talent, run by the omnipresent Ray of course, but in partnership with the others to varying degrees. To Ray the label and studio provided a physical base for his activities as well as an intellectual focus, while to the rest of the band it offered rare opportunities. With the several fledgling acts coming onto the label, John Gosling and Dave went into business with each other. "Together we formed a production company and we produced a couple of the Konk acts," he recalls. Despite the on-stage antagonism, the conglomeration wasn't that bizarre. "Dave could be quite volatile at times, but off stage we got on quite well. We both liked the same sort of music, same sort of movies, so we used to socialise a bit. It seemed logical for us to work together."

The first batch of clients at Konk included Tom Robinson's early band Cafe Society – "we did that album with Ray" – Andy Desmond – "he had a fantastic voice" – and Claire Hammill, which Ray worked on alone. The results, it has to be said, were not good, despite the excellent studio facilities and high-class skills of all involved on the musical side, and at the end of the day some of the clients might just have regretted ever entering the building. "Andy Desmond didn't do very well, Claire Hammill fared slightly better, and Tom Robinson I don't think will ever speak to Ray again after his treatment," Gosling surmises.

Clearly there was a problem somewhere along the line and most of that could be traced to the fact that Ray ran a studio and a label and a band; there just weren't enough hours in the month for all three to be attended to properly, and in the end no one of the strands received adequate attention. The acts suffered because Ray used so much studio time for his own means, although not enough time for The Kinks to have a new album ready that year; and the label hit problems every time Ray was distracted by the other two projects. "The label was like a toy which he played with for a while and got bored of," Gosling notes, "and consequently none of the acts got any proper promotion."

Of all the acts under the auspices of the brothers, Tom Robinson in particular came off worst, eventually retaliating to the extent that even now Ray can react unfavourably to his memory, depending on his mood. "There was always some sort of friction there," John Gosling suggests. "I think Ray saw Tom as a threat, and I think Tom saw himself as the new Ray Davies." Perhaps he was the new RD; certainly his temperament and paranoia reached Daviesian heights on occasion as the relationship wore on. "He thought Ray was deliberately postponing their tour dates and recording times and not promoting them enough," Gosling continues, "which was true. He couldn't be bothered. It came to a head when Ray went to see Tom play in a pub and Tom dedicated 'Tired Of Waiting' to him. Something happened there and ever since then they've been sworn enemies."

Konk the label may have been doomed from the outset, but the studio's life was more happily blessed. A few lean periods aside, it has continually found favour as a professional studio, and the fact that Ray's name can be found on the user roster more than anyone else's means that there has always been at least one client. "The main problem was Ray and the fact that he was using up the lion's share of the studio time," Gosling states. "Other paying acts had to be turned away because we were always in there. A few acts made it through, though: The Bay City Rollers and Bert Weedon came down and did albums, but really, because we were in there so often there wasn't much time for other people."

Twenty-five years later, there remains at least some room for outside utilisers, most notably in 1995 the brilliant indie pop sensations Elastica, fronted by Justine Frischmann, ex-girlfriend of Damon Albarn of Kinks enthusiasts Blur. Small world. Then there was Erasure and... "Oh we've had lots of people in there," Dave boasts, not without some pride since the entire complex, although Ray's second home, is his pride and joy. "It was always well equipped," Gosling admits. "Dave always ensured it had all the state-of-the-art stuff, best desks, monitors, speakers. It's been kept up to date ever since." "Yeah, we've got one main studio and two control rooms," Dave enthuses. "There's an old Neve mixer in one – which everybody seems to like to lay their back tracks on, depending on whether they're using real drums or not. The other room's all hi-tech with an SSL and all the usual things. We've built it up from a demo studio in 1972 to a modern-day place, and it's very up to date now."

Due to Dave, the studio has always been well equipped, making it a technical pleasure to work there. Too much of a pleasure for some however as work on the new album in 1976 dragged on and on and...

"It was very tedious because it took so long to record," winces John Gosling. "It probably took the longest of the lot because we were going over each song again and again, just because Ray had the studio at his disposal. He kept wanting another take but you get to the point where you can't see the wood for the trees and I don't think he could, either."

The mood in the sessions was not aided by the departure of John Dalton in November. Finally succumbing to the rational half of his brain, he decided that the neverending cycle of drawn-out recording stints and harrowing tours had to end. "It got so bad for him that for years after that he never picked up a bass," close friend Gosling reveals. "He just wanted a quiet life and for a while had a transport cafe by the side of a road."

"It's true," Dalton concurs. "I packed up playing for two years and bought a cafe, which was something I'd always wanted to do; I did that for about a year." Such a total break from everything related to his old life seems to indicate John trying to purge his memory of the past horrors but, of all the band members, he is the least battle scarred. He remains adamant today that the political climate of the band was the last reason for leaving.

"I think really it was several things," he relates. "For a start, the money wasn't really there. And I was away from home a lot of the time, and with three young kids that's not easy. Basically, everything just built up and the outside pressures got too much." Surprisingly, to this day Dalton denies the brothers' behaviour drove him to his exodus. "I always got on quite well with them both, Dave and Ray. I was never involved in the fights. I was pretty much left out of that sort of thing, I don't know why. Maybe they thought they'd get a clump from me. They just seemed to leave me alone."

If proof were needed of his commitment to the band, even though he knew he would soon cease to be a part of it, John couldn't leave them in the lurch: "I'd decided I wanted to leave, but to be fair I made sure I put all my bass tracks down before I left. Obviously the album wasn't finished because Ray hadn't put his vocals on, but all the backing tracks were ready and all my bass lines were done."

Hanging around to help Ray out of a fix certainly doesn't sound like the behaviour of someone who hated his time with The Kinks. Little wonder, then, that Dalton was begged to stay by the group's leader. "Obviously, Ray wanted me to stay," he recalls, "but I'd made up my mind. It wasn't like an argument where you come out with something in the heat of the moment, it had obviously been thought over for a long time and he respected that. I had to wait till I'd finished the tracks, so I was still around for a while, but it was all decided and I didn't change my mind."

For someone as seemingly untouched by the degree of disquiet forever surrounding the group, the break was a hard one. Had he hated either one of the Davies duo, the resolution would have been more palatable for him. As it was, he knew he was closing the door on a source of endless good memories. "Others have hated their time with the band," he sums up, "but I loved it, every moment of it. I just took the rough with the smooth – you've got to in everything in life. To actually say I've played at all the top venues in the world – Carnegie Hall, Albert Hall – the biggest stadiums, and to be able to say I've seen most of the world and met some great fans who've stuck by us all the time is very nice. I've got great memories."

Replacing John was a priority, obviously, but not one to be laboured over, according to Ray. He never fully believed that Dalton had finally gone; after all, he'd already returned to the group once, he could do it again. And so it was that when Andy Pyle arrived to swell the ranks back to five, he was met by repeated advice of wariness. "Ray Davies believed John's departure to be a momentary lapse and that he would return when he came to his senses," Andy recalls. "Mick Avory and John Gosling knew that Nobby had gone for good and took pains to warn me of the consequences should Ray eventually decide that my position was no longer temporary."

Hardly anything seemed straightforward with Ray, but to say that personnel management was probably his weakest area is an understatement. John Gosling's status within the group from the moment of audition was nebulous to the point of mental cruelty, and for Pyle it was no better, despite his impressive pedigree. Tenures in Blodwyn Pig, the Alvin Lee band and Savoy Brown had seen his bass playing tested beyond question, but still his accession into the band was strained. From a muddled audition that had consisted of taking part in recording sessions for the album (along with several other low enders – as part of an ingeniously frugal way to get the work done on Ray's part perhaps?) to the ensuing weeks of recording, not once was he officially accepted as a group member.

Fortunately Andy had an ally in one of The Kinks' staff whom he'd known from Savoy Brown. "It was actually on the recommendation of one of the crew members, Brian Wilcox, that I was asked to come in on the recordings," Andy recalls. Once in, he could count on the support of John Gosling, who knew of his reputation as a fellow Luton-area player. "Andy and I got on immediately," he reflects. "Mick was all right, of course, but I don't think the Davies brothers accepted him. I knew he was a damned good player because of the things he'd done with Rod Stewart, and so I wanted them to give him a chance because I needed some companionship after John left."

Despite playing at Konk for several weeks, once the album appeared and the songs had been whittled down from 20 to nine Andy found himself on only one track, 'Mr Big Man'. The rest the exiting Mr Dalton had put down before his departure.

The album, *Sleepwalker*, finally appeared in February 1977 at the height of the punk era. Perhaps in tune with the mood of the moment, Ray pared back the showbiz excesses of recent times and the band were presented once again as a five-piece act on record (six-piece if you count the duality of bass players). For John Gosling, this was the smallest compensation. "The good thing about it was it was back to the five-piece again," he remembers, "but the rehearsal sessions alone were gruelling. I think Ray lost his way completely with that album. We did the whole thing twice, because when we got back from our holidays we found he'd written about seven or eight new songs and junked everything we'd recorded. That was when I started to really lose my temper in a big way and it was never really the same after that.

"I forget the song we were doing, but we must have done it in every key, it just went on and on. I've always been one to say that if it's not working in ten takes then move on to something else, but that's not Ray. Because we had unlimited studio time, he just used every hour he could get, and it wasn't a good idea; if we'd had to rent a studio and pay for it, we wouldn't have used that much time. He ironed out all the nice little things we'd started off doing in the songs and they sounded very lifeless."

Lifeless compared to the original takes, perhaps; but up against the wieldy concept dinosaurs of earlier, quite refreshing in their straight-ahead honesty. By no means a work of greatness, *Sleepwalker* was notable for its lack of Mr Flash and its inclusion of riffs. The title track leads by example: Dave cranks out the simplest of chord sequences and – bang! – it's game on and Ray's insistent vocal (about social parasites) has everything to do to make up the ground. 'Sleepless Night' finds the same filial hierarchy only this time Dave handles lead vocals himself. Instantly recognisable, his shrill style reaches raucous heights as voice does battle with guitar. Result: one memorable song.

Sadly such musical moments are limited, although lyrically Ray gets to slip in a few smile-inducing interludes. 'Life On The Road' threatens to be a continuation of *Show-Biz* but halts no further than being a *London A-Z* put to a (so-so) tune. 'Juke Box Music' is an interesting commentary on the superficiality of pop, and 'Brother' is also worthy of comment. In the final analysis, a welcome break from the rock theatre of yore; but a clear way from a return to form. UK audiences failed to buy in droves, although rock-hungry Americans were more receptive, eventually propelling *Sleepwalker* to Number 21 in the *Billboard* chart.

The American sales at least were some reward for Ray as well as an indication that his latest approach in the studio was paying off. Andy Pyle: "We recorded live, with no guide vocals, from chord sheets written and amended by Ray. He would later reassemble his personal selection of parts drawn from the limitless supply of takes and, together with subsequent overdubs, achieve a finished product which bore no resemblance to what we thought we'd recorded. Vocals remained unheard by the rank and file until the whole process was over."

Aside from concealing his patchwork-like construction, Ray also went to some lengths to entice a semblance of bonhomie by encouraging active input on a creative level. John Gosling remembers the familiar pattern: "Ray claimed that he was open to suggestions from everyone in the band, but we'd normally go back to the way he'd envisaged the songs in the end. The only creative input I had was when Ray used to come to me and we'd try and work out keyboard parts for the songs. Things like the intro to 'Apeman' I came up with, and a couple of others with keyboard fills we worked together on. So some of my ideas were used, but not an awful lot. He'd come in with music and lyrics and ask us for ideas and at first we liked the notion of creative input. But he never really listened to what we had to say; he pretended at first but then didn't bother."

What seemed a plus point for Ray on the man-management scale was soon lost, impairing the final result. "It just got on everybody's nerves in the end," Gosling continues. "We were just going in there and being very mechanical, playing the same old thing take after take. Session men would have done a better job because you can almost hear the dissatisfaction on those tracks. There was no invention on *Sleepwalker* or the album that followed it at all."

With *Sleepwalker* available in the shops, even Ray had to concede that a decision was needed on Andy's long-term involvement in the group. "By the time the album had run into extra time and there was still no Nobby – or anyone else, for that matter – an American tour was becoming imminent," Pyle reflects. "I agreed to the terms offered, though they were rarely adhered to, and was welcomed as one of 'the five Kinks', as Ray called us in times of stress. When *Sleepwalker* entered the US charts, though, the emphasis soon shifted away from the five to the one or two Kinks."

The American tour was something of a revelation for the new boy and a rude initiation was soon under way. "Andy could see what the atmosphere was like and he got fed up very quickly and so we started talking about our own band," John Gosling recalls. "I tried to warn him about the group but he wasn't prepared for the American tour. One night he was sitting on the steps outside the building while we were having this food fight inside. I think Dave and I were throwing things at Ray. But then the room went silent as the door opened and Dave handed Andy his bass because he knew he didn't like to be parted from it – then the noise just started again. I don't think he really enjoyed it from the outset."

Andy concurs. "Although I was continually being briefed on the more unsavoury aspects of the legend I had entered into," he admits, "nothing could have prepared me for the real thing. Suffice it to say that an uncomfortably high percentage of the stories, however bizarre, are true." Stories such as fist fights on stage, drum-toppling escapades, drunkenness and mental violence towards the hired hands with one playing them off against the other..? "Bizarre but true."

To the audience at large, it was business as usual in The Kinks. They were used to the paradoxical existence of a band that hated itself and the world by turns and yet could produce the sweetest of music, the finest of ballads. At the centre of the confusion, naturally, Ray Davies commanded the keenest attention. One moment the loud rocker the next the vaudeville crooner, but always the Englishman, whether he was leading the group through another rousing encore of 'Lola' or spitting at a band member for getting in his spotlight. Ever the London dandy of his earlier song, he came often to be compared to that other master poet, Noël Coward. But there the likeness ends, for while Coward was blessed with the "talent to amuse", Ray's gift was far more sinister. "The talent to abuse" would be a more pertinent description of the occasionally spiteful singer's persona – and certainly as another album and tour episode drew to a battered close and a new one presented itself, it would get few arguments from Dalton, Gosling, Dave, Avory, Robinson and Pyle.

16 GLAD TO BE PUNK

Fashions ebb and flow and leave their mark on all sectors of culture, but nowhere is their trace so defined as in the capricious world of so-called popular music. The late '70s was a period dominated by change. The decade had begun with the abdication of the reigning monarchs of music, The Beatles. Immediately, a host of young pretenders had swamped forward to fill the void, but the mood had changed and the single-voiced autocracy of the Fabs was superseded by a less defined coalition of pop government, as various competing factions emerged to rule at once.

For the first half of the decade, the top slot was shared among a worthy few, most of them wielders of the glam banner. Gary Glitter, Mud, The Sweet, The Bay City Rollers, Slade, Wizzard, 10cc and T Rex all made their respective marks on the time, augmenting their musical push with the stunning fashions of the glam ideal. Bacofoil suits, painted faces, high-rise footwear and songs you could chant along with linked the groups to the era, and the era to success. If you weren't in, you were out. It was that simple. And The Kinks weren't in...

The audiences wanted misspellings ('Cum On Feel The Noize'), posturing ('I'm The Leader Of The Gang') and pure nonsense ('Shang-A-Lang') – tight, three-minute gobs of fun. What they got was repeated lectures on the disintegrating state of Britain packaged in epic theatrical rhetoric. The only time the band came close enough to the mood of the time was to mock it, as John Gosling recalls: "At the height of the glam period, we were doing *Soap Opera* and dressing up in these big fright wigs and matching suits; red suit, red wig. Dave had an outrageous pair of boots about three feet high. But it was all a piss-take of the glam thing; the whole *Starmaker* thing was about that."

The occasional oddities aside, those who sold records in the '70s were the ones who made the effort to embrace the mood of the record-buying populace. The Kinks didn't. They never even tried to keep their old fans by playing the hits. But then a strange thing happened: the world grew up. Suddenly, all that glittered was no longer gold, the heels were toppled and fans looked to a new god for guidance. Its name was punk.

With new blood pouring into the industry from every under-rehearsed corner of every dingy club, the glam casualties were high. The only silver on the new performers' costumes was on the safety pins through their noses; the only heels they cared about were stamping on somebody else; and the only gobs of fun they were interested in were saliva and snot bombs inflicted on the front rows of their audiences.

It was a period of revolution in the charts and in the country as tracks like 'Anarchy In The UK' became political cries and The Sex Pistols for a while really looked set to change something. They certainly succeeded in overhauling a stagnant music industry and caught more than one record company napping when it came to calling the shots. And at last, here was something Ray Davies could relate to; people were finally writing songs about things, real things that mattered to other people. At last the world had caught up.

But of course the other side of the punk manifesto was its youth: old was useless, young was everything. Respect became extinct and yet again The Kinks found themselves on the outside looking in on a trend that they had partially pioneered both musically and off stage. Not being a fashionable band in the first place meant they hadn't become one of the fatalities of the period, but the mere fact of their age and semi-revered status meant they were anathema to punk's angry new brooms. Yet again, they were going to have to fight just to survive.

Ironically, given half a chance, The Kinks were the perfect role models for the new wave. They had been spitting at each other while Sid Vicious was bunking school; they'd shocked the establishment with their outrageous dress sense back in the early '60s while John Lydon was still using safety pins for their original nappy-tying use; and when it came to causing havoc on the road, they'd written the book…

"Things got so bad," Gosling admits, "that we were hard pressed to find anyone who'd do a support for us on tour because of all the fighting. They knew what went on; we were bad news at the agencies. Having said that, we had quite a few names over the years: Elton John, Yes, Tom Petty, Nils Lofgren and Little Feat all in the States, but in England no one would touch us. There was even a fight with Yes' roadies and with Steve Harley's Cockney Rebel; Steve was another Ray. They were just walking in circles backstage, watching the other one and preening themselves."

Whereas the glam aspect had been fair game for the master cynic, Ray genuinely felt an affinity for the ungainliness of the punk spirit. "With the punk era Ray, went all the way with the spiky hair and everything," Gosling remembers. "But this time he wasn't parodying it, he was trying to become what he'd once been a long time ago, but without the costumes, obviously. Their music had always been a bit punky in the early days, although a bit more in tune, and it'd certainly been done with the same attitude that the punks had. But here he was at that age looking faintly ridiculous; they'd lost that charm the band had had in the beginning and now looked like a sad old rock band. It used to be fun; a few wrong chords, bad keys – the audiences seemed to love that, especially in America, where they loved the Englishness of it all – but that all stopped. The bawdy asides and the fun stuff went and they became just another rock band, which is where they've stayed."

Wanting to join in yet being restrained by something as ethereal as age worked on Ray's psyche, and the feeling of resentment which he seemingly never left home without was further fuelled. Around the same time as the punk movement was growing, so too the career of his protégé, Tom Robinson, was taking off. The break with Konk still rankled, despite Davies ending up with publishing rights on Robinson's early hits, and Christmas 1977 saw Ray finally put into song the feelings he was still plagued by. 'Prince Of The Punks' contains many a swipe at the writer of 'Glad To Be Gay', ranging from attacks on his commercial campness to put-downs on his overall talent. The fact that Robinson was an accepted young punk didn't help matters.

In one song, Ray comes across as a bitter, angry individual who would like to disembark the world at the next stop, yet flip the record over and the essential dichotomy feeding his existence is revealed once again. 'Father Christmas', the disc's actual A-side, deals with the exploitation of the season and calls for a return to the values of charity; giving to the poor, helping the needy and shunning the commercialisation of the whole event. The cry comes from the heart and he is at once huggable and sad; he only wants what's best for his children, but he hankers for a world long gone.

Back in the real world, of course, the record failed to make an impression on the charts that were cluttered with the punk tracks of the time. Didn't people realise that without The Kinks...?

"We were one of the original punk bands, I think," John Gosling asserts. "We acted like it and we sounded like it for a while. But that wild element went missing, which was a great shame. He couldn't do it at the shows in the '70s. Early on, the shows were too structured, but towards the end, he was bored of it all; he'd come on and go through the motions for an hour and a half, which wasn't fair on the people who'd paid for tickets. We were up there looking bored and wishing we were somewhere else. And when it stops being fun even on stage, then there's something wrong."

For Andy Pyle, it never really became fun, and after a while the stage shows which he had originally joined the band for were the lowlights of the day. Another chance for the brothers to pull him between them, one spitting, the other kicking his shin, was not what he looked forward to when he thought of rock 'n' roll. "I don't think Andy ever really fitted in," Gosling explains. "He didn't get on with Ray that well and I don't think Dave liked him much either." And Dave, it transpired, was the one to watch. "He was a bit of a wild one then, especially when he got angry, whereas Ray was more of a sulker. I used to see a lot of Dave off stage and we got on. I sometimes used to share a room with him; they'd stick us down the end of the corridor and call it the noisy room and we'd get on great together. But he'd flare up on stage."

With the actual performances becoming things of dread, the band looked for other outlets for their talents. John Gosling: "What we used to do, which was great fun, was stay at these Holiday Inns in America and just get up and play with the house bands. That was fantastic because they were just used to churning out the standards and when we came along they got a chance to rock. Ray never liked us doing that because he liked us to be his band and his band alone, but it was very often the only way to get through the day."

"On stage at the hotel was the high point," Pyle agrees. "That was our compensation; that was sad. We had some fun, but it was never when the two brothers were together."

While keeping a distance on tour, when the studio routine became too much even Ray couldn't ignore the pleasures of the impromptu jam. Only once, mind, but he still joined in, as Gosling remembers: "The rest of us used to play at weekends and occasionally during the week when we didn't have anything to do. Once, we were in the middle of a recording session and nothing was going right so Ray said, 'Sod it, let's go over and play at Nobby's pub.' And we did. We just chucked some stuff in a van and went and played this rock 'n' roll set – a whole Chuck Berry and Little Richard set – to a very astonished bar. That was the first and probably the last time that Ray enjoyed joining in with something like that. He never liked us playing with other people – he made that quite clear – but we still did it, particularly in America. He frowned upon it but that was the only way we kept on top of things."

Things finally got too much for the put-upon Andy Pyle and he told Ray in late 1977 that he was leaving the band. Coming so soon after Dalton's departure, Ray felt that the group's solid core was at risk if things weren't nailed down. Whatever misgivings the singer had (and these have never been articulated), he was determined to keep a solid foundation on which his brother and he could stamp; he had to, if The Kinks were to survive. Studio work on a new album had already been gained from Andy, but if he would just stay that bit longer then the whole band could tour at Christmas and everyone's Yuletide bonus would be forthcoming. Pyle conceded and the tour went ahead.

Yet again London's Rainbow Theatre was to host a pivotal part of The Kinks' history in the making. For once, the hits were trawled out, with Ray delving into every period of the band's past for the material.

Radio 1 disc jockey Alan "Fluff" Freeman held proceedings together as the evening's MC and the whole event went off smoothly. In hindsight, certain members of the band and many of the music press half expected another farewell to song from the mercurial frontman; in reality, they had to make do with a better-than-average show in front of happier-than-average punters.

Ending the year on such a high gave the band new impetus with which to go forward; much-needed time off at the start of 1978 gave them space to reflect. From outside the group, John Dalton observed Ray's decision to play the hits at the Rainbow: he was taking control of destiny again as he had done so all along. Everything, from early success to recent flops, had been Ray's engineering, whether he admitted it or not. "It was down to Ray," he affirms. "He was hell bent on doing these concept albums, like *Schoolboys In Disgrace*, and he never tried to sit down and write a proper single like 'Waterloo Sunset'. He wrote some good songs in that period, but they were all part of a larger plan; he never wrote a single for the sake of it. For about six months after each album, we'd go on tour and perform pretty much that album; he wasn't interested in anything else. If only he'd taken a bit of advice. But he had to do everything himself. He got so wrapped up in the studio and everything became a blur. I don't write songs myself, but I'm sure sometimes it helps if you have someone to say, 'Well, that bit's all right, but the rest needs work.'" But he was on his own.

"In the studio, the song was written by Ray. He knew exactly what he wanted, and so you worked at that. There wasn't much room for you to get involved or contribute beyond just playing your parts. We'd sit round his house, round the piano or something, and he'd bang out some chords and we'd fit in with some other chords. Often we wouldn't know what the song was, we'd just put our bits to it. In the studio, we'd play as a rhythm section without the vocals. Ray'd be on guitar and sometimes he'd put down a guide vocal, and then it would have to be worked on. Some songs you'd finish in a couple of takes and others would take months. I remember 'Lola' took a long, long while to finish; I can't remember why, apart from flying back to change the lyrics."

The post-Rainbow lull gave everyone time to assess the band's situation. Andy Pyle never again saw Ray, not even when he was officially "fired" from the line-up, and after eight years it became John Gosling's final appearance with the band, although even he didn't recognise this fact at the time.

"The Rainbow Theatre was the last show with that line-up," he recalls. "It was a Christmas show and we dressed up in some sort of costumes as usual. It was a good gig. The BBC recorded it and they broadcast it every so often on the radio. But I couldn't believe it when I first heard it. Everything was played at breakneck speed, as if we couldn't wait to get out. It was ridiculous. But I went back to the Rainbow recently for a TV show; the BBC asked me for my favourite gig and I said that one and I'd do the interview there if they could get it. The woman said to leave it with her, then she rang back and said, 'We've got the Rainbow. When can you make it?'"

The suddenness of John's exit from the group surprised even him, although the thought had been there for a while, planted by the monotonous drudgery of the recording cycle. "In England, we'd mostly be doing sessions," he remembers, "especially in the late '70s, when Konk Studios was running. Ray would just have tape running all the time and we'd spend whole days and nights in there, go to bed and come back and start again. It was very wearing; Ray was trying to produce everything himself, and so in the end he couldn't see the wood for the trees, and he just lost all track of what sounded good and what didn't and we'd just play the same songs over and over again. This is where the rot started to set in for me."

As usual, the story is not quite straightforward, and in true Ray style, his reaction was designed to cause the most damage. "I knew I had to get out during the *Misfits* sessions, where I had done so many songs so many times. I think Ray had got wind of the fact that Andy and I had been rehearsing with our other band, but we hadn't actually told him because we had been planning to leave a little later than we actually did. I left and Andy got the sack as a result.

"It was about midnight. I was doing a keyboard overdub during the week and I'd had it up to here because he was really making things difficult for me, making me go through the song over and over again, not doing an awful lot different. But he was stopping the tape every five seconds, saying, 'Oh, I think you missed a B flat there' or, 'You didn't put the bass run.' This was really getting up my nose and I thought, 'Much more of this and I'm going.' Of course, there was much more, and so I went. He'd asked me to try it yet again but I just slammed the piano lid and stormed out. I told him if he wanted to do it he could do it himself – in so many words – and went into the control room, where I poured myself a drink. He followed and tried to calm me down but that didn't work and then he lost his temper and tried to get me to sign a contract for the next tour which was lined up already. But I said, 'I've never signed anything for you yet and I'm not going to start now.' The row carried on and nobody else said a word, in defence or otherwise, which was very strange, and I just walked out. I went out the front door, shut it behind me and never looked back. That was it.

"Mick rang me up a couple of days later saying, 'Ray's asked me to give you a ring' – which was typical. I told him not to worry about me and that was that. In the end, they got a guy from The Pretty Things called Gordon Edwards for the tour. I rang Andy and said, 'Look, we're out of a job; let's get on with our own band,' which we did. We did an album very quickly for Phonogram and lots of gigs, but really it was all a bit premature. We'd planned to leave but not so soon; my temper just got the better of me. You can't go back after that."

The new group was called United and they did indeed have a record deal waiting for them. Sadly, despite a successful tour of Germany and a decent album in the can, record company policy changing meant the record never saw the light of day. Eventually the band folded; Pyle went on to other bands, Gosling became a manager of a music shop. Neither would have it any other way. Andy Pyle sums up his time with the band: "We raced through the hits and laboured over the concepts. Fans were all ages, all persuasions and all sexes. Many would follow the band to every show in case it was the last. Three US trips and a short European jaunt later we were back in the studio for the aptly titled *Misfits* album. It was time to go. But not before I'd been cajoled into yet another Stateside excursion. We returned for the 1977 Christmas show at the Rainbow, a particularly memorable occasion for me, as it marked my final appearance with the Muswell Hillbillies."

John Gosling is equally phlegmatic. "It's silly, having an axe to grind after all these years, but they were horrible times at the end. In the beginning we'd all had a lot of fun, and that was great. But looking back, if Ray had been a bit more reasonable and if we'd all kept our tempers a bit more, then I could see the band still going today with that line-up. As it is, you look back on a wasted opportunity; we could have been up there with the Stones today if we'd behaved back then. In many ways, it ended at White City. When your leader stands up on stage and tells everybody apart from you that he's retiring, that's not the best feeling in the world. After that, it was downhill all the way, and when John Dalton left, that was the end. But looking back, there's never been another band like that. Still..."

17 ...AND I'M HERE IN MAIDA VALE

With members falling by the wayside at every turn, early 1978 should have been the perfect time for the Davieses to look at their own behaviour with a critical gaze. "They share what I'd call brotherly hate," John Dalton suggests. "What the one wants, the other doesn't; it can be that childish."

And that simple. What must never be overlooked when considering their behaviour is that Ray and Dave are that most dangerous of pairings: they are brothers. Jagger and Richards have only themselves to blame for their destructive differences; the Davieses have genetics to contend with. All siblings fight, and it's not as if the brothers used to be close and were violently divided by fame; what they began as boys they have continued with a vengeance as men. But at the end of the day, blood is thicker than water: they may not often like each other, but neither would consider leaving the group, not like the various interlopers that have come and gone.

One such interloper cites the problem as stemming from an exaggerated sense of rivalry between the brothers. Bluntly put, Dave resents Ray's hold on what was his group. "I think that was a lot to do with it," John Gosling opines, "because it was actually Dave's band and Ray only came in as rhythm guitar player and did a bit of singing. When Robert Wace left and Ray took over, that's when it stopped being Dave's group." Throughout the '60s, the relationship and tantrums played second fiddle to the band's career, as they should have, but with more success came greater dissatisfaction from the younger brother. Matters weren't aided by Ray's behaviour, particularly after one encounter. John Gosling: "There was a significant moment when we went to see Elvis in 1971. Once Ray had seen Elvis in his white suit, that was the start of a huge rift between him and the rest of the band. That was it – it was Ray's dressing room, his bottle of champagne, his limo. He'd obviously got it in his mind that he was going to be like Elvis and the rest of us were his band. When I first joined, we were a tight five-piece, all pretty much equal. Everyone was working equally hard. But that all stopped."

The situation had never been ideal, but from that moment on it was worse. Ironically, in trying to deal with Ray's ego, Gosling undoubtedly made it worse. "One night, he was coming over a bit strong, so I started playing 'Mr Wonderful' on the piano. It started off a bit tongue in cheek, but from then on it got less of a joke as he set himself above everybody else." Worse still, from Gosling's point of view, the song was made an official part of the set.

The brothers' antagonism towards each other, exacerbated by Ray's increasing hold on the group, has dominated the band in each of the four decades they've existed together, but in the '70s the rest of the band were treated to some shocking displays of fraternal feuding. "Dave had had it from Ray from the very outset, anyway," Gosling continues, "but then it just got worse. Dave would start singing 'Death Of A Clown' and Ray would walk right in front of him and start 'Dedicated Follower Of Fashion' through Dave's first verse. Little things like that." Possibly revenge for an earlier occasion? "In the early days, Ray apparently jumped off stage into the audience with his guitar, doing his frontman bit for one of the first times. Anyway, he was trying to get back on stage and Dave just put his foot in his face and he fell flat on his back. Not nice."

Bad enough for the brothers, but at the centre of the trouble were the hired hands, paid to play and not, you'd think, fight. "Mick was always getting his drums kicked off the riser, mainly by Dave," John Dalton remembers. "It wasn't safe even for him up there." "We all got played off between them, even Mick," Gosling agrees. "We became pawns because we were stuck in the middle; we were getting the flak."

John Dalton: "During the *Preservation* period, we had ten people on stage and it all got confusing. There were so many of us that you'd get cliques and three or four would do this, others would do something else. But as for the fights, it'd be Ray against Dave, Dave against Mick, Mick against Ray; there'd be arguments after most of the gigs, but that was just The Kinks. Someone would just say something, a beer would be thrown and off they'd go. It didn't matter who started it."

The fact that both brothers are so obviously astute makes their behaviour all the more unfathomable. But at the heart of it remains their blood relationship, as Ray confessed to Ira Kaplin in the *Soho Weekly News*. It's not always serious, it seems: "He sees bits of me that he hates and it just starts. I don't know how much of it is serious from his side. Me, I try to look at it light heartedly and say it's a joke. I get the feeling from him it's real, because Dave is a real tight guy and he can turn just like that."

Whatever the truth of their feelings towards each other, their very public displays of hatred had the effect of alienating those close to them. Ray suffered more than Dave. Ray was the ringleader, the authority figure, and so it was him the others took an impish delight in ignoring. When the sessions for the album that was to be *Misfits* were announced, he found it next to impossible to motivate the troops, to the extent that Nick Trevisick was employed to play drums until Avory could be persuaded to join in. Mick would soon return, but Pyle and Gosling were lost before completion.

John Gosling on his last recording sessions: "We'd normally put the rhythm track down; occasionally we'd put it all down in one go then re-dub certain things – like the bass and the drums and the piano. Quite a lot of the time we'd play the whole thing through as a band, and only rarely did we put the bass and drums down first like a lot of bands do. Generally the whole band put the track down first; it was just what you took out and replaced that altered things. Then we'd overdub various bits, like my piano part, if he was unhappy with the original. Of course, as things got worse between us he became increasingly unhappy with my parts; he really did make my life a misery in those last few months."

May 1978 saw the release of *Misfits*, ten tracks that had nothing to do with Mr Flash. For the first time in years, the band had managed two consecutive albums without mentioning their leader's alter ego, and it must be said that the results spoke for themselves. Although selling fewer than *Sleepwalker*, the album went Top 40 on the *Billboard* chart, proving that the American fan base was still there. While Great Britain was in the grip of The Sex Pistols, The Kinks provided a palatable version of this thing called punk for the less extreme Stateside purchasers. Whatever the reason, the band were happy to be heard.

The LP cover depicted Ray stretched almost beyond recognition in a Daliesque distortion designed to imbue the "misfit" idea. Inside the sleeve, the record contained some of the band's finest work, scattered among the typically average fare that typified the period. Some spectators felt the album's title and slant to be aimed at Tom Robinson, but that seems unlikely. Given the "bastard father of punk" status that meant Ray was despised by the generation he was in part responsible for, it is his cultural displacement which seems aptly summed up in the title. Fortunately the songs failed to emulate his annoyance, taking shots instead at (randomly) transvestitism, tax exile, racism and, er, pollen.

Of the bunch, 'Hay Fever' is probably the weakest, not because it's actually that bad, but because one feels there was probably a better song dealing with a better topic that was kept off the album for it. Mention of pollen counts, sinus pains, allergies, tissues and sniffing do not make the best lyric, despite being perfectly timed for the sneezing season. If any one song seemed to cry out for a concept album to call home, this was it. Fortunately, it remains homeless on an otherwise well-balanced selection.

Of the better tracks, Dave's contribution shines through where 'Hay Fever' falters. Dismissing the trite and irrelevant, Dave cuts to the quick of life and deals with important issues, displayed by the title alone. 'Trust Your Heart' is about visceral responses where Ray would rather wax lyrical over the logic of a situation. In two brothers we have the split which divides Hamlet so fatally: man of action versus man of thought; in this instance, the passionate man of action triumphs with Dave mustering as much from his guitar and own lead vocal as he can to do justice to the lyric.

Elsewhere on the album, the title track proves to be one of Ray's finest contributions. A tale of losers, mad-eyed gazers, loonies and sad-faced failures, it champions the man afraid of himself who is unable to make the world work for him. Every dog has his day is the refrain; how well that applies to Ray Davies in the '70s is open to debate – as is 'Get Up', apparently "a song for the little men who get forgotten" which deals with the same theme of alienation and missed opportunity.

So successfully does Ray deal with society's oddballs that Arista, eager to carve a market niche for their new signings, pushed him out as Mr Misfit, king of the unaligned, spokesman for the off beam, friend of the lonely. Car slogans, ad campaigns and even a cartoon strip were mooted and gradually forgotten.

Better success was had by probably the best song on the album, Ray's 'A Rock 'N' Roll Fantasy'. A mixture of self-analysis and mourning, it takes up where *Show-Biz* left off, exposing the same life led in 'Sitting In My Hotel' with the warning not to take it too seriously. At the same time, there is the reminder that even the star is human – Elvis Presley, Ray's hero for many years, had died while the song was being written. As the song says, "the King is dead" – and there's nothing anyone, not even a million cheering fans, can do. Better turn the record player up a notch...

The song's mood and decent tune suggested it for a more selective audience and so it was released as a single. Increasingly typical of the times, the UK ignored the release while the *Billboard* Top 30 welcomed it with pleasure; The Kinks' international reputation was keeping them alive for the rest of the world, enthusing them to continue with every chart success.

English ears may have been deaf to the charms of The Kinks' own single, but they still broke the UK Top 30 anyway in Trojan horse fashion. In this instance the vehicle was a young band called The Jam, three angry young men with persuasive rock tunes to match their Mod sensibilities; tucked inside were The Kinks, delighted that their song 'David Watts' was a hit for the new group.

The new-found kudos proved insufficient to sway the increasingly critical music press; *Misfits* was dismissed as out of date and, worst of all, irrelevant. But if The Jam's celebration of their work didn't win the critics over, another cover version, this time of the almost prehistoric 'Stop Your Sobbing', sent revitalised hacks rushing to canonise the band they claimed they'd loved all along. The new devotees were The Pretenders, fronted by an outspoken young American woman, herself a former *NME* writer. Chrissie Hynde's treatment of Davies' song propelled both singer and songwriter into the minds of those who matter and the song into the place that mattered – the Top 40. It was a success that both were extremely grateful for.

Suddenly, the respect Ray had been working for since the '60s was forthcoming as a new generation began to take interest. In turn, it became a very lucrative interest as songwriting credit and royalties started to seep through. These two songs didn't exactly make him a fortune, but examined in context, 'Stop Your Sobbing' and 'David Watts' highlighted very clearly the long-term advantages of being a songwriter. Sitting in his very comfortable central London flat, Dave Davies told us the fiscal difference between the brothers. "Ray's been fortunate because he writes the majority of the songs," he explains. "That's why he lives in his mansion in St John's Wood with the McCartneys of the world and I'm here in Maida Vale."

Songwriting, clearly, was where the elder Davies brother earned his crust. Take that away and he was on the same wage as the rest of them, according to John Dalton. "There were times when we found it very hard on the money we were getting," he admits. "But everyone was on the same, it was quite fair. It's not as though Ray was getting more than us. He got all his money from the songwriting." John Gosling continues: "We were all on wages apart from the company, which was Ray, Dave and Mick. They just paid us a flat rate whether we were on tour or in the studio."

Outside the everyday working, important decisions that could affect everybody were made without consultation. "Changing record labels and things like that were decided by Ray," Dalton explains. "Well, him and his lawyer. We never got any extra money from something like that. Whatever there was went straight into the company and we never saw it." The company, and its studio, were strange affairs, seemingly all encompassing yet selective as well. John Gosling recalls the original plans for the band's studio: "Konk was meant to be between the whole group, but I never signed anything and so I never really got anything. The years slipped by and it turned out that just Mick, Dave and Ray earn from it."

Doubtless the paucity of money made available to the band members – Ray included – when it continued to remain a serious money-making concern exposes the brothers' renowned stinginess once and for all. The legendary money borrowing scams of the '60s hadn't been forgotten ten years on, as Gosling recalls: "Ray asked me to lend him ten dollars once on tour because he said he was broke. Dave quite often used to take me and my wife out and he'd foot the bill, but Ray always had this pretence of poverty all the time. I don't know what it was, but he was trying to hide his wealth. He is very rich, but not blatantly. He doesn't flaunt it. He's not interested in material possessions, and when we used to rehearse at his big house in Cobham, Surrey, there'd be about two items of furniture in each room. For a while, he'd walk around with his wage packet for that week in a carrier bag. He used to try to pretend to the rest of us that he wasn't wealthy and he was very sparing when it came to handing it out; always left his wallet in the dressing room and never bought a round of drinks. When you know the guy's loaded, you expect him to be a bit more forthcoming.

"There was a song we used to do called 'Money Talks' and he'd dash around doing his Max Wall impression as Mr Flash stuffing fake five pound notes in our pockets as we were singing – that used to get right up my nose. And he used to look quite angry as he did it, as if he really meant it. We certainly weren't in it for the money. It was the songs and the enjoyment of being with the others when it was all going well. The money was the very last consideration."

It had to be. Andy Pyle had earned twice his Kinks wage with Savoy Brown, and that was five years earlier.

But the money emphasised the changing definition of the band. John Gosling: "Ray and Dave got worse with each other and grew away from the rest of us. You've now got the rest of the band as wage earners, and it ends up just as Ray and Dave instead of The Kinks, and those two are totally different. It has changed drastically, probably since about 1973."

Dave and Ray occasionally, usually just Ray, but hardly ever The Kinks; the perception of the core of the group still fluctuates today. But in the '70s it was mostly Ray's group. That was obvious in everything they did, from checking in at hotels at different times, as Gosling recalls, or just the travelling arrangements. The truth of the matter is that Ray found the others' company too rowdy to be among very often and so he distanced himself; but it was yet another sign of the singer being different and therefore "better" than the rest.

John Dalton: "He was always there with us. I've got to own up, we were always a bit noisy so he'd sit apart on planes and things. We'd all be together and he'd be with the managers. He'd always be there with us – just a few rows back." Gosling agrees: "Very occasionally, Ray would join in the fun with the rest of us, but mostly he set himself very apart on the road, more so in the last few years. Even Dave became the same towards the end."

As well as different mentalities, Ray had work to do at the back of the plane. With the band constantly touring when they weren't in the studio, he needed to grab every opportunity to come up with the next concept album. *Show-Biz* had to come from somewhere, after all...

"Everything that was in his mind was writing," Gosling remembers, "and that can make somebody a boring person. He was fun to be with sometimes and came out with us once or twice, but generally he was very difficult to relax with. I couldn't unwind with him and I don't think anyone else could do either. He wasn't interested in anything other than work; he just wanted to sit on the tour bus with his notepad, staring out the window, completely detached from everything going on around him."

"He works every day," agrees Deke Arlon, who became manager of The Kinks in 1996. "He's not a holiday person. I keep imploring him to take breaks, but he just writes and creates. He has ideas all the time. Not a day goes by without him having at least the idea of part of a song or project, and sometimes these won't come to fruition until five years' time, but it doesn't matter. He has bits of paper everywhere, notes which nobody else can understand, but he does."

Occasionally, the prospect of being one of the lads proved too great for Ray and he would join in with the others – of a fashion. "Well, he tried to pretend," Gosling continues, "but in reality he wasn't like that. He had everything planned out. It was a shame because he couldn't really come out with us and relax because he had to keep himself together for the shows, whereas the rest of us were a little more devil may care and, if it worked, it worked. He became distant in that way. He wouldn't come out clubbing with us when we went to LA or New York, and in the end I think he became a lonely person. He got some good songs out of it, but I don't think that was any way to live."

Ray's commitment to work had cost him his marriage to Rasa so he knew the penalty for shutting himself off. But by his diligence, the rest of the band were kept in employment and, if anything, it was surprising he tolerated the behaviour of the rest of the group as well as he did.

"He obviously went through phases, especially when he was ill, but he was never really into all the drinking, not like the rest of us," Gosling recalls with some relish. "In the States they used to call us The Juices because we really used to tuck it away. We once did a thing in Central Park which was promoted by this beer company and they just lined the dressing room with cans of the stuff and we managed to finish most of it off. We took it back to the hotel with us and filled the bath with it and made our way through it and then had to have two days off."

As well as pretending to join in with the band off stage, on stage Ray had mastered his drunken image, pioneered during 'Alcohol' years earlier, and still going strong today. Gosling: "The rest of us earned our reputation, and of course Ray picked up on that and made a big thing of it, balancing the beer bottle on his head and pretending to be pissed all the time. But somebody had to hold it all together and so he couldn't do it really. Not like the rest of us."

With a clear head, it was left to Ray to replace the missing personnel for the next album. Jim Rodford, ex of Argent and Phoenix, came in to play bass; keyboards became the jurisdiction of The Pretty Thing's Gordon Edwards. The group back to its optimum size, hastily arranged gigs were lined up and performed to trumpet the release of *Misfits*, and for a while the band enjoyed something of a mini-revival during 1978. The inclusion of a blistering cover of 'You Really Got Me' on a young American band's debut LP topped the year for the group; on their way to becoming one of the biggest heavy rock names of the '80s, Van Halen's tribute to The Kinks' anthem ensured that the legend of Ray Davies was not going to be forgotten just yet. Nor ever. Almost two decades later, Ray remains grateful for the plug which without doubt introduced, if not his name, then his work to a new generation. "On many occasions, I've had 18-year-old girls come up to me after shows," he told us, "and they thank me for playing the Van Halen song. But that's life, it happened and you can't change that."

Despite being the writer, Ray wasn't precious enough to not appreciate Van Halen's treatment of the song. "The great thing about them is that they took 'You Really Got Me' up a tone and played it in A. That allows you to thrash the chords out more, and it changed the sound of the whole thing – playing an open G and then slamming your hand down to the A. Whereas we did it in G and had to play barre chords and slide them. It was a great idea, more no-nonsense than our version."

If the success of his songs through other people was beyond his control, then the line-up of the band ran it a close second. After a short spell with the band on the road, Gordon Edwards quit the group on the eve of the next album, the blunt *Low Budget*. Without a permanent pianist, Ray took on the job himself, attacking with enthusiasm the role he often made it seem he wanted many years earlier. But a full-time replacement needed to be found, and eventually Ian Gibbons, on Jim Rodford's recommendation, began to appear at the studios. Jim and Ian had worked on a session together and Ian had recently completed a tour and album with The Records; but since he wasn't an official member he easily found himself with time to help out The Kinks. Although not credited, he allegedly handles a couple of chorus vocals and possibly a keyboard part or two on *Low Budget*. A massive American tour was his proper introduction to the band and he was to stay for more than ten years.

Low Budget in several ways lived up to its name. While so many of the decade's concept projects had slow boiled any signs of goodness away during interminable sessions at the band's own recording studios, the new album was completed relatively quickly – at another studio, which had to be paid for. For the first time, The Kinks recorded outside England, finding the atmosphere of Blue Rock in New York more conducive to a gutsier performance. With a renewed sense of urgency the group thundered through sessions, often accepting the earliest takes on the backing tracks. Ray seemed keener to move on rather than labour too many points, culminating in a completed album that was a relative joy to make – and it sounds like it, too. If only Gosling and Pyle had been around to see it.

September 1979 saw *Low Budget* set before the public. The UK reacted with its customary blend of disdain and dismissal; the US, however, responded favourably to the band's obviously American-orientated rock slant and, possibly, thanked them for deigning to record the album in their country. Whatever the motive, while Great Britain's charts remained untouched by The Kinks' presence, the *Billboard* listings had it reach an amazing Number Eleven – their highest ever placing for a studio album.

Slices of Americana thrown into the lyrics and big riffing chord-driven songs obviously touched the US public; namechecks for national heroes like Captain America (Marvel Comics' patriotic freedom fighter is alive and well in 'Catch Me Now I'm Falling') and Superman (DC Comics' father of all heroes gets his own song: '[Wish I Could Fly Like] Superman') kept the band's Stateside syncopation active. The latter song as a single release even charted in the lower 40s.

Yet while the welcoming arms of America were obviously being courted, Ray couldn't quite give up his roots. 'National Health', although not exactly about the UK's once-glorious NHS, does hint strongly at one of his home country's finest institutions. Closer inspection finds its lyrics concerned with nervous tension and various pleasurable antidotes: Quaaludes, Valium and cocaine are dismissed as palliatives by the thoughtful Ray while a little bit of exercise is recommended. The slant is humorous and the tune catchy, a return to form.

Still with his tongue seemingly in his cheek, the Puckish bandleader vamps his way through the album's title track. 'Low Budget' centres on a fairly well-to-do character whose pecuniary frugality bears no little resemblance to a certain RD Davies. Ill-fitting clothes are bought because they're cheap; he sucks mints rather than buy cigars; and, most illuminatingly, he asks not to be called "tight" if he doesn't buy a round. As if... Put to a striding rock track the song cracks along with the singer never so truthful in his interpretation of the lyrics.

Of the album's other highlights, 'Attitude' seems sung once more from the heart, with Ray the quiet obvious character being described. The song takes a thrilling ride through his own life, hilariously slipping in just about every criticism that he's ever been subjected to. Tightness, looking like a queer, alienation – all charges to which he would be found guilty. Finally, as if there were any doubt at the start, the song ends with him admitting he's used up all his old licks which only a change of attitude can get him out of. Again, musically the band play what is a fine song well.

As if to illustrate the Atlantic divide which affects the album, Charles Spencer, for *The Daily Telegraph*, wrote in 1995, "It's a deeply depressing experience listening to some of The Kinks' later albums, hard to believe that the gormless lyrics and duff tunes come from Ray's pen." For his proof, he cites several lines from "a lamentable LP called *Low Budget*", not even dignifying the song with identification. It is, in fact, 'Moving Pictures', a deft if unimaginative sequel to 'Celluloid Heroes'; not brilliant, but not worthy of castigation almost 18 years later.

While not the greatest album of their career, *Low Budget* did pave the way for future success in America, a territory that had caused their careers such great damage in the '60s. England might not have responded so faithfully, but the wearing works of Mr Flash needed some time to be forgotten. Restoration for the band in their native country would one day come, but not in this decade. Perhaps the '80s would be kinder.

18 A STRANGE WAY OF WORKING

The 1980s saw a big change in pop music. Punk had done its best to eradicate what it saw as the dinosaurs of rock – mainly groups like Led Zeppelin, Queen, The Who and even Status Quo, although there was no reason to suspect that The Kinks would not be targeted, too. On that score, at least, it failed miserably. During the years 1976 to '80, Led Zeppelin sold more records than all of punk put together. And for whatever reason – their acknowledged weirdness, their refusal to follow fads or even their relative lack of success – The Kinks emerged from the safety-pin tirade with considerable credibility. Several punk (or at least punkish) bands had even covered Ray's tunes and various compilations in the coming decade would try to capitalise on this. So, as far as the post-punks of the early '80s were concerned, Ray Davies and his boys were okay.

But in the '80s, a new threat would emerge, in the form of the synthesiser bands and the new romantic movement. Where punk had shouted, "Bollocks!" (or never mind them), new romanticism pitted one-finger keyboardists against the most tour-hardened and work-fit bands in the world. Bands just like The Kinks. In fact, the synth groups would come closer to wiping out dinosaur rock than punk ever did: sales of guitars reached their lowest for decades; Casios, Rolands and Yamahas ruled the roost; and groups with names such as Depeche Mode, Orchestral Manoeuvres In The Dark and Spandau Ballet threatened to do their worst. Many rock fans would say they did exactly that.

As it was, the Davies brothers, Avory, Rodford and Gibbons rode out the storm and went on to make the '80s a great decade for The Kinks. Albums such as *Sleepwalker*, *Misfits* and *Low Budget* had already broken the American album chart barrier and almost all the coming LPs would do the same. There would, however, be personal casualties.

In the first February of the new decade Pye released a coupling of the band's two most raucous early hits, 'You Really Got Me' and 'All Day And All Of The Night'. Although seriously marketed as product which suited the post-punk afterglow, the single failed to chart. Two months later came another compilation; this time in the form of the LP *You Really Got Me*. Not one of Pye's budget Best Ofs, this time the record was released as a full-priced album, designed to appeal to new listeners; those who had been turned on to the band by artists such as The Jam and The Pretenders, whose success with 'David Watts' and 'Stop Your Sobbing' respectively had assured Davies' songs of the ear of a new generation. To this end, both tracks were included, as was a selection of the group's lesser known early material. Although a clever marketing strategy – The Kinks were indeed becoming something of a cult – *You Really Got Me* stayed out of the charts.

The first "proper" Kinks album of the '80s, *One For The Road*, marked a significant moment in the band's career. Having established themselves as a serious stadium attraction in the United States, they could afford to release their first full live album since the disastrous *Live At Kelvin Hall* in 1967. (*Everybody's In Show-Biz* had been only half live.) And what pleased Ray the most was that it would be tied in with a simultaneously released concert video.

The Kinks' live repertoire at this time contained a lot of recent material, as well as a few old favourites. Ian Gibbons was present on all the gigs from which tracks were used on the album. Here he describes its making and hints as to why *One For The Road* failed to make an impact in the UK while reaping significant successes in America (where it reached a healthy Number Eleven in *Billboard* magazine's weekly rundown) and Europe: "Originally on these gigs we were promoting *Low Budget* and also doing stuff from *Sleepwalker* and *Misfits*. Quite recent stuff really. Of course, from about the mid '70s the band had been concentrating on America and building it up, just doing a couple of weeks each year in the UK. For some reason, the Americans seemed to understand the new stuff much better than they did in Britain; I think the British audiences wanted – and indeed still do want – just the '60s stuff. Obviously Ray has never stopped writing and the new material had a much better chance of being listened to in America than it did in the UK, or even on the Continent.

"So we did this very long tour, at the end of which a concert video was made from a show in Providence, Rhode Island. After we'd recorded this video, we came back to Europe and did Scandinavia and Germany, etc. Then, after Christmas 1980, we returned to New York state and did a series of theatres; Ray recorded quite a lot of the shows on a mobile studio and he put together this double live album, *One For The Road*. The video that we'd recorded in Providence was released simultaneously. That live album was very successful all over Europe and America."

A rather different affair from *Kelvin Hall*, *One For The Road* was taken from almost a year's worth of Kinks dates and benefited from a tight band at the top of their form, and of course from some judicious overdubbing at both Konk in England and Blue Rock Studios in New York. Originally to be called "Double Life" and released several months earlier than the eventual date of 1 August 1980, the album included several staples, with raunchy versions of 'You Really Got Me', 'Lola', 'All Day And All Of The Night' and 'Till The End Of The Day', plus the rejuvenated 'David Watts' and 'Stop Your Sobbing'. Numbers from the band's more recent albums were also included, such as 'Low Budget', 'Misfits', 'Prince Of The Punks' and several established cult classics, including a moving version of 'Celluloid Heroes'.

On one of the concerts for this tour, Ian Gibbons' Yamaha keyboard went up in smoke – literally. "This was in Austin, Texas," grins Gibbons. "We had these overhead explosives – maroons, I think they call them. They had them hanging off the lighting gantries and one night one of them didn't go off, didn't bang in the air; instead it fell off and landed right on top of my Yamaha CP70. There it was, at the top end of the keyboard, fizzing away. When those plastic keys catch light it's a really black smoke which stinks like mad. So I turned around to play the organ, because I wanted my back to the smoke and to the thing itself, in case it actually went off, while Kevin the keyboard chap tried desperately to put it out. But the whole of the two top octaves melted together and all this molten plastic was dripping on the floor and catching the carpet alight. That was one of many interesting evenings."

Shortly after *One For The Road* came the surprise release of the year – in fact, of the last 13 years. Finally, Dave's solo album – commonly known as *Dave Davies* or by its catalogue number *AFL1-3603* – hit the streets and it proved, to many fans at least, to be a disappointing heavy metal pastiche. Having originally used session musicians from The Kinks' *Misfits* album, Dave suddenly decided to erase their work and record more or less everything himself, including drums, bass, keyboards, guitars and all the vocals. The album sold respectably well but reviews were generally unfavourable, pointing out that there were heavy metal bands – most notably Led Zeppelin, those darlings of the American stadium circuit whose drummer, John Bonham, died that same year – that did it a whole lot better. The next year, Dave would release the follow-up, *Glamour*, which fared worse from a sales point of view and no better with the critics. Many would point out that Dave's vitriolic lyrics – particularly in 'Move Over' – were clearly directed at his brother, although the guitarist denied this. "I could never write anything that obvious," he retorted.

Dave felt that his current record company, RCA, had failed to put their weight behind the album, and so he decided to move. After some considerable struggle – no one wanted to sign a solo artist who was also committed to such a major group – Davies was picked up by Warner Brothers. The following year his third solo outing, *Chosen People*, was released. This was a happy time for Dave, and the album, despite one or two slips back into the heavy metal of *Dave Davies* and *Glamour*, shows the younger brother as a gifted writer and performer.

Meanwhile, Ray's own private project took up much of late 1980 and the early part of '81. This was a theatrical adaptation of Aristophanes' *The Poet And The Woman* and showed Davies in collaboration with playwright Barrie Keefe. *Chorus Girls* proved a more successful bonding of theatre and rock than almost anything that had gone before it, owing to Davies' legitimacy as a contemporary composer and Keefe's acknowledged abilities as a theatre writer. Put together during a solid month in a Portakabin in London's Stratford East, the show opened in early April. As a political drama which featured Prince Charles being kidnapped while attempting to open a new job centre, the play was not kindly received, although both Keefe and Davies were more than pleased with the results.

During this period, Ray was living with the Pretenders singer Chrissie Hynde (she was cited in Ray's divorce from his second wife, Yvonne). Hynde had not only brought 'Stop Your Sobbing' back into the public eye but in November 1981 gave Ray another Top Ten hit with one of his finest early songs, 'I Go To Sleep'. Hynde and Davies had a child together, Ray's third daughter Natalie. They were also nearly married, in a farce which highlights the often ridiculous life of a Kink. Having named the day and booked the registry office, the pair decided, literally moments before the knot was due to be tied, that marriage was a state of mind and not the proverbial piece of paper. According to Ray, they then reconsidered, deciding to go through with it after all, by which time the registrar had other ceremonies to conduct and dutifully refused their pleas.

Like a latter-day Yoko Ono, Hynde accompanied her Kink whenever she could, a situation which bred resentment – perhaps even jealousy – in brother Dave. On one American show, she was ushered to the stage and introduced by Ray to the audience, to Dave's obvious disgust; he threw down his guitar and left the stage, only to return and spit in the face of his brother's consort in a childish gesture of defiance.

Spitting, cursing and the occasional airborne guitar were the basic stuff of Kinks tours. It had gone on in the early days and was hardly going to stop now, as Ian Gibbons relates: "When I first joined the band, I was blissfully unaware of all that. I'd been warned, but I didn't really see much of it until a gig in Santa Barbara, when there was a bit of an altercation with a flying guitar. I thought, 'Hello, best keep my head down.'"

Despite the ever-present squabbles, The Kinks maintained their busy tour schedule through the decade's early years. Gibbons: "It wasn't constant touring but we were working on a pretty regular basis. There were definitely two or three months in America every year, then Europe and then some in this country. Between 1980 and '83 we also went off to Japan and Australia, so it was pretty hectic. And when we weren't off touring, we were at home putting new albums together – *Give The People What They Want* was next and then *State Of Confusion*. We managed to put a few singles out too."

In fact, the next Kinks single broke the Top 50 barrier in Great Britain for the first time in nine years. But 'Better Things', although still owing something to the British pop group of a decade or so earlier, hinted strongly at the Americanisation of the band – which Ray consistently denied, although it was plain for everyone else to see.

1981's *Give The People...* did almost as well as the group's tearaway live album, reaching 15 according to *Billboard* and hanging around the chart for a full nine months. Ian Gibbons was present for the duration of the recording sessions and recalls his experiences in dealing with the unusual studio practices that Ray had evolved over the years. "He's certainly got a strange way of working," exclaims the pianist. "With most other artists, I've found that there are usually two ways of working: you either come in and record the song as a group – and in that situation you obviously know what the song is because you're all playing the arrangement; otherwise, the keyboard player can be brought in towards the end of the recording, when the song is almost finished, for overdubs etc, and in that case you can hear what the number is because there's usually a rhythm track down and a guide vocal too. But with Ray, you'd all go in the studio but you wouldn't know what the melody was, what the lyrics were going to be or anything; he'd keep that pretty close to his chest all the way through the recording. Basically, he had an idea for a song and reams of lyrics and we'd all go in and jam around chord sequences that he'd written. I'm sure he had an idea in his head of the finished product. It was just that he wanted to try out as many different approaches as possible."

Give The People What They Want was released in August of 1981 in America, but the UK had to wait another five months; proof, if proof were still needed, of where the band's audience, and allegiance, now seemed to lie.

Gibbons describes the group during this period as one of the great live rock bands. "When it cooks, it really cooks," he exclaims. "Because of those great songs, it's difficult not to groove. I suppose it's a bit like the Stones, really, where nobody's playing anything that amazing, but there's always some really good stuff going on." Gibbons goes on to say which tracks from *Give The People...* provided the most musical pleasure on stage. "'Art Lover' was a great one to play, as was 'Give The People What They Want' itself. Both those songs had great grooves and so these were the ones that worked well on stage. One of my favourite songs on the album was 'A Little Bit Of Abuse', which was great to record but we tried it out a couple of times on stage and it didn't really work; perhaps it was a bit too subtle. 'Better Things' was a great pop song too – typical Ray. I have to be honest and say that I hadn't really kept up with what The Kinks were doing until I joined a couple of years earlier. Obviously I'd grown up with their music, but through doing your own stuff in different bands, you lose contact, so I hadn't realised that they'd been gaining this huge American audience and just how good it would be trying out the new songs on them."

Between each record release the touring continued virtually unabated, with the band playing bigger and more prestigious venues. By the end of 1981, The Kinks had gained enough clout to fill New York's Madison Square Garden. In spring of the following year the American guitar virtuoso Eddie Van Halen added to the band's considerable credibility by including 'Where Have All The Good Times Gone' on his group's album *Diver Down*. David Bowie had covered the same track on his Number One album *Pin-Ups*, nine years earlier.

In spite of all this success and admiration, the tensions that had always existed between the various members, and which had traditionally shown themselves during the making of records or during long stints away from home, naturally surfaced again. It always seemed that Dave was in the middle of it all, whether in another bout of sibling rivalry or attacking whichever unfortunate band member happened to be handy, should Ray not be around. Tales of fisticuffs and flying guitars abound and several Kinks, past and present, have intimated to us that enough has been made of this feuding – which often erupted into mindless but spectacular violence – elsewhere. Others, with jobs still to protect, feel that discretion is perhaps the better part of valour.

Ray's love of film and theatre, until this time mostly frustrated or thwarted, would soon find a worthy vehicle in the still relatively new and largely unexploited medium: video. When 'Predictable' was released at the end of October 1981, it was accompanied by a brilliant Julien Temple promo. This showed Davies in full command of the screen, capitalising superbly on his apparent failure to accomplish the simplest of everyday acts; in salting a bag of chips, for instance, he empties the entire cellar onto his dinner. The newly launched Music Television (MTV) made great use of the video and the track was a visual, if not a commercial triumph. Ray told us how he believes the potential of MTV to make art out of music videos was squandered: "In the early '80s, when MTV was really beginning to happen, there was a chance to become an art form, but now the art is in marketing." If 'Predictable' was art, then its follow-up, the musically trite but lyrically perceptive 'Come Dancing', would take The Kinks back into the Top 20 on both sides of the Atlantic.

'Come Dancing' sees Ray doing what he does so well: milking nostalgia for the old England; ruing those salad days when his sister and her boyfriend would dance every Saturday night away at the Atheneum ballroom. Parking lots have replaced bowling alleys, which have in turn wiped out the local palais.

"I just wanted the record to be a little tribute to my sisters, who were big fans of the dance halls," Ray told *Guitar World* in 1997. "It was inspired by a photograph that my sister showed me of her dancing at the local hop on Saturday night. It's just about her and her husband."

Again Davies exploited the video format, this time blending himself into the role of his Uncle Frank, a spiv character from the '50s whose facial features were not unlike those of his nephew. Ray slicked back his hair and acted out the part to a tee, with striped suit and a pencil moustache. Gibbons' Caribbean-style keyboard riffs add an up-beat, happy feel which belies the sadness implicit in the lyrics – his other sister Rene had gone dancing and died of heart failure the day she presented Ray with his first guitar.

Ray Davies (left) in full flow with an uncharacteristic semi-acoustic on an appearance on TV's *Ready Steady Go*.

A more staid performance in traditional '60s Shadows-style. L-r: Ray Davies on Telecaster, Pete Quaife on Rickenbacker bass, Mick Avory on drums and Dave Davies on Vox Phantom.

Kinky by name. Modelling the latest '60s fashions, (l-r) Mick, Pete, Dave and Ray.

Still dedicated to fashion in the late '60s. As usual, Dave and Pete are the most comfortable with the "dressing up" aspect of success, as well as the band's perceived campness. Mick remains the least impressed.

Above and below: the changing faces of The Kinks. John Dalton (top right) replaced Pete Quaife on bass in 1966 and again in 1969 after Quaife's slight return. John "The Bishop" Gosling (bottom right) added permanent keyboards to the four-piece line-up in 1970.

A gold lamé-suited Dave models the new Gibson L-6S.

Ray confounds American audiences with a "fag" between his legs.

Everybody's a star – The Kinks embrace the stadium age.

Mr Wonderful.

Schoolboys in disgrace, catapulted to obscurity in 1975.

Dave may have invented heavy metal riffing, but Ray knew the clever chords (F♯9).

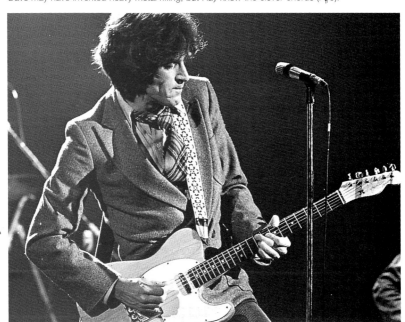

The line-up for the promotion of *Phobia*, 1993. L-r: Bob Henrit, Dave, Ray, Mark Haley and Jim Rodford. Haley would soon be replaced by the returning Ian Gibbons.

Performing at the Rock 'N' Roll Hall Of Fame in Cleveland, Ohio, 1995.

The Storyteller mid anecdote, 1995.

Dave Davies solo star, late '90s.

A man for all generations – the inspiration for Blur, Oasis, Pulp, The Jam, Van Halen, Reef, Wheatus, Kirsty MacColl, The Pretenders and who knows how many more to come.

The song plays out with a jaunty horn section, echoing those dance band days and perhaps even alluding to Ray's own time with The Dave Hunt Band. Ian Gibbons tells how Ray liked to use the same session people for these parts. "He'd often call these guys in to overdub horns and things, like on the end of 'Come Dancing'. He'd call them the 'Jazz Dads' and he's used these same players on most of the albums I've done." A track recorded at the same time as 'Come Dancing' was 'Don't Forget To Dance', which brother Dave and several other pundits preferred to Ray's happier choice. 'Don't Forget To Dance', while perhaps a superior song, was far less commercial as a single and proved this point when in late 1983 it failed to dent the BBC chart. (A reissued 'You Really Got Me', released on the same day, beat it by an embarrassing eleven places.) The track only just scraped into *Billboard*'s Top 30.

Although 'Come Dancing' eventually provided the group's biggest UK hit since 'Lola', it nearly flopped completely. The release, just prior to Christmas 1982, ensured that it was lost among the tide of torrid pap that pervades the British Yuletide charts – that year's Number One was 'Save Your Love' by Renee And Renato. But when Jonathan King later showed some clips from the American charts on *Top Of The Pops* – including 'Come Dancing' – fresh interest was shown, the single was re-released in April and it made Number Twelve in August 1983.

Years later, Ray is still critical of his label boss' hopes for the song. "Was I surprised when it became a hit? Clive Davis was."

A decade after its success, Ray explained how videos had been good to the band. "I like videos," he told us. "'Come Dancing' was a hit because of a video, but I tend to think that a lot of film is too two-dimensional. Videos are fine, but they do tend to take away that magical moment when you close your eyes and listen to something like 'Waterloo Sunset' and think, 'I imagined it would be like that.' Everybody has their own picture of it."

Ray had spent much of the previous year involved in another solo venture. This was a film that was to be made for Channel Four, called *Return To Waterloo*, which plotted the fantasies encountered during the daily train journey of a London commuter between Guildford and

Waterloo. The project eventually garnered not only serious financial support but also a talented team of professionals to complete it, but the length of time spent by Ray on the project irked Dave, who refused to offer any contributions. Gibbons explains: "When Ray got involved with *Return To Waterloo*, it took up quite a lot of his time. I was involved with the soundtrack, but Dave didn't want to perform on it; basically he felt it was a Ray Davies film and he didn't want it coming out as a Kinks project. I think what he meant was that the music was being designed to go with Ray's film, rather than there being a Kinks album from which the songs were going to be taken. So there was a bit of controversy over that." An album of the songs from the film would be released in the US and Canada in July 1985. The soundtrack, imaginatively titled "Return To Waterloo", included three tracks that by then had already been released on *Word Of Mouth* – 'Going Solo', 'Sold Me Out' and 'Missing Persons'.

1983's album was *State Of Confusion*, a title which suited The Kinks as perfectly then as during any time in their 20-year career. With Dave and Ray only just making up after the controversy of *Return To Waterloo*, Ray's relationship with Chrissie Hynde on the verge of collapse (she would marry Simple Minds' Jim Kerr within a year) and Mick Avory in private turmoil over his own position in the band, the description was more than apt. Although *State Of Confusion* is peppered with decent tracks, the overwhelming feeling is that Ray was tailoring the music to the AOR tastes of America and that, as his William Grimshaw school report might have said, he "could do better". The title track transparently deals with his neuroses, from the crumbling fabric of his house and its contents to a fear of the unknown and, of course, a constant paranoia about money: "Am I going overdrawn, am I going in debt? It gets worse the older you get." Ray's increasing disillusionment with socialist Britain comes over in 'Clichés Of The World (B-Movie)' while 'Young Conservatives' describes the growing complacency of the young elite in the ever more money-minded climate of 1980s England.

As had by now become the norm, *State Of Confusion* stayed out of the British charts but crashed into the *Billboard* Top 100 at Number

Twelve. If Britain was shunning The Kinks, then perhaps it had something to do with their pandering to American tastes and touring the UK erratically and with obvious indifference – in spring of 1984, they treated their home fans to all of eleven dates. The band castigated British audiences for treating them like a '60s nostalgia act, but was that really surprising? Hadn't they barely been here since the early '70s? Of course, as any Devil's advocate would firmly interject, The Kinks would probably not exist at all had it not been for their transatlantic rollercoaster ride. Without momentum, however, even the tallest and most exhilarating fairground ride slowly accedes to gravity; its speed decreases and the trajectory falls, leaving the riders back at the bottom, dazed and not a little confused. With pop groups, such momentum is created by regular albums and nationwide concerts in support of the product – a stable band is usually a help. It may have been 18 months since their last record and the brothers had taken the band off the road to concentrate on other projects, but at least The Kinks' line-up was as solid as a rock. Wasn't it?

19 A BIT OF HISTORY

As all connoisseurs of the group will attest, triumph in The Kinks camp inevitably leads to disaster. And in what could easily have been the band's *coup de grâce*, Mick Avory, their long-serving and even longer-suffering drummer, decided to quit. He'd had enough. Sessions had already begun for the new album, *Word Of Mouth*, when Mick, whose 20-year battle with Dave had apparently got the better of him at last, announced his resignation. Dave himself had recently been admitted to a nursing clinic suffering from "mental fatigue and exhaustion", which his later autobiography would admit was comparable to Ray's breakdown a decade earlier; although a big American tour was cancelled, he was soon back on stage with the band. But tensions were obviously running high. Avory had been a stalwart Kink, a fine and solid drummer and the acquiescent butt of a million jokes and jibes. As a quarter of "The Company", Mick did not leave the picture entirely, instead accepting a position as manager of the band's state-of-the-art studio, Konk, in Hornsey, North London. He also went on to do odd sessions and played in a low-key pub band (The Bullets) with fellow ex-Kinks John Dalton and John Gosling, as well as joining a re-formed Creation with original guitarist Eddie Phillips.

Not since Quaife's departure in 1969 had an event so rocked the camp. It would have been easy for the brothers to call it a day; both had solo careers that could more easily be nurtured without a monolith like The Kinks towering over it; Rodford and Gibbons could simply have been let go – they were only hired hands after all; life could be quieter and sweeter without the stresses of the road. But no, The Kinks were on a roll, their albums were selling well and their tours raking in the money. A new drummer was the only solution.

Bob Henrit joined the fold in July 1984. Henrit had played in singer Adam Faith's band The Roulettes (Number Ones 'What Do You Want' and 'Poor Me'), as well as enjoying stints with Unit 4+2 ('Concrete And Clay') and Argent, the band he formed with Jim Rodford and Rod Argent (Top Five single 'Hold Your Head Up'). Bob had also worked with Rodford in The GB Blues Band with members of The Mike Cotton Sound, Ray's erstwhile horn section. Having additionally played on Dave Davies' last two solo albums, *Glamour* and *Chosen People*, there really appeared to be no other choice. So Henrit was in. But where Davies R, Davies D, Quaife and Avory had been a foursome of supposedly equal share, the brothers were now in total control; The Kinks had become a two-headed monster. But as in all such genetic quirks, one half of the duopoly would eventually emerge as the dominant force.

Word Of Mouth was a US flop by comparison with the band's recent output. In fact, it fared worse than anything for years. Perhaps the change of personnel unnerved the US record buyers; or maybe their recent lack of touring had kept them out of America's public eye, just as it had done at home. Whatever the case, when the band went back out on the road again things had taken a distinct turn for the worse, as Ian Gibbons explains: "There was a long time – over a year, I think – when we didn't do too much as The Kinks, mainly due to Ray and Dave's solo projects – *Return To Waterloo* and *Chosen People*. But then we did *Word Of Mouth* and *Think Visual*, and that's when we started again. But because we'd had all that time off from touring America, the audiences had gone down and we found ourselves playing in smaller venues again. With the States, I think you have to keep working on a regular basis and have new product out every time you go over there." The Kinks' problem was that they went back to America with material that the fans had already heard or seen the group perform. "Plus there hadn't been anything in the charts for a while," adds Gibbons. "The next single, 'Do It Again', didn't even make the US Top 40. So the audiences simply weren't there to the same extent. It was still good, though, and obviously the die-hard fans were always around."

Word Of Mouth came out on 19 November 1984. Across eleven tracks the band again demonstrated their diversity with the title track, 'Do It Again' and the elegiac and, some would say, prescient 'Going Solo'. But for many the stand-out track was 'Living On A Thin Line', one of two numbers on the album written by Dave ('Guilty' being the other) and one originally, he told us, intended for his brother to sing.

"Over the years 'Living On A Thin Line' has become a bit of a Kinks fans' favourite, alongside 'Celluloid Heroes'," Dave told us. "That was a song which I specifically wrote for Ray to sing for The Kinks. But we got in the studio and Ray did a version of it, we talked about it and he thought that my version was more appropriate for some reason, so we went for that one."

Whatever the reason, Ray either wittingly or unwittingly thwarted one of Dave's ambitions. "It's always been a bit of an unfulfilled ambition of mine to write a song for Ray to sing with The Kinks," Dave told us. "I know it sounds a bit sentimental and it's not meant to be, but one of the first recordings we ever did was a song called 'I Believed You', which we did when we were still The Ravens, just prior to being The Kinks. It was a song that Ray sang but I wrote, and I always felt it was a big, big stepping stone for me, and I felt it was a big musical step for us."

Before *Word Of Mouth*'s worldwide release, a UK single was put out to alert buyers that new material was imminent. Two Ray songs, 'Good Day' and 'Too Hot', were chosen as the respective A- and B-sides, and 10 August was set as the release date. Despite both "summery" titles appealing to simplistic radio DJs and a twelve-inch format featuring an extended mix of 'Good Day' plus a bonus track of 'Don't Forget To Dance', the song failed to chart.

The first US single emerged on 4 December. Backed with Dave's 'Guilty', 'Do It Again' reached Number 41 in a ten-week run in the *Billboard* chart. Eventually released in the UK on 19 April the following year, the same day as a twelve-inch version featuring the bonus track 'Summer's Gone', the single failed to trouble UK chart compilers. For the German version of the extended single, the song 'Long Distance' was included instead, making its debut on vinyl, having been previously only available on cassette.

For America's second single, Arista chose the UK's bonus track. 'Summer's Gone', with 'Going Solo' on its reverse, was released in March 1985 and failed to chart. Although they probably didn't realise it, The Kinks had seen their last hit in America. For all their later industry, they would not "do it again".

Various Kinks, including John Gosling, John Dalton and Ian Gibbons, have told us of the strange recording practices at Konk. Having worked on all the '80s albums, Gibbons is in the perfect position to elaborate. For instance, is Ray good at extracting a performance from his musicians? "Yes, sometimes he's very good," admits Ian, "but other times I can find it a bit frustrating." The main problem, as Gibbons has already stated, is that there is usually no melody to work from. "And you don't even know where the gaps in the singing are going to be, so it can be a bit vague. Sometimes I'll try a little idea out here or there, because maybe the chord has given a hint as to what's going on, but normally there's little or nothing to go on." Gibbons adds that Davies likes to get the bass and drums recorded first – "to give a basic structure to the song as he sees it in his head and then build on it from there." Not surprisingly, a huge amount of material is usually committed to tape. "There's always an excess amount of material recorded for each album," stresses Gibbons. "There's always 15 or 20 tracks, and the ones we continue to work on end up on the album while the others are put into storage. That's the luxury of having your own studio."

The main frustration, apparently, is hanging around and waiting to be called to do your part. "There is a lot of time sitting around while someone else is doing their overdubs," confesses the pianist, "so you'll be watching telly or playing snooker, waiting for the call. And that might take ten hours or never come at all. The same could happen at home. Ray would call and say, 'I might need you tomorrow', so you'd sit in and wait, phone in at midday, phone in at four, etc. That was the main frustration, hanging around, but that can happen in any recording situation, and of course with The Kinks I've had the great privilege of playing on some wonderful songs."

While the band toured through the '80s, they would often be supported by other artists, including some who have since risen to the highest heights. "John Cougar Mellencamp used to open for us quite a lot," tells Gibbons, "as did Ian Hunter [Mott The Hoople], Blondie, INXS and even the young Bryan Adams. The relationship between us and the support bands has usually been pretty good, because I think most groups feel it's a bit of a privilege to work with The Kinks – it's a bit of history, really, isn't it?"

As has already been seen, life on the road with The Kinks can be a volatile experience, but some things occurred which were outside even Ray's control. "Like the time a bloke came through the ceiling in Seattle," laughs Gibbons. "We were performing in this building which had scaffolding all round the outside because they were doing some work on it," he explains. "The building had quite a big dome on the top and they'd put a false ceiling in, with these walkways across it that had lights and things attached to them for their regular functions – it was an ice hockey rink and they played basketball there and all kinds of stuff. Anyway, this bloke decided he was going to climb up the outside of the building and get in to see the show, but while he was on one of these gantries going across the false ceiling, he was spotted." The errant music-lover made a dash for it over the flimsy panels, which he clearly didn't realise weren't made to take the weight of an absconding intruder and, startled, crashed straight through the ceiling onto the audience some distance below.

"The funny thing was," continues Gibbons, "Kevin Brown the keyboard technician had been playing practical jokes, which he did all the time. When John Cougar was opening for us, he used to do a song called 'I Need A Woman Who Don't Drive Me Crazy'; Kevin had fitted up one of these blow-up dolls and they were raising and lowering it behind John. Of course he couldn't see it, because he was facing forward. But anyway, we thought that this person who had fallen through the roof was one of Kevin's blow-up dolls, because it looked so weird. But in fact he landed on these people in the audience and the whole show had to be stopped; he was lucky, because the people he landed on broke his fall, but there were some quite horrendous injuries to people's necks, and that was terrible."

While the new material struggled to get itself heard, 1984 saw The Kinks' 20th anniversary celebrated by various compilations. In the States, the aptly named *20th Anniversary Edition* double LP and cassette assembled an odd mix of hits – 'Sunny Afternoon' and 'A Well Respected Man' – and covers – 'Dancing In The Street', 'Louie Louie' and 'Beautiful Delilah'.

Meanwhile, in the UK, 'All Day And All Of The Night' was re-released as a single on 2 November, almost 20 years to the day of its first chart appearance. The full "hits" album, called *The Kinks – Greatest Hits*, followed three weeks later, but the celebrations didn't end there. 30 November also saw the UK release of *The Kinks – Kollectables* featuring tracks like 'Rats', 'I'm Not Like Everybody Else' and 'Polly'. Notably, of its 14 tracks, six are written by Dave.

Ray's contribution to another album released the same day was even less. Called *The Kinks – Kovers*, it compiled 13 of the songs the band had covered on record over the years: 'Milk Cow Blues', 'Bald Headed Woman', 'Long Tall Shorty', 'Long Tall Sally', 'Cadillac', 'Dancing In The Street', 'Louie Louie', 'Naggin' Woman', 'Too Much Monkey Business', 'Beautiful Delilah', 'I've Been Driving On Bald Mountain', 'I'm A Lover Not A Fighter' and 'Got Love If You Want It'.

Another project, *Kinky Music*, saw the Davies brothers restored as writers but their musicianship replaced by session players. Originally released in 1965, it was by The Larry Page Orchestra and featured players of the calibre of Jimmy Page, John Paul Jones and Clem Cattini. Ray, having publicly slated the original album, was erroneously credited as "arranger" on this version.

After a career founded in music but interspersed with various attempts at reaching a theatrical audience, 1986 saw Ray given a marvellous opportunity to achieve a new crossover. Julien Temple, one-time pop promo director for stars like David Bowie, Judas Priest and of course The Kinks, was making his feature film debut, adapting the '50s retrospective novel *Absolute Beginners*. A star-studded cast led by Bowie was swiftly assembled, a soundtrack LP produced and chart success abundant for the album in April. But while most of the film's tabloid column inches were devoted to the presence of new sensation Patsy Kensit (starring as Crepe Suzette), singer with pop band Eighth Wonder and former child star of certain root crop television ads, and while music papers lapped up the garrulous media presence of the Thin White Duke, there was another serious pop star making a decent contribution to the film's soundtrack.

In a marked contrast with his rebel image, Ray Davies, as patrician guardian, smoothly fills the part of father figure to the lead. His song 'Quiet Life' sits comfortably on the film's soundtrack, striking a perfect one-hit balance of wry comment and catchy tune. Of course, his mere presence in a film set several decades ago adds a note of veracity to the picture; Ray somehow fits into the era in a way few of the main stars can fake. And, like Bowie's title track, his song doesn't seem out of place in either mood or style.

'Quiet Life' finds Ray reflective and tired. Omnisciently, he oversees the generation below him growing up, making the mistakes he warned them about, then bringing their problems to his door. In the charming but defeatist lyric, he admits to preferring the image of senseless idiot rather than be bothered by the trials of other people's daily grind. He speaks as a father of children, but he could be voicing the concerns of someone saddled with explaining every shortcoming of '60s pop.

Most interestingly, from a lyrical analysis standpoint, after a song of wilful denial he ends each chorus with the admission that he's on top of it all. As in life, he appears to bump from one project to the next, ignoring the views of everyone from his family to his public, blissfully working on the following goal with little heed to the needs of others. And as in life, he just may be sitting back and smiling at the furore that surrounds every album release that doesn't contain a replica of 'You Really Got Me', safe in the knowledge that even if things look like they're going wrong, it's okay, he planned it.

As a footnote to the episode, a showbiz irony can be located in the cast list. In *Absolute Beginners*, Ray Davies stars alongside Patsy Kensit, who used to be married to Simple Minds lead singer Jim Kerr, who used to be married to Chrissie Hynde, who nearly married Ray Davies.

Another major part of the soundtrack was The Style Council's 'Have You Ever Had It Blue', fronted by ex-Jam singer Paul Weller, of course. The soundtrack aside, 1986 saw the release of another Kinks album. Inspired by his close involvement in the film world and the success of 'Come Dancing', November's *Think Visual* offered several comments on the perils of melding song with pictures. Keeping up with the theme, the liner notes introduced us to the "cast" rather than musicians. For this outing, the five-piece arrangement of Davies (times two), Henrit, Rodford and Gibbons was augmented by the slight return of Mick Avory. Keeping up his involvement with Dave, Mick plays drums on one of the younger brother's tracks, the bracing 'Rock 'N' Roll Cities'.

Prior to the album's release, 'Rock 'N' Roll Cities' was issued to American record shops as a taster track. The single actually marked a fairly significant milestone in Kinks history as it saw a Dave Davies composition on the disc's A-side for the first time. For once, Ray's track was nudged into a supporting role, giving the young guitarist a welcome boost in confidence. (In the UK, however, another track by Ray called 'How Are You' was selected for single release.)

Dave's track excepted, the rest of the album shows all systems normal. A new bluesy route is suggested in the US single's B-side, 'Welcome To Sleazy Town', a song that was set to play a prominent part in later tours. The core of the song reflects Ray's long-aired despair at the thundering process of modernisation. Rather than an unfriendly ghetto, Sleazy Town is a place from Ray's childhood that he remembers fondly, warts and all, from a time before the bulldozers arrived. Interestingly, his cherished video age is also criticised – forget the remote controls, the pause facility, the play-when-you-like convenience; for real life, step outside your home for a while. Visit 'Sleazy Town' – if it's still there.

The video age is again the subject of 'The Video Shop', but once again the idea of industry-driven urban decay prevails. With unemployment rife due to a lack of investment, Ray opens a video store and fast becomes the peddler of dreams. Like the drug society encouraged in Aldous Huxley's *Brave New World*, Ray sees the fantasy offered by a two-hour cassette as a way out of modern life's stranglehold. Escape the drudgery of life, he advertises in this charming piece, for just £1.50 a day.

He too could do with a break, if the opening track, 'Working At The Factory', is anything to go by. At first it sets up the album's concern with industrialisation and the dehumanising advances in production. But deeper than that, the song makes a striking admission that Ray's own life has been a desperate slog, as much like working in a factory as any job screwing on bottle tops or pasting stickers nine to five. Stating that he clocked on at his factory in 1963 (the first real year of The Kinks, remember), his life since has been a laborious, humourless slog, less gratifying than the most menial manual tasks. The music business, he weeps, has become a characterless production line and what was once a dream has turned into a nightmarish reality.

Both Ray's pet gripes on this album come across in the title track. The recurring buzz words of "productivity" and "profitability" tie the song immediately to those before it, but its concern with image hones its relevance tightly in on the pop star's role. The musical production line of 'Working At The Factory' is extrapolated here: it's no longer good enough to pen a decent song, he bemoans; acts now have to be marketable in a fashion sense. For a man in his awkwardly dentigerous position, the order to "flash those teeth" must doubly hurt, but the command to smarten up his act if he wants to make it in the business is soul destroying.

After the honour of leading a 45's onslaught on the US market, Dave Davies had another burst of kudos in October 1987 as a compilation of his material was put out by their first record company, Pye. Effectively stripped of any rights to his proposed solo album from the early '70s, they still maintained ownership of his first few singles, and so the record, entitled *The Album That Never Was*, collated several A- and B-sides plus two of his prominent Kinks creations, 'Death Of A Clown' and 'Susannah's Still Alive'.

December 1987 saw the near release in America of the band's next album, a proposed double live set called *The Road*. Not for the first time, Ray envisaged a full live video accompanying the release to consolidate the band's success in the visual medium. And not for the first time, his record company said no. MCA, the band's record company in the US from 1986 (London Records took over the UK and the rest of the world), also balked at the size of the record and ordered that a single disc would be sufficient for a live album. As a consequence, tracks like 'Lola', 'You Really Got Me', 'All Day And All Of The Night' and 'A Well Respected Man' ended up on the studio room floor to make room for recent cuts like 'Art Lover', 'Lost And Found' and 'Living On A Thin Line'. In the end, only two hits make the final grade: 'Apeman' and 'Come Dancing'.

That final grade was the single album *The Road*, released worldwide early in 1988, although dates varied from January in the US to May in Great Britain. (In the UK the album was scheduled and re-scheduled for release several times in the first five months of the year.) The album consisted of eleven live cuts recorded almost entirely at the Mann Music Center, Pennsylvania (although 'Lost And Found' was taped from a gig in Maryland), plus one new studio track born at Konk the previous September.

Called 'The Road', the new track remains an often hilarious, overtly autobiographical account of life with a touring band. Structured with a bouncy new line / title refrain / chorus, the song works as a live track; although of course it was the only one put down in the studio. Dealing with the long slog of his life so far, "greasy spoon" eateries and "motorway" over-familiarity, the highlight comes in Ray's precise naming of his band's original members. Pete Quaife, Mick Avory and Dave the Rave are all presented and corrected (while long-serving current members are ignored). But the killer line is reserved for the singer as he deals with all the rumours surrounding his effete stage presence by admitting he strummed away with "a slightly limp wrist". The song was released as a single ahead of the album in the UK but failed to chart.

The Road also premiered another new track, although it remained a live cut. Entitled 'It (I Want It)', the song is an experimental rock-ballet piece that had been aired during the tour of 1987 to occasionally bewildered response. It has never been attempted in the studio; we can probably live without it.

It may have had to make way for a newer cut in 1988, but the live version of 'You Really Got Me' intended for *The Road* eventually turned up in September 1989 on the B-side of the band's latest single, the pessimistic 'Down All The Days (To 1992)'. (Another track, 'I Gotta Move', would emerge on the B-side of 'Did Ya' in 1991.) Ray would get his double album out one way or the other.

Rare twelve-inch formats of 'Down All The Days' featured a second B-side, called 'Entertainment', on which there hangs a tale. Not a new song at all, it was actually first mooted for inclusion on *Give The People What They Want*, but intervention from Arista meant that the single 'Better Things' was put on in its place. Never one to waste a good song, Ray put it forward two years later as the title track to the band's next album, which would be a concept work centred around the activities of a dance hall ('Don't Forget To Dance' and 'Come Dancing' were already written). But as quickly as Ray came up with the idea of a supporting video linking all the songs and starring the same characters, the project was aborted. At the same time, a new song called 'State Of Confusion' found its way into the set and something had to be dropped to make room. Exit 'Entertainment'.

The story doesn't necessarily conclude there. 'Entertainment' finally made its way onto the band's last album of the '80s, *UK Jive*, but via another twist in its already circuitous route. Not surprisingly, *UK Jive* wasn't the original title planned for the album; that honour went to the track 'Million-Pound Semi-Detached', which was originally going to head the list. Its eleventh-hour removal from the set, however, following London Records in the UK voicing concern over the song's merits as a single, meant that a place was available for another number. Enter 'Entertainment'.

Ian Gibbons left the group in 1989, at the end of the recording of *UK Jive*. "It was never easy recording with the band because there were lots of pressures from either side; Ray would want one sort of thing and Dave might want to go in another direction. And the album seemed to be going on for so long that I felt like I was burning out. I needed to have a break. They were great gigs though. We started off in this club in Dallas as a couple of warm-up dates and the shows just started getting bigger and bigger until we got up to New York, where we were doing these gigantic ice hockey rinks and things." Ian's replacement was a young piano player called Mark Haley, whose band, in a strange twist of fate, had been playing on tours organised by Hal Carter, The Kinks' early stagecraft mentor. Haley had previously worked with Hal's great idol Billy Fury, shortly before the singer's death in 1983, and played with The Monkees when three of the group – Davey Jones, Mickey Dolenz and Peter Tork – reformed for a comeback tour; he had also been the jobbing keyboard player with visiting American artists such as Brian Hyland and ex-Brit Eden Kane. Haley added one or two keyboard overdubs to *UK Jive* but only lasted as a full-time Kink until the end of 1990, when his services were used only occasionally on the road. Haley left in 1993 after a souring of his relationship with the band. "I spoke to him on the phone and he said, 'I don't know how you took it for so long,'" confesses Gibbons. "But I think he was so much younger than the rest of the band that he didn't really understand what was going on, and generally Kinks shows are so off the wall that you never know what's coming next. But who couldn't get something out of playing those songs? All the raunchy rockers like 'You Really Got Me' and 'All Day And All Of The Night' and the gentler, subtle numbers like 'Days' and 'Autumn Almanac'. They were the archetypal British '60s pop songs. He wrote the book on it, really, didn't he?"

20 THE ONLY THING THAT KEEPS US TOGETHER

Taking a perusal of any local theatre listings these days can often be like winding back the years as you turn over the pages of the local paper. Names of acts you'd thought long finished or, worse still, dead can be found populating the music venues in most towns on most Saturday nights. And why not, of course? The band members still have a living to make, even if none of the original line-up are left; and the packed halls prove there's still a sizable market for retrospective acts to pander to the wave of new-millennium nostalgia.

In that way, The Kinks weren't alone in the 1990s chalking up their fourth decade on the road. Any number of acts, from Gerry And The Pacemakers to The Searchers, can still be caught live after more than 30 years in showbusiness. But where The Kinks retain their credibility is in their prodigious churning out of new material. By no means innocents on the "Greatest Hits" trail (they have been the subject more than most of lucrative back-catalogue reissues), they had had, by 1993, 28 serious new releases in just 29 years; quite a feat. Where others are content to live comfortably off the fruits of labours long gone, treating live audiences to the same set year in and year out, The Kinks have never settled for the old joke where a new one would do. The reason for this can be summed up in two words: Ray Davies.

Ray's belief in his own powers has rarely faded since his first faltering steps at songwriting many years ago. Two-minute pop songs in the '60s, lumbering concept albums in the '70s, thematic rock projects in the '80s – the hits may have dried up, 'Come Dancing' aside, but the intention was there. By releasing new material virtually annually, Ray was staving off defeat; remember, his character won't let him lose while his body is still capable of trying, and while there was the competition of other acts scoring Number One successes, he was going to carry on.

But carrying on in the '90s, a new decade and a new chapter in the band's career, was not going to be that straightforward. It was not destined to be a time of musical growth for the band and they would release only one studio album plus another quasi-studio live project. And yet, come the middle of the decade, the name of The Kinks and, in particular, that of Ray Davies would be as well known as during any time since the late '60s.

The groundswell of Kinks worship ostensibly started by The Jam and carried to greater heights by The Pretenders and Van Halen in the late '70s would reach new levels some two decades down the line. Ray Davies, semi-forgotten legend, the man interviewed by the *NME* in the '70s under the banner "Well Neglected Man", was at last to get a hint of the respect which he – along with most decent-thinking music-lovers – had long felt he deserved.

Certainly when one considers the fates of his closest early contemporaries he deserved – and deserves – more than he achieved. Indeed, the three biggest bastions of British pop from the '60s were being treated very differently. The Beatles, despite splitting up in 1970, had never lost their command of the marketplace (as 1995/6's *Anthology* TV series and CD collections testify); John Lennon's death had in many ways only served to increase the lucrative mythology surrounding the band. On the other hand, The Rolling Stones, despite a reportedly far-from-salubrious lifestyle, had succeeded in maintaining, through little more than their reputation, the imagination of the public on the live circuit. The *Steel Wheels / Urban Jungle* tour of the late '80s had broken their own concert records; a feat they repeated with the *Voodoo Lounge* world blitz in 1994/5/6, despite poor album sales throughout the last 15 years.

And The Kinks? The brief UK resurgence during 1983 aside, they had seen their world-wide grip slowly slip, especially in America where the Top Ten excursion of *Low Budget* had never being equalled; the lower hundreds, already a formality in Britain, were becoming a familiar sight for the frustrated band even in their biggest marketplace. But hope was at hand through secondary sources, as a generation of musicians born during The Kinks' boom period began to start repaying the debt they'd accrued through just listening to Ray's lyrics and music. Many artists had covered his songs, but this was something more: fragments of what would become a whole musical movement were amassing independently, using the flavour of their heroes more than their actual songs. And soon they would rule the world.

Britpop – the cute jingoistic tag attached to a growing mood in the UK indie scene – was on its way and Ray Davies, through no solicitation of his own, was to be the genre's so-called "godfather". Unlike most godfathers, Ray was absent from any christening; the first he knew was when he became aware of his own name cropping up in the *NME* once more – and for positive reasons. Blur, the Essex group fronted by major Ray fan Damon Albarn, would become the prime motivators in re-introducing The Kinks' name to the media and the world. Other major acts such as Pulp, Supergrass and the ex-Madness star Suggs would not be far behind in their public admiration, nor would female stars Aimee Mann and Kirsty MacColl.

That was all still to come. During the early '90s, The Kinks found themselves somehow in limbo. Touring remained sporadic and new releases non-existent. But that wasn't to say the band weren't busy. Ray had written the next album, for an as-yet-unspecified record label, and recordings at Konk were, of course, under way. Only a core unit of the brothers plus Jim Rodford and Bob Henrit was present at the sessions, the smallest retinue since the '60s. Mark Haley's one-track contribution to *UK Jive* was to remain his total studio output with The Kinks. It became clear he was only required on a touring basis as Ray took it upon himself to deliver all keyboard parts on what would become their next album, *Phobia*. (His role would be even further diminished in the spring of 1993 during promotion for *Phobia*. An "incident" between Haley and Dave Davies in Switzerland on 10 July led to his departure from the group two days later; Ian Gibbons stepped back into the breach to replace him.) Ray, of course, balanced his time between the studio floor and the control booth like a practised tregetour, leading the troops from the ground as well as directing the war from on high. Work went well, but the results weren't to emerge until 1993.

A new year then, another record company and, finally, a new album. 1993's offering, *Phobia*, released on the massive Sony-owned Columbia label saw the band treated to the most serious treatment for years. Now they were stablemates of Bob Dylan, Bruce Springsteen and Michael Jackson their future looked almost as bright as their past and no expense was spared on the album. Top engineer Bob Clearmountain, a name more usually associated with the likes of Mick Jagger and David Bowie, was drafted in to give several of the tracks that '90s sheen, and the whole project was put together with a serious stab at chart action the goal.

With the aims set out, it's time to assess the potential. Ammunition-wise The Kinks were firing some of the deadliest bullets yet, with a high proportion hitting their target. *Phobia* sounded sharp, loud, riffy and big, with the band really performing as a well-trained rock unit. The album had actually been ready for some time, some of it recorded two years earlier and only seeing the light of day now due to the record company situation being sorted out; but whatever the history, the result was a well-groomed effort at regaining lost ground, and therefore one deserving greater attention than many of the earlier *oeuvre*.

From the first cut, *Phobia* nails its colours to the mast: rock is to be the name of the game. 'Opening' sees Dave striking up a brief guitar reveille, playing one speaker off against the other in his declaration of the band's rocky intentions. It's the perfect introduction to 'Wall Of Fire', an excellent riff-based grinder. Gruff vocals from Ray and looping harmonies from Dave add to the powerful production sound, the tune is instantly hummable and the band play like they've been on stage all night.

'Drift Away' offers more Grizzly Adams-type vocals from Ray, again backed by his brother who chips in with some well-paced, mature guitar playing. The other instrument of note is a charismatic swirling organ sound, played by Ray. The hard numbers continue with the title track, one of Davies' finest songs so far. Everything about 'Phobia' screams Led Zeppelin – it just needs Plant and Page performing it, because it already contains their energy and idiosyncratic change of rhythms. With a suitably pessimistic lyric insisting that everyone has their demons somewhere, the song shines; things end with Jimmy – sorry, Dave – widdling into a feedback frenzy. Excellent.

Despite scoring high on the riffometer, *Phobia* still finds room for more than a couple of ballads, although few of them match the heavier, faster numbers for immediacy or even warmth. 'Only A Dream' probably comes closest, sounding like 'Holiday Romance' (from *Soap Opera*) mixed with the untouchable 'Days'. The lyrical observation that life is like an elevator – it takes you up and brings you down – goes some way to explaining the song's balanced efforts at cheering and moving its audience. Compared to the ease with which he handles the harsher vocals, Ray's voice seems ill at ease on this track, not quite reaching the required levels on occasion. When the song calls for a spoken word, his accent becomes most confused and the mumbled singy / talky effect is probably not that which was hoped for.

Another balladic departure from the rock-tinted album is 'Still Searching', a poppy smooch number with affairs of the heart and looking for a home at its core. Prominent bass on this track comes as usual from Mr Rodford, proving ever more stable as the years wear on. Also showing signs of calm in the '90s is Dave, who on 'Don't' gets to show he can still produce a nice, clean solo when it's called for. On this occasion it proves to be a lifesaver, clawing the song back from going over the edge into the pit of non-description.

Speaking of which, 'Over The Edge' itself offers another instrumentalist the chance to shine – this time Ray as he grapples for control with some great synth playing. As the title is blurted out forcefully by the brothers in unison, a familiar topic subject-wise raises its head. Suburban pressures manifested through garden barricades and Union Jack-garbed fascist extrapolations of the neighbourhood watch theme meld with the pitching vocal delivery – another success. A well-crafted pop song, then, presented with solid musicianship and particularly nice high BVs from Davies the younger serves as another highlight on an album which had more than its fair share.

Where 'Over The Edge' succeeds quite humorously in its third-person depiction of the war-torn suburbia, another song achieves even greater comic results through hand-on-the-heart type first person honesty. The title: 'Hatred'. The theme: the same. Sub-titled 'A Duet', the song is a vicious dialogue between Ray and Dave, the one spitting out his lines in riposte to the other's asinine claims. Based, it is impossible not to suppose, on the real relationship between the brothers, the lyric spirals in its rapacity. However sad it is that hatred is the only thing they have in common, the frenetic pace of the track, Dave's excellent playing and the superb juxtaposition of some of the lyrics make this the funniest song on the album; if not in the whole Kinks catalogue. Modernist readings of literature absolutely forbid the interpretation of lyrics as relating to the author's life, but for the most part the accuracy with which the song maps the brothers' real relationship cannot be ignored. Ironically, it sounds like Ray and Dave had such a hoot recording the track that the veracity of their lines could easily have been weakened with every take. No proof, just a feeling...

"It was very funny," Dave told us. "It was also great fun to do because it was kind of like a mini-exorcism because of all the tension that sometimes builds up between Ray and me. There's a lot of tension there. There always has been. But I'm sure it's helped us a lot as well. It's been very healthy. I don't believe that creative art of any kind is always easy – although that's not to say it has to be this difficult. But sometimes it has to be difficult to get anything done.

"But yeah, I enjoyed that song. It kind of started from a line from a Charles Bukowski film, *Barfly*, which you should see. It's very funny. It's about this guy who's a writer, and I think it's really based on Charles Bukowski's life. It's this drunk who's a great writer but all he wants to do is be a drunk. He has writing ambitions, but he's such a purist he doesn't want to have any success at it, so any time he makes some money he drinks it. It's a great perspective and there are some great lines. He has to get a job, but he doesn't want one; he comes back to his regular haunts and says to a barman, 'Why is it that everyone's gotta do something or be someone?' It's a view I can relate to. There's another scene where he wakes up listening to this rowing couple next door. And he laughs to himself and says, 'Hatred – it's the only thing that lasts.'"

...Which obviously inspired the Ray line, "Hatred is the only thing that keeps us together."

"I think in a lot of ways it's helped. Look at the Gallagher brothers. People like it when you argue. They like it when things go wrong. Ray and I have had a lot of problems, but I do think that people blow it up out of all proportion. To be honest, I think Ray and I have had a very difficult life – I know it sounds daft, and how can someone who's made a certain amount of money have a difficult life, but believe me, you can. You can condense a lot of experience into those few years, and for what you've got to show for it at the end, it's not a lot."

Back to the album, no sweep of the songs of note on *Phobia* could omit 'Somebody Stole My Car', which again highlights another slice of oft-shrouded Kinks humour. Stepping over the matter of the track for a moment, it concludes with a car alarm followed by a familiar-sounding "beep beep, beep beep, yeah" from The Beatles' 'Drive My Car'. Ironically, for all the earlier antagonism between the groups, when the chance arose, there was no question of not doing it as a tribute to that other, now-defunct pop outfit from the '60s. As for the rest of the track, the lyric once again finds comfortable ground in the experiences of an underdog, this time the honest Joe hit by the increasing crime wave. Ray Davies didn't like the effect of industrialisation on housing in the '60s; the conurbations of the '70s little improved matters and the grand metropolises of modern times, nowhere better demonstrated than in Tokyo – home of many of the band's most ardent later fans – seems proof of a world gone mad.

The next track on the album, while listed towards the end, actually was the starting point of the whole project.

"The first song we started working on was one of mine, one called 'Close To The Wire'," Dave revealed to us. "I tried to inject ideas into that based on what was happening in England at the time – like the decline of the Yuppy – but at the same time keeping it personal, about what was happening to The Kinks: we're still surviving but it's touch and go. Those were the thoughts and feelings I wanted to inject into it. That started the ball rolling for the whole album, so it was an important song in that respect.

"As usual, it began with me selecting a few ideas I'd had that I think would be appropriate for a Kinks album. Then normally Ray and I sit down and play through them, just me and Ray getting together round a keyboard or guitar or whatever, thrashing ideas out."

While a decent track on most albums, alongside a dozen or so others written by one of the greatest songwriters of his generation, Dave's contributions can seem slight. It's a problem he's aware of, which makes the success of his own songs all the sweeter.

"There was a song we had out on the *UK Jive* album called 'Perfect Strangers' which I always thought should have been a single," Dave reminisces. "Our then manager agreed – this was in America. But that was an obvious song. That had to go on. Sometimes it has been a bit of a battle. I mean, Ray's such a prolific writer he'll almost go and write ten songs just to spite me. It'll be like, 'Oh great, you've got five songs.' Then next day he'll come back and it's, 'Here's ten songs I've written overnight which I think should go on,' and it'll be, 'Oh, I like that one, and I like that one…' and it can get a bit silly."

On the plus side, of course, is the fact that, in the face of such competition, if one of Dave's goes the distance, it has to be a great song. "Yeah, I suppose so. But it does mean that a lot of songs don't see the light of day. I think it's an important lesson for any writer, not to throw any ideas away, because you might be writing a song, scratching your head for a line or a bridge, and you'll remember that song you wrote ten years ago which you've got on tape somewhere."

With the '90s under way by three years, the fact that *Phobia* was only the band's first album of the new decade made it something of a temporal oddity. The same period in the '70s resulted in an astounding five albums being produced (one of those a double set); even the '80s had produced three new additions to the back catalogue during its opening years. The very exclusivity of *Phobia* condones serious assessment of the work as a whole. In 1993, The Kinks had clearly fallen off the treadmill to the extent that their next venture became, once again, something of an event and not just the next turn of the wheel.

While critical response to the album was on the whole positive, sales did not repay Columbia's apparent investment. Barely an impression was made on the UK charts while *Billboard* registered a mild fluttering just inside the Top 200; not a success by any means.

"I really liked that album and I don't know why it didn't do better," Dave told us. "I think one of the problems The Kinks have had historically – apart from all the different record companies – is that a lot of companies haven't really understood what The Kinks are. I think Clive Davis at Arista knew, he got it. He really, really got it [groans at his own pun]. I think Sony tried, but it was a case of too many cooks: they kept saying, 'Why don't we try this?' or 'What about doing that?' and Ray and I would look at each other and go, 'Here we go again...' They didn't really know what to do with it. I think *Phobia* was a fabulous album, but the record company didn't know what to do or what to promote first. It was almost like having too many good songs on it so one A&R guy would say, 'God, we've got to put "Scattered" out,' and someone else would want another one, so it wasn't focused."

Deke Arlon, manager of The Kinks in 2001, has his own theory on the album's demise. "*Phobia* was made for a very commercial record company – Sony," he says. "They pressed the buttons and either got a response to the buttons or didn't. Each act only has that small window, and if there's another act at the time getting better a response, you've missed your chance. In those days, you had to sell a million albums to be successful; these days, you have to sell eight million, because the marketing men have taken over and you need to sell that many just to break even. Ray comes out of an era where you made a record, you put it out, radio liked it so they plugged it on their shows and if you sold a million copies you were a big, big success and money was made."

Commercial disappointments aside, *Phobia* proved interesting in other ways, not least of which was for its inclusion of Ray's trademark guitar, the famous National steel acoustic, on 'Scattered'. As a great-looking instrument, its fame can partially be put down to the album cover of Dire Straits' *Brothers In Arms*, which featured such a marque; as a great-sounding tool, though, look no further than old Kinks classics like 'Lola's intro for just how good it can sound – how good and how irreplaceable. "On 'Scattered', I've used it to make the sound bigger," Ray told us. "They're great but very difficult to record, but I wouldn't want to put pick-ups in because it would sound awful. I still have the original National that I bought for 80 quid which I think was made in the 1940s. I don't know how much it's worth, but to me it's invaluable because of the sounds I've got and the things I've done with it."

Sadly, for the album's accompanying tour, the National wasn't removed from its case at Ray's home. Instead he found himself sporting a selection of other makes. "On this tour, I'm using a Gibson Victory which has more top end than any guitar I've ever played," he reveals. "Then there's a beaten-up '60s Gibson Melody Maker that I acquired in America about 15 years ago and a Les Paul which I've taken to very late. I had a wonderful Telecaster that I bought with my first earnings from 'You Really Got Me', but that was stolen, which is sad because it can never be replaced. I've also got a Martin, my National, and a Gibson semi-acoustic like the old, original Chuck Berry guitar. But my favourite is a Sears-Roebuck guitar which I got in America because it has an amplifier in its case." Being the lead guitarist, Dave's needs are more basic than his brother's; not for him all that alternating between electric and acoustic instruments. "Guitar-wise, Dave uses a Fender Telecaster Elite," revealed his guitar tech Geoff Horne. "He has three of them but only two on stage. There are also a couple of Gibson Artisans which he used in the '70s. We tried them out again but he prefers the neck on the Telecaster."

Live in 1993, The Kinks put on a show of some diversity and much merit. Harking back to the days of the band actually supporting themselves, the shows commenced with the now-typical sight of Ray strolling on stage unaccompanied, save for his trusty acoustic (not his National). Wearing a peaked cap and tan, raincoat he looked for everyone like the bloke off the street who'd stumbled in by chance, happening to find an audience. Arguably a real interloper would have had greater command of The Kinks' back catalogue as Ray wilfully accepted requests from the surprisingly ecstatic throng. On one memorable night in Cambridge, a burst of 'Dedicated Follower Of Fashion' quickly led into the opening lines of 'Plastic Man' – which soon faltered as Ray stumbled over the song's peculiar lyric. "You'll have to help me on this one," he grinned at the female requester. Then, giving up, "I'm sorry, but I tried..."

For many ardent supporters, this new style of jukebox entertainment supplied the best slices of the night's enjoyment. The rest of the show, fluctuate as it might, could never be as freeform as Ray's spot on his own. Real obscure numbers could be thrown at him and, depending on his memory and his hearing, some would be played. The possibilities were endless, although, as Andy Pyle reveals, not entirely revolutionary.

"Originally I went in to help them finish the album," he recalls of his '70s experience. "Then they said, 'We've got this tour coming up...' so Ray gave me a pile of albums with the songs that I had to learn ticked off on them – about 200 songs. The thing with Ray was that, if anybody called out a song, he'd play it. The band didn't want it note perfect, but I had to be aware of the songs. Not exactly the best way of working."

By 1993, though, Ray had pared down the risk element of the show, taking the bulk of the chance on his own shoulders during his acoustic set. But even during the main event it sometimes turned out that his caprice was far from satisfied.

"We have a notional set pasted up which is just what we've been doing the last few nights," Ray told us. "But that is just a guide and it changes. I don't often look at it because it's all in my head."

For the most part, he remains in control, but the 1993 tour, like many before and since, saw another factor playing an important role. "A lot of it depends on what the audience want to do," he admits. "The audience is and always has been an important part of what we do live and I think that the drawback of being in a studio for two years making an album is that you lose contact with them."

The audience is put forward by Ray once more as the prime decision-making force at a Kinks gig; but endless punters and a succession of ex-members would disagree. What about the song selection that omits the hits? Ray, it seems, has a selective memory, or perhaps his viewpoint is slightly aslant. He believes his own rhetoric for a reason; scilicet from a mildly off-centre standpoint compared to most commentators. For example, the one part of the 1993 show which unanimously invited – almost encouraged – criticism from audiences because of its inaccessibility is championed by Ray as the pivotal proof of audience sovereignty.

"I like narratives but I also like to create a load of images," he begins. "That's why I like this thing 'New World' we do, because it's just a lot of ideas drawn together; it doesn't lead anywhere and it leaves the audience free to reach its own conclusion."

'New World', to explain, involves Ray, a harmonica, the rest of the band in blues jam mode, some atmospheric blue lighting and two dancers who perform silhouetted against the stage's backdrop (as they also do during 'Aggravation'). It's a far cry from 'You Really Got Me'; in fact, it seems the '70s circus troupe approach to touring never really went away. Certainly, Ray's need to play ringmaster is as profound as ever, crystallised during one soundcheck at Cambridge's Corn Exchange by his attempts to balance instructing the band, playing harmonica and directing the dancers through their sequence.

"I was only helping them out," he suggests. "We haven't got the depth here to get the effects we want, so I had to get the girl to angle herself so it looked more representative of the position I wanted to see out front. The thing with the band was me trying out this little harmonica thing for the beginning of 'New World' which we are playing – it's just a freeform sort of jazz jam-type thing. I wanted a harmonica bit to go over the front of it so Dave had to work out its odd phrasing. I didn't even know if I'd do it on the night because harmonicas are sons of bitches to work with – they sound great at soundcheck but in the show the notes don't blow properly."

With the choreography hinting at past glories, Ray reveals how close the entire *Phobia* project came to not being an all-out rock band album at all: "'Don't', which was my provisional title for the album, I wrote as a nine-minute opus which was like a mini-musical because it had so many chords. I didn't know at that time whether I wanted this to be a conventional rock album – whether it could be performed in a conventional rock environment or in a theatre. I had this idea of putting The Kinks in the background and making the music secondary to what's happening on stage..." – in a similar vein to the live achievements in recent years of Pet Shop Boys (successfully), Erasure (less so) and David Bowie (hardly at all). Fortunately for straight-ahead fans, Ray was turned back on track: "I lost that mood after a few weeks and decided it was not the right way to project the band. Normally, people associate the music with the people on stage, and with the original version of 'Don't' I wasn't prepared to do that."

The concept may have altered, but there remained a nine-minute opus to be dealt with. "There were too many chords for an ordinary rock song on an album," he reveals, "so I changed it. But I'm glad I did that first because it opened up the choices for me."

Songwriting for a master craftsman such as Ray Davies is not the mystical experience it can appear to other writers. He works at his art rather than let it come to him. And for all his personnel communication problems, when it comes to penning a lyric he knows better than most how to reach out to a thousand different ears. And backing up his libretto, of course, is the music, the tunes whistled by generation after generation. The results may have varied down the years, but Ray's processes remain consistent. The man is the consummate professional, forever writing, always creating. And more than just a singer, he's a musician; he knows what he's writing about. Taking *Phobia* as our example – as the band's most recent studio offering, it seems most pertinent – Ray guides us through his constructional thoughts.

"Depending on the project," he begins, "whether it's an album or a show or just a song I've been commissioned to write, I like to think about whether I use guitar or keyboard. The difference between them is obvious to anyone who understands songwriting. Songs like 'Phobia' were obviously written on a guitar because of the chords I wanted in there; I write on piano and guitar but people tend to downplay my role as a guitarist. I'm very aware of what instrument I'm writing on because I do a lot of my songwriting in my head; you have to put a lot of information down. Whatever instrument is closest to hand I write the chord sounds on."

For such an inventive spirit as Ray, sometimes keyboards and guitar aren't enough to get his song across. "With 'Phobia', I knew I wanted strident chords. Then I wanted a different rhythm section and I wrote that on a computer. Computers are amazing to work with. Say you're jamming. You have the computer on all the time and it's that wonderful thing where everything you do is saved on disk; it's MIDI [Musical Instrument Digital Interface] and all that, and you can play everything through to the end, start to finish. Anyway, after the computer, then I went to the ordinary keyboard and wrote the next bit, and then I made a home video of all the sections, and I played that to the band as a demo and we did it all in one take. That was important to me because the attitude has to come across." The video on this occasion substituted the standard way of writing down the dots for the musicians to read. "If I write things down, I like people to learn it so they can play it without looking at the sheet. I like them to play it in their heads, so I would rather we rehearsed more and remembered the song."

Back on the songwriting trail, another one written on guitar was 'Only A Dream', released in the UK as the album's first single. (It failed to chart.) "I used open D tuning to write that, but on the record I've used conventional tuning. There were some chords that I put in and then switched. I met Ry Cooder a while ago and he has all these different tunings himself and he wanted me to write him a song like 'Low Budget' because he felt that he could do that. But I kind of got seduced by all the guitar tunings and we never really took it any further. I love all these G and D tunings, and I think the way I tune the guitar helps the melody evolve: 'Wake up in the morning, da da da da da da da da' – that's quite a nice guitar shape. I barre the E string into the [sings] 'F sharp, A, E, A, open A, everything I do for you...'"

Singing the guitar part is one thing; playing it is a different matter. Perhaps another reason why Ray shouldn't be overlooked as a guitarist is for his peculiar left-hand shapes. "Playing, I use my thumbs a lot, which is a bad habit," he admits. "I started playing classically, but over the years I've developed some habits because I've had a couple of injuries; I hurt one of my fingers about ten years ago so I've had to adapt my style accordingly. I use my thumb a lot to do barres from above rather than do the whole thing because this tendon hurts. My strumming hand has an odd quirk to it: when I'm doing strong strumming, before I hit the string with the pick I do a pre-hit with my finger and get a sort of slap. I've got all these bad habits which I suppose have added to my style."

Without question, Ray Davies' style of playing makes him a player to be reckoned with. And not just on the guitar; songwriting aside, he played keyboards throughout *Phobia* to recreate the days when '70s player John Gosling left and Ray filled in. For the tour, however, Ian Gibbons was called back for his familiar role to stand alongside Rodford and drummer Bob Henrit. On their first decent tour of Britain for eight years and with a new record available, The Kinks seemed to have little trouble filling the halls with fans of all ages. Old followers arrived for their umpteenth tours, often bringing their enthusiastic kids, who had been raised on the band's music. Other fans turned up for the nostalgia aspect, oblivious to the fact that the band weren't just another sad cabaret act; their children were often there under duress, patently wishing they were somewhere else. Why couldn't their parents like a proper group – like Blur?

21 RAY'S A VERY INTERESTING MAN...

For a man who has suffered full or partial breakdowns more than once in his life, Ray has emerged fairly unscathed on the professional path. Pressure at home, problems in his personal relationships or fears·for the band's future have all contributed to his occasional black spots. But where he has usually stood firm is on the writing side; in fact, often it has been the excessive songwriting which has caused troubles elsewhere. Rarely is he stuck for inspirational prompts.

"I thought it was fun, having this string of big hits," he told *Mojo*. "It instils a kind of...not competitiveness, but it makes you want to write great things." Rising to the challenge has rarely been his problem, as he told us: "My creative crises come from having to deal with an environment where I know that the music won't be presented properly. With *Phobia*, I was working in a situation where I suspected from day one that the people I was making the record for didn't understand what they wanted. So I couldn't help them." Those people sadly were his record company, the Sony-owned Columbia. "We had terrible problems with Sony," he recalls. "They just didn't understand." The *Phobia* experience had not worked as well as either partner had hoped and ties were severed forthwith.

But not all was lost. Certain other very influential people had got the point, and the first signs of a revival – a credibility thing rather than a sales-driven renaissance – became apparent in the UK music scene. Blur had started the work with their 1991 hit album, *Leisure*; in 1993, they continued the vicarious promotion for their favourite band to accompany their second album, the obviously Kinks-ridden *Modern Life Is Rubbish*, eventually appearing on the same bill as their heroes in, of all places, Sweden. Ray remembers the youngsters' performance well, perhaps reflecting on The Kinks' own presence when they first broke: "Everyone in the band was saying, 'They're loud. It's great. They're loud.'"

There the early similarities end, according to Ray, who, rather than look in his own closet, airs that of another: "When I played with The Beatles and I watched them from the side, I could tell they had problems," he recalls. "They were performing great, all the songs were great, but they were fighting over the count-in. In between songs, John would shout something at Ringo and he'd say, 'Fuck off.' There was tension there, but when I watch Blur playing, it just felt like it was a really together outfit, a good team."

These early meetings between Davies and Blur would become more important later as Damon's hold on the British scene tightened, but for the moment Ray welcomed the attention from yet another fairly successful modern band, as well as other sources. BBC 2's highly respected serious music show *Later With Jools Holland* invited The Kinks along to its studios to play the same venue as other luminaries like Oasis, David Bowie, Elvis Costello and Van Morrison. Coming during their *Phobia* tour, the show found them in fine form and ready to make the most of their TV exposure. A selection from *Phobia* was respectfully received by the other musicians in the audience, and as the main act on the bill, Ray got to lean on Holland's piano for a rather jerky interview.

Another act on the show that night was rising American singer / songwriter Aimee Mann. Generally known for her worshipping of Elvis Costello, she holds another English idol up as inspiration as well. "Ray Davies is a great songwriter," she enthuses in her soft-spoken drawl. The feeling is apparently mutual. "He invited me to tour with them and then we met up again on *Later* together. For me, it was thrilling to be performing there. Usually, it's such a sterile experience: you're performing to the camera or to a studio audience that's made up of just random people off the street who don't know who you are. But to play in a room full of my peers – people like Ray Davies – and colleagues is what it's all about for me." Almost the typical fan, Aimee is honest in her appreciation of Ray. "I don't like everything of theirs," she begins, "but what I do like, I really like."

Obviously falling into the latter category, 'Dead End Street' was performed by Mann as part of her unplugged appearance on MTV's *Most Wanted* show in 1993, the same year as the *Later* appearance. Similarly, her live shows have been known to feature 'This Time Tomorrow', while in 1995 she included a song called 'Ray' on her *I'm With Stupid* album. So was it about the leading Kink? "Ray's a very interesting man..." she says, diplomatically.

Ray's personal attentions, prompted without doubt by the weekly music press digging out his records again and realising what Damon and co knew all along, resulted in more high-profile media slots. Among the regular stack of interviews for TV and radio, he also found time to play again with Jools Holland, this time on Channel Four's excellent if chaotic holiday quiz *Don't Forget Your Toothbrush*. Given a rapturous welcome by the show's host, former Radio 1 disc jockey Chris Evans, Ray rattled through a knockout version of 'You Really Got Me' as well as taking part in the quite surreal section of the show where a celebrity's wits are pitted against those of a "Superfan" on the specialist subject of the celebrity. Humouring his supposed Number One Fan somewhat, Ray stalled on virtually every answer for maximum sympathy from the raving crowd (sympathy he dearly needed, having forgotten to bring a personal treasure from his home to give the contestant – even Cher managed to fulfil that requirement when she was on the show). He lost and gave Tracy Noonan one of his Doc Martens. Forgetful or tight?

Elsewhere on the programme, his penchant for hamming up a part overcame him when it fell on his shoulders, as the celebrity, to "blow up" a member of the audience with a mock detonator. Faking a yawn and pretending to accidentally lean on the plunger as though tired, his comic subtleties sadly looked slightly out of kilter among the show's frenetic abandon. Similarly, when it came for him to duet on 'Bring Me Sunshine' with the charged-up host, Ray's inability to share the spotlight left him somewhat adrift of the song's purpose as show-closer.

Sharing a spotlight, of course, has long been Ray's weakest area. Relinquishing his grip on the control of any situation seems anathema to one who has railed for much of his life against outside influence. This, if anything does, provides the largest single psychological backdrop to his so-called "unauthorised" autobiography, finally published in 1994 after years of postulation and more often procrastination. Wittily entitled *X-Ray*, the book's name leads the reader to expect its subject held up to the light to see what internal make-up makes him tick. In truth, this is not what happens. What at first seems like a personal treatise awash with memories and honest introspection appears, on closer analysis, to be a brilliantly woven tapestry of invention mixed with reminiscence for the aim of entertainment as much as enlightenment.

Ray's approach to recounting his own life seems to be similar to that of another performer who has led the last five decades of his life in the public eye. The Australian caricaturist and author Barry Humphries sees only one objective which must be sought after when undergoing any type of probing journalism: "The object of the interview is to obfuscate the truth." If this can apply in interviews, there remains no impediment why it can't also be true of memoirs. Ray appears to concur. Even the book's structure seems designed to assist confusion, with its protagonist – the character blessed with first-person narration – somebody other than Ray, something quite inexplicable for an autobiography. Instead, a scenario unfurls whereby Ray is tracked down and interviewed for the purpose of a biography. Combine this knowledge with the fact that it's set in the future so we are witness to Ray's funeral, his recollection of The Kinks ends in 1973, and throughout there is as much sub-plot involving the journalist's life as that of Davies and we are left with less of a hand-on-your-heart autobiography than a work of excellent fiction.

Either way, it's a cracking read and first reports on its hardback release through Viking were very encouraging. The bold writing style was alternately branded crass and remarkable, but never plain. No reviewer went away unentertained; a few grumbled that they knew less about Ray at the end than they did before they picked the book up, but it was a critical success. Miles Kington in *The Independent* summed it up as "excellent", while his colleague at *The Times*, Alan Jackson, had this to say: "Pop biographies rarely come more inventive than this, an enjoyable mix of true confessions and quasi-fictional scene-setting. The eye for detail is as precise as in the best of his 1960s music work, and his creativity is sharply evident throughout." Tom Hibbert, writing in *The*

Mail On Sunday, agreed: "*X-Ray* is that rarest of things: a rock star autobiography that is engaging, entertaining and well written, to boot."

The level of critical success surrounding *X-Ray* should not come as a surprise. The book deals with the same topics that Ray had been focusing on for the last 20 years with lesser success; at last he had found a medium where in-depth analysis on certain matters close to his heart was not deemed too unwieldy by a soundbite-orientated rock audience. No, the book's strengths should not have come as any surprise, but what should have raised a few eyebrows was the very fact that it had got written at all. In the foreword to his biography of The Kinks, *The Sound And The Fury*, Johnny Rogan noted how Ray had turned down applications for assistance on the grounds that he wanted to pen his own version of events; he had apparently been in the process of doing so for about seven years. This was in 1984 – *X-Ray*'s publication some ten years later means that Davies was toying with this project for at least 17 years.

In his autobiography, the central figure is not Ray but a young journalist (who happens to share a lot of Ray's memories and grows more like him every chapter). Even Ray is not Ray; rather it is "Raymond Douglas" who is interviewed about his life. Finally, the only other character of note is the mysterious "Corporation", a futuristic amalgamation of City Fat Cats gone mad. The themes of loneliness, smallness, disenfranchisement and impotence, prevalent in so much of his music throughout the '70s and later, are all wrapped up in those two words: The Corporation. If there's a problem, the Corporation probably caused it; if they didn't, then they're probably making it worse. George Orwell's *1984* doesn't paint a bleaker picture than the future Raymond Douglas envisages for the UK.

Spurred on by the book's success, and possibly creatively drained by the writing process, Ray's next musical project saw him back with The Kinks reliving some of their best-loved material. If the title of *X-Ray* was evidence of the veracity on offer therein, the album's name, *To The Bone*, indicated what lay at the very heart of a band now in its fourth decade together. Perhaps fittingly for such an achievement, the album's liner notes are attributed jointly to Dave and Ray, and both share copyright on the whole record.

After their disappointment with the world's largest record company, this release found the band on their own Konk label under the auspices of an independent company, the industrious Grapevine. While this smaller set-up was sufficient in the UK, the world market still isn't ready for such a scale of production, as Ray knows too well. "This country can't really handle independent distribution," he told *The LA Times*. "You can't do it. It's too big." As a result, *To The Bone* failed to be released in America in 1994, finally emerging as a different entity entirely in 1996.

In Britain things were very different and it became another critically acclaimed release from the man of the moment and his merry troupe; Tom Hibbert (again) writing in *Q* magazine gave it a deserved four stars at the end of his glowing review. After so many modern groups coming up through the ranks and displaying signs of listening to The Kinks' Pye catalogue, it was refreshing to hear the songs' originators giving them a '90s spin. 'Apeman' in particular is subjected to a total calypso overhaul, while other tracks, like the opener, 'All Day And All Of The Night', display a sheer rock power that was absent even on the originals.

Although a live album throughout, *To The Bone* consists of a couple of different postcard-like concert scenarios. 'All Day...' kicks off the proceedings with a heavy rock rendition lifted from the average Kinks live show; after that things get mellower with a select audience at Konk being treated to slightly calmer versions of 'See My Friends' and 'Tired Of Waiting'. Ray throughout is in good form, as is the whole band. Introducing his brother's party piece, Davies Senior says, "Okay, this is Dave doing his 'Death Of A Clown' piece one more time," and off they go on a tasteful excursion down memory lane led by a prominent acoustic guitar, and helped out by careful harmonies from Ray.

The album wasn't the only project intended to come out of the session, as Ian Gibbons told us: "Ray actually wanted the gig filmed for video release, and so we had cameras buzzing around us on the night. We went through a batch of The Kinks' best-loved classics and threw in a couple of album tracks that Ray wanted to try in a different way. It was a really good night, although to this day the video hasn't emerged."

The point of *To The Bone*, as much as there is one behind its obvious role as a collection of superlative music, is that the song is all, and the hype very little in the final analysis. No better is this proved than on 'Waterloo Sunset', a song alone in its unquestionable beauty; a genuine pop classic. But tell Ray you admire the song and you're likely to receive a discourse on the power of production in blurring your mind: "There is a big difference between the song and the record," he told us. "'Waterloo Sunset' hasn't really been covered by anyone so people only know that recording of it. It's like with Phil Spector: the song became the record to everyone and the two are kind of inseparable and so nobody else's versions sound like the 'real thing'. When people say something is their favourite song of all time, it's the record they're talking about. 'Waterloo Sunset' was one of the first records I totally produced and I was more interested in creating a kind of effect on the record than just making a recording of the song. Through the sounds, the clouds and shapes and what I call colours, you get a kind of impressionistic record – so I'm surprised that people say it's good, but perhaps that's the art of making great records."

Taking a song out of the context of its record can have unsatisfactory consequences. For one thing, that constant struggle that Ray as an artist has balancing his words with appropriate music can be affected. "One of my best friends died and she had the lyrics of 'Days' read at her funeral," he recalls. "Without the music it just didn't seem right and I just wish I could have done a rewrite for the spoken version."

The song then, to the writer, has a separate life on stage to that it was originally given via the record. But whatever Ray's feelings on the matter, 'Waterloo Sunset' is such a superb pop song that the version on *To The Bone* for the few minutes it is on, is absolute perfection, and all notion of another recorded version ever being available is forgotten.

The same goes for other songs: 'Better Things', 'Muswell Hillbilly' and 'Don't Forget To Dance' all cross the gap between original version and live rendition with some aplomb. But if 'Waterloo Sunset' still works even when stripped of its studio icing, then the perennial success of Ray's traditional solo stints is more remarkable. On this album, 'Autumn Almanac', 'Sunny Afternoon' and 'Dedicated Follower Of Fashion' are all treated to the Ray-on-acoustic treatment. Each song adopts an honesty which perhaps the other instruments would have hidden, showing Ray's audience control at its peak. The busking element is highlighted by his call of "That's enough of that!" after several choruses of 'Almanac'.

With Ray's solo spot given such prominence on the record, the tease that "I think the Kinks have just entered the building" which precedes 'Dedicated Follower' gives a glimpse of his view of himself as perhaps outside the band. It's a line he'd been peddling for a while, of course, but putting it on record seemed the final proof. When the band do come on, it is to 'You Really Got Me', and for a time the internal troubles are dissolved as sheer professionalism meets abject enjoyment for some musical magic.

With *To The Bone* in the record shops and *X-Ray* on sale in book stores all over Britain (again America would have to wait more than a year for its sniff at the cherry), the merchandising stands at the band's 1994 tour were packed with goodies particularly aimed at the passing Kinks fan who had come along on the off-chance of a good nostalgic night out with a blast from the past, and had actually enjoyed the show enough to be seduced by new product. The concerts themselves went off as well as ever with the dancers employed for another season and the customary sight of Ray shuffling on first, looking not unlike the comedian Benny Hill's Fred Scuttle character.

Bearing in mind the autobiography on sale in the foyer, the inclusion of a track called 'X-Ray' points people in the right direction. A new song called 'The Ballad Of Julie Finkle' goes even further to drag audiences into his book's world – Julie is, after all, not only the mysterious love interest in *X-Ray* but also, it is suggested by the devilish author's text, the "girl" in 'You Really Got Me'. Whatever the true origins, the song comes across well with a decent chorus and deft acoustic playing from RD.

The amount of himself that Ray puts into songs is open to debate. He often maintains that they are vehicles for his musicality and not diaries – "I don't like to give too much away" is a common phrase – but careful arrangement of various parts of the band's back catalogue will lead you to his entire life in music. One memory from the 1994 tour indicates that he is, in fact, rather precious where his more personal songs are concerned. Using a reminiscence about his past to introduce 'Julie Finkle' at a show in Brentwood, Essex, Ray was encouraged by a member of the audience (although some reports say it was Dave) to "Get on with it." Far from getting on, Ray's response was to get off. He threw down his guitar, swore at the heckler and flounced off stage – he'd made the mistake of getting too emotionally involved in his speech and he'd paid for it dearly.

Having made such a flamboyant gesture, the showman could hardly return immediately, and in fact he stayed away for the next 20 minutes. Reduced to a leaderless four-piece, the rest of the band eventually muscled their way through 'Death Of A Clown', with roadies sent to coax the fuming Davies back. A second song followed – still no Ray. Then a third and finally another, by which time the band's knowledge of Dave's repertoire had probably been exhausted.

Ray's return found him still smarting and obviously wounded. Sarcasm reigned for the rest of the evening, with one song leading quickly into the next and any rare remaining introduction curtailed by the line "Oh, but I'm not allowed to talk, am I?" To have been stung by the crowd's shouts was not uncommon, but the measure of the singer's hurt can be estimated by the length of his time off stage. John Gosling recalls a similar occasion from the '70s: "We managed to get through half a song once when he'd refused to go on and Dave just said, 'Fuck it, let's go on without him,' but Ray was on stage before the end of the song because he could hear how well it was going down and he didn't like it; so I'm amazed they managed to get through that many without him. He must have mellowed a bit. He was always one for the big I AM act. He'd make us all sit outside the hotel waiting for him on the bus; then he'd be the last one off the bus as well. At airports he'd be a step ahead."

Despite years of Ray's impromptu absences and their joint on-stage dust-ups, Dave remains surprisingly phlegmatic, if not dismissive, about the angst behind the behaviour, as he admitted to us.

"Sometimes we do it for a bit of fun, but most of it was real," he says. "I think sometimes Ray used to provoke me just because I'm easily provoked.

"There was a story a while ago about this band with two sisters – I can't remember their name but they had a quirky little hit in America. They used to go and see The Kinks in the '80s and they went to their first show and thought it was great because me and Ray were fighting, throwing guitars and stuff. They thought, 'We've got to see this again,' so they came back. Anyway, they saw us three times and the same thing happened and thought it was all staged."

Like John McEnroe these days on the senior tennis tour: he might not care anymore, but the punters are disappointed if he doesn't get upset with the line judges. Speaking of which... "Watching us two play tennis or table tennis must be frightening for anybody because of all the insults and innuendo that goes on," Dave laughs. "And the mind games. It's horrible."

Mind games and the occasional bluster such as that at Brentwood aside, the remainder of the *Phobia* tour in Europe passed without hiccough and, despite the success of his autobiography, his growing personal cult status, and the persistent threat of his first solo album, Ray and the band were soon looking at entering another year still together.

1995 saw America, home to a still-significant fan base, dominate the band's summer schedule. From Los Angeles to New York via Washington and all points in between, it became one of The Kinks' largest undertakings in years. With *To The Bone* unavailable at the time for Stateside purchase, there wasn't the same hook on which the band could hang their tour, yet the shows were similar in style to the tour that had ploughed through the UK the previous year. A so-called spontaneous calypso rendition of 'Apeman' caught out many an American fan oblivious to the track's inclusion on the live album and largely the set followed traditional structure. As usual Ray was found appearing first, trotting through a clutch of acoustic readings, among them the customary 'Dedicated Follower', 'Sunny Afternoon' and even 'I Go To Sleep', before welcoming The Kinks to the building. Joined by Ian Gibbons, Bob Henrit and Jim Rodford, the brothers successfully erased most memories of some of their less inspired performances witnessed during the *Phobia* tour two years earlier.

Highlights of the US leg were many. A series of shows at Sunset Boulevard's House of Blues in July found the band in particularly fine fettle. Given the venue's infamous locale, a reference to the British actor Hugh Grant's embarrassing imbroglio with prostitute Divine Brown seemed a perfect introduction to 'Celluloid Heroes': "Success hand in hand with failure" could not be more aptly put, although both parties' subsequent financial gain from the experience alters matters in hindsight. Then there was the famous blues jam. The House of Blues found itself home to a song called 'House Of Blues Blues' – a tune lifted from 'Mannish Boy' with improvised local lyrics (Dave could be heard muttering "What the hell was that?" at the end of the song). Not surprisingly, that particular lyric didn't travel well and found itself superseded at other concerts: the 'Devon Philadelphia Blues' was played at the Valley Forge Music Fair in, naturally, Devon, Philadelphia; 'Buffalo Blues' could be heard in Buffalo, NY; and 'Washington DC Blues' was aired at Georgetown, Washington, different in both lyric and tune – some indication of the fun the whole band were having on stage at the time.

Such wanton acts of self and public indulgence aside, the set lists fluctuated from state to state giving hardened followers a nightly bonus. Occasionally Dave could be found singing vocals of 'Sleepwalker' and again on 'Good Golly Miss Molly', also on 'Too Much On My Mind' and 'Living On A Thin Line' as well as his usual party pieces. 'Low Budget' found its way into the act most nights (occasionally dedicated to the promotions dept at Arista) and the '60s B-side to 'You Really Got Me', 'It's Alright' (rather than Dave's '90s track) made friends whenever it was aired. In fact, whatever the tracks, the band were rarely in anything less than good form, let down occasionally by poor venues and unsympathetic local staff. Indeed, Ray in particular seemed to enjoy himself so much that when his solo dates for later in the year were announced, no one could be surprised.

22 EXPECT THE UNEXPECTED

A lone guitar leans on its stand. A spotlight falls on an open book, its lines matched in number by those on the reader's face, each one capable of a million tales of its own. The speaker coughs, chuckles and smiles a gapped-tooth grin that remains as untouched by time as the rest of his body has failed to be. It's 1995 but it could be 1985. Or 1975. Or 1965. It's 1995, and Raymond Douglas Davies of The Kinks stands before an expectant audience, about to regale his paying guests with tales culled from his autobiography, *X-Ray*. For once the songs that have made him famous play second fiddle to his prose. He orates the recorded passages of his life with a strange dignity, as though recounting the roles played by others in some momentous event in British history and bowing to their superior wisdom. His awe is obvious, and not entirely misplaced. In his hands he holds a collection of reminiscences that go back more than five decades. Reminiscences that are at once personal yet pivotal. They are the stories of his life but they mean so much to everyone who hears them. After being a part of history for so long, he has finally got round to writing his version of it. And about time.

Typical of Ray, the solo shows only came about because he was asked to do something else entirely. Publishers always expect celebrity authors to promote their books via the traditional route of book-signings and readings at larger branches, with members of the public encouraged to attend and, therefore, buy the book. Duly called upon to follow suit, Ray took along his guitar and peppered his reading with a couple of hits. Before long, a full two-hour show, grandly named *20th Century Man*, was ready to be toured in concert halls around the world.

"The show came about because Ray had just written his book, *X-Ray*, which had been very successful," explains Kinks manager Deke Arlon. "He was asked by the publishers to promote it, which basically involves going to various shops around the country and doing readings and signing autographs. He decided that he would do a little bit more than just read from the book; he'd sing a song, talk about it, sing another song, talk a bit more. The book had a very clever structure involving a younger Ray being interviewed by an older Ray, and so he was able to develop this into what became his one-man show."

After a showcase-cum-book launch at fabled London jazz venue Ronnie Scott's, partnered for the night by guitarist Peter Mathison, Ray was booked into the Edinburgh Festival – Europe's leading arts festival, aimed at airing new talent and premiering new shows from respected artists – for a week from 18 August. If these dates went well, he surmised, he would take the expanded show to a wider audience on the road.

If there were any doubts about the viability of an evening of readings and acoustic songs, they were unnecessary. By the end of the Scottish engagement, a full-blown tour was being booked. From Edinburgh to Tunbridge Wells, Folkstone, Wolverhampton, Clacton, North Wales and Norwich in August; then the leap across the Atlantic for a month of October shows in the USA, before spending November in the theatres of Great Britain and December in Australia, New Zealand and Japan.

"It's wonderful how the show developed," Ray explains. "I did the book launch at Ronnie Scott's and Pete knew about four or five songs. Then I did a tour with The Kinks and Pete and I kept getting together, learning more songs. Then I phoned him and said, 'Look we're doing the first show,' and we got in the van together and I wrote down the running order of the songs. It was very easy."

Advertisements for *20th Century Man* carried the banner "expect the unexpected". It was as much a warning as a sell-line, but for long-time concert-goers it offered a rare chance to catch their main man without the trappings of a band. Accompanied only by fellow guitarist Mathison, Ray presented the shows a little like the Rainbow concert he had in mind in the '70s: a history of himself through music, in this instance telling the story of the early days of The Kinks, culminating in the release of 'You

Really Got Me'. Aware that many ticket-buying customers would be turning up on the strength of his Kinks commitments, he usually found time, at least in the opening weeks, to assuage fears of a band split. "The next Kinks record will be out in 1996," he assured nightly, to rapturous response. As the solo dates wore on, however, and '96 became '97, and with still no new Kinks product, there appeared to be a change in policy and the line was dropped. With it went at least the pretence of a cushion which Ray had been holding onto in case his solo forays hadn't panned out. There appeared to be the realisation that, perhaps as he'd expected, he didn't actually need his old band. In truth, seven years after his opening solo night, the promised album would still not be delivered.

Perhaps tentatively carrying a feeling of fraudulence into his early shows – he was, after all, dipping freely into The Kinks' catalogue for his solo tour – Ray soon began to wear the mantle of the carrier of the flame. Despite their solo status, his *20th Century Man* shows were filled with mentions of his perhaps former band, unavoidable as *X-Ray* was plundered again and again to provide tales of childhood, family and hardship by way of explanation for the songs.

"The book's there as basically an extraordinarily well-used prop," Deke Arlon explains. "Ray starts the evening by saying he's going to tell some stories from his black book, and he's away, with hardly the same show two nights running."

Perhaps fuelled by the improvisational aspects, perhaps enjoying the benefits of promoting something for which the profit is solely his, perhaps because The Kinks' American tour had been such a blast or perhaps just because he was revelling in his role as the Godfather of Britpop, the shows for *X-Ray* found Ray in sterling form. Consistently good humoured throughout the entire 1995 tour (perhaps, in Mathison, he'd found a guitarist he got on with?), audiences were treated to a more intense experience as a result of the more focused show. Suddenly the "unexpected" looked like meaning that he'd got his enthusiasm back after so many years of ploughing the same furrow. Certainly without a band to carry him, and without the comfort zone of sharing the spotlight with an equal partner, there was more responsibility on stage than he'd ever known; he had to enjoy it.

Hits stood proudly alongside album tracks and the occasional new song, and for once there was absolutely no hint of going through the motions. From the new cache, 'X-Ray' found itself well-received all round the world. 'Americana' attracted different reactions depending on whether you heard it with American ears, as did 'The London Song', a fairly typical aural map of Hampstead, Highgate and, of course, Muswell Hill. 'To The Bone' and 'Animal' instantly achieved classic status at every show. If these songs were typical of the work currently in progress, the long awaited – and much vaunted – debut Ray Davies solo album, slated for release in 1996, would indeed be something to behold.

From the back catalogue, distant gems like 'Two Sisters' fell like refreshing summer rain on most ardent followers' ears; pure, beautiful and honest, it was a relevant symbol of Ray's relationship with Dave in the '60s and it still is today at a time when they are rumoured to only communicate by fax. Other album greats like 'Village Green', 'Dandy', 'Moments' and 'The Money-Go-Round' found themselves similarly received, but the real applause waited as usual for the hits. 'Waterloo Sunset' found itself regularly performed by the two guitarists, for many audiences their first live rendition. The usual selection that had opened Kinks shows for the last few years again couldn't be omitted – 'Dedicated Follower', 'Sunny Afternoon', 'Almanac', etc – and the total blend seemed to work for most audiences. Very possibly, during those months of solo touring from August 1995 into the next year, Ray found himself met by the most enthusiastic applause of the last two decades. Aside from a couple of shows in Willesden and York cancelled due to illness, he didn't fail to merit it.

Not everyone, however, found it easy to accept some of the songs without the rest of The Kinks being present; this was particularly true of former members of the band who obviously identified with the current line-up being left by the wayside for this tour. John Dalton caught up with the X-Ray double act – a far cry from the travelling troupe he was forced to work among in the '70s – in Borehamwood. "It's just Ray and a guitarist – a very good guitarist," he reflects. "I found it good in parts, but like there are some songs that don't work if you add brass, there are some songs that don't sound right with just two acoustic guitars. Take

'Victoria' – that just doesn't sound right on two acoustics. And he keeps quoting from his book, which obviously is why he's doing the shows, but I found it went on just that bit too long, you start getting a bit bored by it." Perhaps disappointed that night, John still admires Ray as a performer and, most importantly, as a friend. "I went up and said hello to him afterwards, of course, and it was good to see him. I went to his 50th birthday party, he came to my anniversary; we see each other when we can, but you all get on with your own lives. Dave lives in America now so I don't see him that much."

Dalton's gripes aside, the mood from the current Davies camp is far more bullish, and rightly so. "I think you come away from the evening thinking you know a bit more about who Ray is," avers Deke Arlon. "You know a lot more about the Kinks, a lot more about what the songs are about, and why he wrote them. A great example is a song like 'Two Sisters'. When he explains where it comes from, you suddenly realise that it's not about sisters at all, but about Ray and Dave."

One of the bonuses of the two-man set is that there is more freedom to switch course midstream. A responsive livewire at the best of times, some of Ray's impromptu antics on-stage with The Kinks have seen the rest of the band caught out more than once – many's the newly recruited backing member suddenly challenged with playing a solo in a song he'd neither rehearsed nor even heard before. But with Pete there to back him rather than lead him, solo Ray has more flexibility to respond to the mood of each individual audience. All fine in theory, of course, unless, as Deke Arlon was, you were trying to prepare the show for an overseas tour...

"We made the show technically safe by putting a lighting plot around it," he explains, "which means that the lights follow the same sequence every night. This makes it easier to go on tour and use foreign equipment or personnel, because all the moves are programmed in. The problem was, you never knew where Ray was going to go. If he thought the audience needed a ballad or a hit, he might do it; if someone called out a song he hadn't thought of, he might launch into that. Suddenly your lighting plot was up the creek because you had to watch the stage, watch the man and be prepared to go with him.

"Of course, that spontaneity and flexibility has its advantages. We did a show once with just Ray and a full band with a horn section. The promoter decided that Ray had done long enough, because there was another band due on after him, so he just unplugged the amps, which was a disgusting and incredibly unprofessional thing to do. The audience hated it, so Ray just walked back on stage with an acoustic guitar around his neck and sat there entertaining them for as long as they asked for it. He said, 'If you want to get rid of me, you'll have to physically throw me off.' He didn't."

In Pete, Ray had found the perfect foil for his improvisational bent. "I think the contribution of any part in a show like this," Ray says, "is to know about the spaces. It's more about what you don't do than what you do. Obviously it's a team up there, and it's very important to have the right chemistry."

While Ray was beginning to push his solo act around the globe in 1995, the memory of The Kinks was living on courtesy of fresher, occasionally more hirsute, faces. In August, a bunch of tune-drunk kids were witnessed going mad in the audience as the group of enthusiastic youngsters on stage bashed out an exhilarating up-tempo shoutalong number for their encore. A mix of modern social comment, yobbish arrogance and downright fun vibes, the song in question was 'Where Have All The Good Times Gone', written by Ray Davies and recorded by The Kinks in 1965. On 4 August 1995 it was a young band called Supergrass, fresh from Top Ten residency themselves with their vibrant summer hit 'Alright', who were putting one of their favourite songs through its paces.

Supergrass' treatment of the song many attribute to Van Halen or David Bowie was typical of the mood of the mid '90s. Real pop values returned to an arid wasteland of an industry where house music and jungle had looked like leaving many casualties, and once again bands were walking onto stages with instruments rather than equipment. 1995 may have seen irritants such as The Outhere Brothers reach Number One in the UK with little more than a chant ("let me hear you say way-o"), but such events seemed to be becoming fewer. Songs were once again starting to matter again, as they did to Ray then; and, in the mid

'90s, he was beginning to matter again. Kirsty MacColl, fresh from her hit with the track in 1989, reappeared with 'Days' in 1995 to even greater acclaim second time around. (The song's use on a popular television commercial had a slight hand in affairs.) A brand new audience was suddenly heard thanking her for the Davies composition.

(The song would find further fame for all the wrong reasons in 2001, when, following MacColl's tragic death in a sea accident, its sentiment seemed to provide the perfect obituary piece, both on radio and in print.)

Blur remained the main flag bearers. Whether annoyingly for them or by way of compliment, hardly an article on the band appeared without some reference to the influence of The Kinks. Not exactly copyists, Albarn and co cut their own cloth, for sure; but the parochial obsessions, inescapable melodies and their unswerving Estuary English presentation could have been lifted directly from the Davieses' blueprint for pop stardom. That their first Number One single was called 'Country House' and The Kinks had a song called 'House In The Country' (on *Face To Face*) is interesting but not a criticism; that Ray likes the young pretenders is without question. In 1995 he agreed to appear with Damon on Channel 4's excellent music show, *The White Room*, where they duetted on a generation-spanning version of 'Waterloo Sunset', as well as Blur's 'Parklife'. For older viewers it was strangely moving to see the historic and the fresh transcend temporal differences; for the younger members of the audience – Damon's mighty teenage fan club – it must have been an epiphanous moment, seeing their idol with his. For Damon himself it was a dream come true: "I was in love with him for that hour," he mooned after the recording.

Acknowledging Damon's tribute, Ray confessed his own gratitude for the situation. "It's very intimidating to have somebody say that you've been influential on their career," he told us. "It's nice, but I always say it doesn't matter how successful or influential you are, you still sometimes like a pat on the back. You like people to say, 'Can we help you?' It's kind of give and take. I love the idea that I might have helped musicians and writers start and take that first step; it's like an encouragement in a way because it inspires you to go back to your own songs and that's the important thing."

In 1996, *Q* magazine gave away a free CD featuring the televised duet between Ray and his protégé (*Q* 113).

The White Room wasn't to be the end of Damon's public helping hand for Ray that year. In another landmark broadcast for music lovers, he appeared with The Pretenders (whom he'd succeeded as The Kinks' Unofficial Fan Club) to play piano on a chillingly haunting version of 'I Go To Sleep' (commercially available on their *Isle Of View* album). The Boy Who Would Be Ray and The Girl Who Wouldn't Be With Ray finally met up to do justice to one of their joint influences' most sublime moments. Stunning.

Talking to *Flatiron* magazine in 1996, Ray almost admitted his pride at the younger generation's veneration of his work, but typically saw it as more of a coincidence of circumstance than anything that could be attributed to him. "I wrote songs that reflected where I lived, where I came from, and the people that I knew," he explained. "That's been happening with people like Blur, Pulp and particularly Oasis. It's much more rewarding because they are not actually covering my songs, but rather that we seem to be paralleled in our creativity.

"I listen to the new Oasis album [*Be Here Now*] and I hear every song and think, 'Yes I know when I went through that.' And I see a lot of myself in that and I can relate to it. It's very much like the attitude of The Kinks: a gritty, edgy attitude to things. 'Don't Look Back In Anger', for example, is like a Kinks song in that sort of feel. Blur is more similar to the way I would write – sort of observations. And in an odd way, Pulp have the look that The Kinks had with fashion."

Even there the Blur / Kinks link refuses to fade. Elastica, fronted by Damon's girlfriend of the time, Justine Frischmann, recorded their superb debut album at Konk. Ever the paternal shadow, Ray was concerned about the young act's fate. Their big-money backing isn't entirely distant from his own experience with Sony: "I'm relieved that they are a success. Geffen is a big label not to be successful on," he told us.

With Blur, Supergrass, Paul Weller and even The Pretenders taking up most of the Kinks-related newspaper inches, it became increasingly difficult for other devotees to have their say. One person who found himself disenfranchised from his own roots was Suggs, former singer with Madness and 1995 chart star with his rendition of The Beatles' 'I'm Only Sleeping'. "It's very funny with people like Blur," he told the *NME*. "I find it difficult to find my own footprints because their feet are in 'em. Damon turns up doing 'Waterloo Sunset' with Ray Davies – it's me. There's only so much space for all these influences."

What they lack in outright similarities of songwriting style, Oasis make up for in feel (although 'She's Electric' from *(What's The Story) Morning Glory* is melodically reminiscent of 'Wonder Boy'; while the title of their debut LP *Definitely Maybe* could have been inspired by The Kinks' 'Definite Maybe' from the *State Of Confusion* album). In particular, the Manchester group's internal make-up makes for very obvious comparisons between the bands. Two brothers comprise each band's core; in each case, the bands were formed by the younger sibling, but it is the interloper who writes the lion's share of the material; and both pairs appear to hate each other in public. For Oasis, even television shows are not a guarantee of fraternal harmony. Liam Gallagher failed to appear on *Later* in 1995, forcing Noel to take over singing duties. The singer had already pulled the same stunt at a new album release show earlier in the year.

"I think tension between musicians is great," Ray pointed out to *Flatiron*'s Stephen Pitalo, "if it produces creativity. If it's all friendly and suppressed, then you turn out suppressed music. Certainly, with all the new recordings I've done with Dave, there's a tension you feel in the tracks and it's like sometimes there's a musical argument going on and that's what makes people buy the records. It goes right back to 'All Day And All Of The Night' – his aggressive guitars and my sort of small voice popping out over the top – it's like a battle. But that, in a sense, paid off."

A modern spin doctor would be proud of Ray's interpretation, but even he is not blind to the price.

"When it falls apart it's just the most arduous, exhausting situation to be in. It reminds me of one of my favourite quotes from Orson Welles in *The Third Man*: 'Italy has had 3,000 years of wars, fighting all the time, and also the creativity – Michelangelo, what have you. Switzerland has had 3,000 years of peace, never gets committed, and what has it produced? The cuckoo clock."

Speaking to *The Boston Globe* in 1996, he went further. "If it still works on stage, that's all I care about. We're a little bit further along than the guys in Oasis." However, called upon by newspapers to comment on Oasis' touring troubles of that year, Ray declined. "I don't like to do interviews about it," he explained. "I just know what it's like – they can't help it. They weren't taught how to be what they are. They weren't taught to be rock stars. It wasn't until I read some of the reports that I realised the similarities between the two sets of brothers are quite terrifying."

"When Oasis came out," Kinks manager Deke Arlon says, "the media obviously knew that they'd get mileage out of the band by comparing them to The Kinks, just because there were a couple of brothers in each band. There's no question that both Oasis and Blur were directly influenced by The Kinks, and that showed in interviews and on their records. It's a great compliment, of course, because it's good to be associated with good things and you can feel proud if you get the credit for influencing something you like. But it works both ways, and sometimes you can be credited with influencing something that you think is crap."

Less internally flammable, Pulp are another group who have their roots in The Kinks' style, and not just in the fashion-wise sense noted by Ray. Led by the affectatious if brilliant Jarvis Cocker, Pulp have resuscitated the art of detail in an increasingly bland pop climate. Like Ray before him, Jarvis generates tales of humdrum ennui, brought to life by the glorification of the minutiae. Whether it be the raw, slightly edgy Sheffield world of *His'N'Hers* or the London-based angst of *Different Class*, Pulp prove that classic pop music can be centred upon a night at Glastonbury, a date with a high-class snob or comedic drug flirtations.

Their 1998 album, *This Is Hardcore*, even saw the band begin to explore the idea of the linked-theme "concept" album as The Kinks had dabbled with two decades earlier. But although the style shifted away from accessible pop nuggets, the subject matter remained consistently mundane, with lyrics about doing the dishes, filming a home sex movie and, subject of the album's first single, helping the aged.

Ned Sherrin speaks here of The Kinks, but it could be – and perhaps one day will be – said of Pulp: "It's always a question, it seems to me, of honing in on the quite often small. And suburbia is almost just another word for small. These lives behind net curtains are more interesting than world events." Both Jarvis and Ray are social voyeurs; the new Neighbourhood Watch.

Tom Robinson concurs: "You don't need to have worked in a steel town in New Jersey to appreciate Bruce Springsteen, and you don't need to have played cricket on a village green to enjoy Ray Davies. But the fact that he knows his own particular world gives his work a universal appeal; I think what the Americans have liked about The Kinks over the years is the fact that they are so rooted in English society – not British, but a particular kind of English."

Ray is English, Jarvis is English, Damon is English. The rich vein of talent runs cleanly through them all. Yet not everyone will admit that new ground is still being covered. For some, like John Gosling, the excavatory work of Ray Davies in the '60s uncovered everything of value in music; modern fans are just scratching at the surface. "I feel sorry for these groups like Jarvis Cocker and Blur etc, because it's all been done before, really," John opines. "I can't imagine trying to emulate the groups that my parents listened to and it's very odd that they do. I suppose there's nothing else to do these days except rehash old styles. Some of it's all right and melodic, but most of it's just second-hand."

Second-hand or not, it serves a purpose for the average Kinks fan who will accept any consequence if it means their favourites are in the public eye again. For one event in 1995 they needed no other reason than their own history. The Rock 'N' Roll Hall of Fame, long an itinerant academy of huge kudos but no fixed abode, finally opened its permanent site in Cleveland, Ohio – and long-time members The Kinks were honoured to appear. Alongside such luminaries as Bruce Springsteen, Bob Dylan and Sheryl Crow, the band tore through a couple of numbers while Ray displayed the continent-linking charms of his wardrobe, wearing both his Union Jack and Stars and Stripes jackets that night. The final act of repentance from the country that banned their progress in the '60s was both sincere and public – viewed by millions of fans the world over.

"That night was amazing," says Deke Arlon, "because so many

people saw how good the band was. Away from the showbusiness world, Dave and Ray don't really have much to do with it, but both of them have got it in spades and they can really turn it on when required. There were some really major acts on the bill that night in Cleveland, but when The Kinks came on-stage, with Ray in his reversible jacket, they just blew them away."

The event came five years after the band's actual induction. Speaking in 1998 to fellow Canada resident Martin Kalin, Pete Quaife recalls playing at the 1990 event. "I was down in New York when we were inducted," he said, "before they built the museum in Cleveland. I've been down to Cleveland a couple of times since and it's magnificent, as is the Kinks exhibit there. The four of us got to play together at the induction. My wife has a home video of Mick jokingly turning over furniture in our room at the Waldorf Hotel because The Kinks were famous for destroying hotel rooms when we got pissed off at each other. We were banned from so many places for that in the early days."

While the Hall of Fame honoured its new residence with a display from some of the music business' most celebrated acts, another of those honoured by the Hall's beneficence was busy sweeping its way round the globe, in a style vastly differing from that of The Kinks. The Rolling Stones' world tour of 1995 became the highest grossing musical event ever. By comparison, Ray's solo tour is still slipping around theatres and smaller venues of the world seven years later. Both acts experienced phenomenal success in the '60s, both have had harder times recently, and both continue to sell out on tour. But the Stones sell out bigger capacities. Ray is phlegmatic about the comparison. "I think it's because I'm quite difficult to market as a person," he told *The LA Times*. "We've never done high profile publicity whereas Mick Jagger is a very good exponent of PR. I think the PR has overshadowed the music in recent years, but you've got to give him credit." Arguably the difference in sales is as much down to Jagger and co selling out, and playing the hits for the last 20 years. "You're not going to see The Rolling Stones really," Ray concludes. "You're going to see Disneyland."

It's a view that Deke Arlon confirms, citing the fact that Ray and Dave's priorities lie in different areas. Where some acts are prepared to milk the publicity cow for all its worth, others, like The Kinks, are more comfortable – perhaps in themselves, too – with being away from the spotlight. At a time when a musician's worth can seem to be judged in column inches attracted, Ray in particular shows a healthy disregard for his reputation.

"It is a shame for many that Ray isn't actually 'bigger' than he is," Deke says, "but it's just a different take on the same game. Bowie and Jagger have contributed no more to music than Ray, yet they are closer to 'household' names than he is because they're different people. A lot of your really successful people – the David Bowies, the Paul McCartneys, the Mick Jaggers and, to some extent, the Paul Simons – have all got PR companies keeping them out there all the time. Part of their function of being successful, part of their focus on their career is making sure that the public are aware that they're out there, that they're doing things, that they're still part of the structure of success in music. To that end they employ people around them to feed that machine. Whether you're Andrew Lloyd Webber or Paul McCartney, that machine is fed. Meetings take place with your PR company and you discuss what you'll be doing in the next six months: 'Are you touring, do you have product out, what do you want to draw attention to?' There's a whole campaign with calls to journalists saying he's doing this and would you like to come to this. This approach never happens with Ray.

"If Ray has a book out, the book publishers have a PR department to promote that book and they go out and work for that book. They'll arrange interviews with Ray for *The Times* and all the major newspapers and magazines, because all these people want to speak to him about new projects, and Ray will go along with it. But Ray does not spend time on self-congratulatory PR campaigns. He's very similar in this respect to a great friend of mine, Tom Stoppard. He doesn't pay thousands of pounds a year to ensure people know he's 'Tom Stoppard'. He writes plays and film scripts and screenplays and the PR department launching those plays or films ask him to help promote the project. This, of course, he does, but when that project has launched, Tom goes back to writing another play and you won't hear where he is or what he's doing until the next project is ready.

"Ray Davies is the same kind of person. He does his day's work, which involves writing, informing, soaking up aspects of life for public consumption, and only when there's a release of a book or a play or a record do you hear from him. He'll stand by the company launching the project and help out on the PR side, but he doesn't promote himself for himself. The book or record is the product being promoted, and not 'Ray Davies'.

"Another comparison is the case of two of the best record producers of all time. One of the most promoted, successful and hugest talents in the business is that wonderful darling of a man, George Martin. George is thought of, quite rightly, as one of the greatest record producers ever. A brilliant musician, knighted, the winner of all sorts of industry awards, all of which he justly deserves. Even if he did nothing else – and of course he did – he produced those wonderful Beatles records. But there are other people, like Glyn Johns – who produced Eric Clapton, The Eagles, The Who, the Stones, The Doobie Brothers, Cosby, Stills, Nash And Young, Joan Armatrading, Joe Cocker and many more – you never hear of. That's not because Glyn and co aren't talented or haven't paid their dues and made the great records. It's because they don't have, by choice, a PR machine or business structure around them to promote their work. Most of the top producers in the world could walk into a room and no one would recognise them. I wouldn't and neither would the public. You could stand up at a music industry dinner and introduce some of these people, and even that audience wouldn't know what they looked like. Mutt Lange is a prime example of this.

"It's a different take on how you promote your career. Neither is wrong and neither is right. It's down to your personality. If Ray Davies did something terribly important to him, it would only attract PR if that was necessary to achieve its end. When his theatre show, *Come Dancing*, comes out in 2002, the producer will employ a PR company to turn the PR lights onto the project to get the public's attention. It won't be Ray saying, 'I've got to have press.' Some people like the burden of being recognised all around the world, in every restaurant they go to, although it might get on top of them from time to time. But it is part of the overcoat of success that they wear, and they take it on. Others don't.

"There's a story about The Average White Band turning up late for a gig in Canada and not being allowed in because no one recognised them. As a publisher, I represented Chicago for more than 20 years and they've sold 40 or 50 million records, but there's no one in the band who you would recognise. If the bass player from Iron Maiden walked into the room, no one would recognise him. But if George Harrison came in, everyone would know him.

"Some acts have their photograph on the front sleeve of every record they make, as part of the marketing tool; some acts have never had their faces on the sleeves ever. They might have a blue splodge, a red splodge or an arrow going through the bag with Chinese writing and that represents Cream or Zeppelin or whoever. They're just different marketing approaches."

If The Rolling Stones are, as Ray suggests, Disneyland then there's a good case for The Kinks being Euro Disney. The same component parts are there, the same initial popularity is there, but one will always be an attractive proposition in the media while the other – EuroDisney, Disneyland Paris, Ray Davies or The Kinks, call them what you will – just can't seem to compete. As both Ray, Dave and Deke are quick to point out, the differences are the results of choices made. But for outsiders, including some who were once within the fold, giving the public what it wants, to cite the old album, has to be the way forward.

"In the old days, on the *Preservation* tour where we did two separate acts," John Gosling explains, "people preferred the support band because they just wanted the hits. America was a little more tolerant but it was a long show to sit through if you didn't like that sort of thing.

"The problem is that people our age are still expected to play the hits; even Paul McCartney. At the beginning of Wings he'd maybe do one Beatles song and that was it. On his last tour it was almost a whole Beatles set. It's expected of them to go out and do what they became famous for and anybody who steps out of line and tries to do something new at 45 or 50 is really pushing their luck. Even Dylan is getting round to do greatest hits as they sound on the record."

The demand for well-remembered favourites percolates everywhere, to the extent that otherwise august media are in danger of subverting history. In December 1995, for example, BBC 2 broadcast a revealing look-back on the band's career. *I'm Not Like Everybody Else – The World Of Ray Davies And The Kinks* was an entertaining hour's television made all the more palatable by cogent interviews with the brothers and Mick Avory among others. It also featured footage from the group's earliest '60s shows, right up to Ray's solo tour; sadly, 'Come Dancing' aside, virtually everything in the massive interim period was overlooked. Consequently, what could have been a definitive biopic resulted in as haphazard a portrayal as possible, depicting Ray as yet another has-been on the '90s nostalgia circuit. No wonder *The Daily Mirror*'s television critic was perhaps misled into concluding: "It all felt rather sad and depressing, as '60s pop icons tend to be. Ray, like the rest of them, looked as if he needed a good steak and a year's sleep."

The television production focused heavily on Ray's solo jaunt of 1995 – how else would they secure his involvement in making the programme (as he told the *LA Times* on tour with The Kinks in the same year: "I wasn't going to do any interviews because we don't have anything to sell"). Obviously, to both artist and producer, the full band's own lengthy concert programme around the USA earlier in 1995 was not worthy of coverage – an oversight hopefully at least addressed in print.

23 SCHIZOPHRENIA IS NORMAL

With Ray seemingly firmly cocooned within the shell of solo success and his solo album imminent, 1996 offered little hope of a Kinks reunion. Hopes were raised, though, on 12 April when, lecturing at the Rock 'N' Roll Hall of Fame, he announced that The Kinks would be playing a brace of Scandinavian festivals that summer – although, ominously, he said that one of the band would not be able to appear. As billed, Stockholm's 12 Timmar 70-Tal duly took place on 1 June, while Oslo's Norwegian Wood followed a fortnight later, and each show proved to massive audiences what they would be missing should the band ever decide to quit the international stage.

For Deke Arlon, on board only recently as the band's manager, these shows provided the first glimpse of what his new charges were capable of. "The first show the band did with me as their manager was the festival in Sweden," he says. "That night they were topping the bill over huge acts like Van Morrison. They hadn't played together for about a year, so we hired a wooden shed somewhere near the venue as a practice hall. They locked themselves in it for an hour and when they came out, you'd think they were halfway through a 150-date tour. They were as tight as hell, and the relationship between Dave and Ray on-stage was phenomenal. They look at each other and they know exactly what's going on at any time. Pure magic."

Untouchable as part of a duo with his brother, Ray was proving himself no slouch partnering Pete Mathison on the *20th Century Man* tour. Admirers were to be found in all quarters, some of them extremely influential. Music station VH1 was so impressed by the show that it signed Ray to perform a televised version. Recorded at one of his Wesbeth Theater shows in New York (a dozen performances between 12 February-3 March), the show saw what international audiences had been enjoying for months, namely the head Kink retelling the band's history inkeeping with his own *X-Ray* account.

Billed as *Storytellers* – an obvious description of the raconteurial nature of the event – the show was broadcast in the US on 2 June. Unusually for a stage production transferring to television, it was successfully and largely faithfully reproduced, a triumph for which executive producer, Bill Flanagan, a former *Boston Globe* contributor and *Musician* magazine editor, and director Michael Simon, must take credit. The reason for its successful transition was the fact that, as current *Globe* scribe Jim Sullivan isolates as the key to the TV show's success, Ray's show was actually the inspiration for the TV show and not vice versa: "This hour-long *Storytellers* debut is not a case of Davies adapting to a VH1 conceit, but VH1 plugging into a masterful, ready-made roadshow."

The truth of the matter was that VH1 had been for some time searching for an alternative to MTV's *Unplugged* series. The station's planners were so moved by the *20th Century Man* experience, that they bought into Ray's autobiographical singalong concept wholesale, leading to his show becoming the first in a series of *Storytellers* events: Jackson Browne was broadcast on 9 June, Elvis Costello and Lyle Lovett in the immediate weeks following.

"Ray's show was the pilot for the VH1 series," explains Deke Arlon. "It was his basic idea and concept which VH1 liked. They saw his show in New York and said they wanted to do a series to follow the *Unplugged* shows, something similar but to do with songwriters. They loved Ray's format so he did the pilot show, which they then showed to the James Taylors and the Paul Simons, to get others involved. The rest is history. It's been hugely successful since."

Having been instrumental in its inception, Ray took steps to maintain his association with the brand.

"Ray agreed to promote *Storytellers*," says Deke, "but then, for the benefit of VH1 and for the benefit of the public, it seemed silly to have one show on TV called *Storytellers* and the same show in theatres called *20th Century Man*, so he changed the name of his touring show."

So much for the concept, how fared the execution? Anecdotes for the evening included the explanation of what made 'A Well Respected Man' controversial in 1968 (the meaning of "fags" in America is not "cigarettes" as in the UK), the inspiration behind 'Sunny Afternoon' ("written when I was overworked, underpaid and in crisis, which is pretty normal for The Kinks") and 'Celluloid Heroes' ("inspired by Sunset Boulevard and some people I knew in that strange country called Los Angeles"). As Jim Sullivan reported, "I only wish the show had been longer."

Storyteller continued to wend its way around the globe throughout 1996, including an extensive two-month leg in America to capitalise on the TV exposure, but before that there was the matter of an intimate engagement at a small London venue called the Royal Albert Hall. Billed as a night of poetry reading, 7 July saw Ray once again alongside Damon Albarn, reciting lyrics to the amassed pan-generational crowds.

Back in the States, however, the next phase in the campaign to build on Ray's reputation was under way. Two years after its UK launch, 15 October finally saw US label Guardian release The Kinks' *To The Bone*, followed by the single of the same name the following January. Perhaps by way of recompense because of the wait, the American edition was a two-disc affair, carrying 29 tracks to its predecessor's 13. More than a pared-down greatest hits compilation, it took in some of the band's lesser bought but more respected efforts, as well as focusing on albums that had particular success in the States. 'Picture Book', 'The Village Green Preservation Society', 'Give The People What They Want', 'State Of Confusion' and 'A Gallon Of Gas' were all not featured on the first album.

Other extras for this version included the recorded debut of new songs 'To The Bone' and 'Animal', both written for the album, but well aired already at Ray's solo shows. According to the singer, the final selection of songs came more down to practical reasons than sentiment. "Dave and I are the only people in the current Kinks line-up who did these songs in the first place," he told *Guitar World*. "The other guys didn't know them so well, so because of the limited amount of time we had it was just a matter of which ones they could pick up the quickest. Except for 'Do You Remember Walter?' which I definitely wanted to record. I think that's one of the cult classics that only real fans know about.

'Set Me Free' was another highlight for him. "I think that came out great on the album," he says. "It's an unplugged thing and it's played through one of those tiny little Korg practice amps, with brushes on the drums. The accordion on 'Apeman' adds a new dimension. I love the accordion. I love cajun music...in moderation."

The genesis for the album, he revealed, was the BBC documentary *I'm Not Like Everybody Else* which featured film of the band rehearsing in Konk Studios. The result impressed Ray and in the end inspired the album and its posited accompanying video. "I thought it looked quite good," he says, "so I said, 'Why don't we just do this with a few people as an audience in the studio?' It worked out okay. We videotaped it as well but I'm not sure if that will ever see the light of day."

Reviewing the US release on website CDNOW (cdnow.com), Ed Hewitt noted the fact that disc one comes in at 37 minutes while its sequel racks up a full 63 minutes. "It's no accident; one is dampened by the sort of moments that cause most live albums to disappoint: inane intros, shaky vocals, even something that approaches a medley, fer chrissakes. Disc two, on the other hand, plays like a great night with The Kinks, from three-minute proto-punk shit-kickers, to jazz-infected, complex compositions and quite a bit in between." At fault for most of the album's failings – mediocre singalongs, half-speaking lyrics, etc – CDNOW points the finger at Ray. "His *20th Century Man* experience has made Davies revere his every brain fart," it claims. "His talents are intact, but his judgement occasionally wavers."

Stereophile's John Swenson argues that, on the contrary, it's the carefully considered ambience of Ray's solo endeavours, based on the fact that he has distanced himself from the shackles of the band, that give *To The Bone* its excellent results. In fact, it's the success of *20th Century Man* which might just have whetted US industry appetites for more Kinks product. Dave, too, is singled out for superb guitar work on 'You Really Got Me' and 'Set Me Free', even winning praise from Ray for his solos on 'I'm Not Like Everybody Else' and 'A Gallon Of Gas'. All in all, a satisfied, if surprised, customer, and one who concludes, like many others, that, "Instead of the end the band thought it was, *To The Bone* now stands as the beginning of a new chapter in the story of The Kinks."

Even the most disillusioned Kinks fan – "and Kinks fans have many reasons to be disillusioned" – would be impressed by this set of poignant, sensitive classics, said Scott Schinder in *Pulse* magazine. In particular, the inclusion of relative obscurities such as 'Picture Book' and 'Walter' in itself, he reckons, is "enough to strip a decade and a half off the band's tarnished reputation". Wading in with four (out of five) stars, the review generously points to a future that may be brighter than anyone suspects.

It's a feeling supported in a review from *CMJ New Music Report* which agreed that the album was a more than worthy addition to the Kinks *oeuvre*: "Their latest release proves to doubters that Ray and Dave Davies still have what they had in the early '60s when, as part of the British Invasion, they helped build the framework that would be used in the '70s and '80s by innumerable power chord bands." Citing inclusion of lesser known classics like 'Picture Book', plus the "two sparkling new songs", the feel is of a band on the up.

In almost predictable fashion, when the building momentum of interest in the band needed to be exploited, The Kinks did nothing; at least, not as a group. Ray, of course, was reaping the rewards at his personal shows, so it was only right that Dave was at last beginning to create a few headlines for himself with the long-awaited launch of his own autobiography, pithily and honestly entitled *Kink*.

If metaphors need to be looked for to explain the differences between the Davies brothers, no better example could be found than by comparing their two memoirs. Where Ray's earlier volume was written in the third person and presented as a piece of cod fiction, almost daring the reader to assume that any of its content was about the author, *Kink* was candour itself. Not only was his book delivered without the smokescreen of pretension or authorial diversion, but he also didn't pull any punches when it came to spilling the beans on his own life. Whether naive or bold, clearly nobody pointed out to Dave that rock autobiographies don't generally reveal too much of the truth.

Dave's impetus was honesty: "I tried to keep it straight ahead," he says. "There have been biographies about The Kinks, and they've pissed me off because they get things wrong." No names...

While *X-Ray* was disappointingly vague on most topics of interest (although still a brilliant work in its own right), *Kink* contained explicit revelations about Dave's relationship with his brother as well as evidence of his open-minded sexual explorations in the '60s, his drug use and, to his credit, his own occasionally less than pleasant treatment of those dearest to him. By way of example of the latter point, "Dave, the silly bugger, went as far as telling his wife in Los Angeles about his wife in London", a flabbergasted Pete Quaife reveals. "He was the wild man out of the lot of us, that's for sure. Dave revealed stuff that was going on at the time that I had absolutely no idea about. I said to myself as I was reading, 'He did that?', 'He said what?' Ray set his book up as though he was interviewing himself. Well, if you do that you can rephrase your answer if you don't like it the first time. Dave's is more factual and authentic, no question."

LA Weekly reviewer Dan Epstein was impressively smitten: "An impossible to put down tale of drinks, drugs and sexual experimentation, with cameo appearances by characters real, hallucinated and extraterrestrial, it's nothing less than you'd expect from the man who came up with the crazed guitar solo to 'You Really Got Me'."

Reviewing for *United Press International*, John Swenson is slightly more restrained: "A lurid and excruciatingly self-revelatory history laced with bitterness about the way the band's affairs were handled. In the book, Dave accuses Ray of stealing songwriting credit to songs he contributed to and thus robbing him of royalty payments." It's a fair summary of an explosive tale.

Describing the book in 1997, *The LA Times'* Buddy Seigel sums up its charm: "He spills it all. The men, the women, famous and unknown, he slept with (or almost slept with); the binges of substance abuse that would kill most ordinary men; the wanton destruction of hotel rooms and public property; his fellow members of British rock royalty; and the notorious, physical and psychological battles with his brother, Ray."

There are many such passages detailing those battles with Ray. "He became so abusive to me, so cruel and creatively draining" is one example; "he displays an almost resentful and sometimes condescending loathing for his past, his family" is another; "he is at times venomous, spiteful and completely self-involved" is a third. Speaking to *Record Collector* magazine, though, Dave denied that his brother had faired unfavourably overall. "I don't think he comes out badly," he says. "I think he comes out really well."

Another aspect of the book of particular interest to Kinks aficionados was Dave's various claims about the credits on some of his elder brother's more celebrated compositions. In particular, he claims he has never been given due credit for his creative role in 'Lola', although, as he told *Record Collector*, "I think that Ray would admit that if push came to shove."

It is to Dave's credit that his natural inclination to look beyond financial and ego quibbles – the traditional causes of most bands' break-ups – has fuelled his life, rather than dwelling on issues that others find unacceptable. But some – outsiders – as he points out, don't really know what goes on. "Other people have said, 'Have you thought about suing Ray?' but it's never really bothered me; it's only a financial thing and money's never really interested me."

One aspect of *Kink* which shocked everyone – not least because it was exactly the degree of honesty which set the book apart from others of its genre – and not just fans of The Kinks, was Dave's admission that while on tour in the US in 1982 he had experienced a spiritual visitation in the shape of voices in his head: "I began hearing these strange voices talking to me, in clear and unmistakable tones. Two of them said that they had always been my spirit guides, and two others were entities that were not of this earth but were involved in missions here as watchers and nurturers of our race." It was a stunning departure to a book which, to that point, was little more than standard rock fare.

"I felt very safe," Dave admits, "I felt in control and that I was going to stay like that forever. When it ended, I was devastated. The emotional effect of it ending was as if I was a piece of shit. Even in my sleep, there isn't a moment in which I don't think about it in some way."

By way of rationalising the experience, he has sought to channel the episode into his work, and to look for ways in which it may already have been helping him. "Schizophrenia is quite normal, I think," he says. "I feel it's a necessary part of the mind. The whole process of writing is schizophrenic. Look at Ray and the imaginary characters in his book. If something creative comes out of it, what's wrong with that?"

As with a lot of projects undertaken by the brothers, Dave's venture into book writing was trumped by Ray's, although neither was aware of the competition. Ray had contacted him in the '80s to discuss an official biography, but Dave had been too busy working on a film script to participate and the trail went cold. Prompted by an LA literary agent, Dave eventually started the agonising process of trying to get his life down on paper. Having a diary helped, but it was a gruelling, lonely process. In 1994, though, armed with a manuscript, he arranged meetings with several leading London publishers and flew in from his home in California. But big brother had got there first. "I got off the plane, looked up and there was an ad for Ray's book," he recounts. "I knew nothing about it. I thought, 'This is going to happen to me until the day I die.'"

While Dave has read and liked X-Ray ("I really enjoyed it but when he got into difficult areas he was a bit more evasive"), Ray maintains that he hasn't repaid the compliment. Dave, however, thinks this is bluff: "Ray phoned up someone at our office and said, 'Have you seen Dave's book? You know, I think this is going to be the end of The Kinks this year'."

In retrospect it could well be the case that Kink was the catalyst for the end of the band, given that there has been no significant group activity since and Dave and Ray rarely see each other. But, since both brothers make a point of denying a split in every interview they do ("the bottom line is that I do have to rely on The Kinks for income," Dave admits, "I'd be a liar if I said that wasn't part of it. But there's another driving force and that's the real Kinks fans. I kind of know what they mean. *I'm* a Kinks fan"), there should be hope of recorded reconciliation. In the mean time, though, there are solo avenues for both brothers to explore.

Prior to the release of his autobiography, Dave had been busy working on the second of his collaborations with horror film specialist John Carpenter. *Village Of The Damned*, released in the US in 1995, was a science fiction movie based on the classic John Wyndham novel about a small town invaded by children with unusual powers. In his sleeve notes to the soundtrack, Carpenter relayed how it was his job as composer to support the drama, unify sequences, and heighten the suspense in the film. With Dave, he was charged with bringing emotional life to a story without humanity, a task aided by the guitarist's contribution. Focus for the project arrived when Dave had sent him a cassette containing a sketch which eventually defined the direction of the album, "eventually referred to as 'March Of The Children'," he says. "Dave's music was beautiful, haunting, dark and somehow heroic. I loved it."

Unusually, the young Davies was suddenly part of a working partnership that was not only fulfilling, but also rewarding in a public sense. He was suddenly in a relationship that was creative, professional and...that's it. There were no mind games and no back-stabbing. "It was pure joy," he admits. "There was no torture or emotional abuse, just the discipline of work." In particular, he was amazed at the generosity of the sleevenotes: "I just cried, I couldn't believe it," he says. "I was so used to doing it without getting any thanks, it felt really odd."

The scene was set when the duo had worked on *In The Mouth Of Madness* a year earlier. When the CD came out, Dave had been refreshingly surprised to find himself with a songwriting credit – admittedly deserved. After a lifetime of fighting for every ounce of recognition, here it was, unprompted: "I thought, 'This is great – isn't this how it's supposed to be?'"

Just as Ray was inspired by *X-Ray* to take a solo show on the road, *Kink* proved just the excuse that Dave needed to make his first foray into solo showmanship. Ironically, given it was his solo career which Wace and co had tried to launch with 'Death Of A Clown', and that he had already released several solo albums, he had never succeeded in treading the boards as just Dave Davies. In 1997, that was about to change.

March 1997 saw Dave's solo debut in New York, at the Bottom Line club. Writing for *The New York Times*, John Pareles found the show a breath of fresh air compared to his brother's reading / playing performance: "Dave Davies just plugged in and played. He was an inexperienced front man but an enthusiastic and endearing one. The longtime second banana who had finally seized his moment." Listing the set, Pareles noted the appearance of recent songs, some from the 1960s and even a few of his brother's which he admires. "Compared with his brother's songs, however, Dave's tend to go to extremes: angrier, sadder, grittier."

Angry, sad and gritty Dave's catalogue may be, but there was also a sense of humour obvious at the Bottom Line when he found time to make fun of his brother's solo *Storyteller* tour. Having performed a 'Lola' medley including 'Strawberry Fields Forever' and 'The Girl From Ipanema', he then produced a copy of *Kink*, and made as though to read from it. "It's not as long as some books," he promised...

A month later the show was ready to start a tour proper in West Hollywood. An early hitch was overcome when the scheduled backing band – three quarters of The Smithereens – had to be replaced by Andrew Sandoval (guitar), David Jenkins (bass), Jim Laspesa (drums) and keyboardist Danny Magu. For the opening gig at Luna Park on 21 April, Dave proved, as he would throughout the tour, that a set list is only there for guidance, although he still appeared to be using a music stand for lyrical help. Where 'Little Queenie' and 'One Night With You' were written on the band's charts, neither was played. 'Sea Of Heartbreak' was another casualty. None of them was missed, however, in a two-hour show that saw the guitarist rip through some of his greatest work, from both solo and Kink catalogues. Non-chart favourites 'Picture Book', 'Wicked Annabella' and 'Love Me Till The Sun Shines' stood alongside more broad-based fare like 'You Really Got Me', 'David Watts' and 'Dead End Street'. 'Look Through Any Doorway', 'Strangers', 'Get Back In Line' and 'Too Much On My Mind' also went down well – what didn't? – but perhaps the biggest cheer was reserved for the pre-'Got Me' encore of 'My Way'. A month into his first solo tour, and Dave was hitting his stride.

A week later at Santa Ana's Galaxy, 'Little Queenie' and 'One Night', although listed, failed to appear, and Dave was still leaning occasionally on the lyrical crutch of the music stand. But, as most fans would agree, when you are premiering new songs, that's forgivable. As with Luna Park, 'Fortis Green', a track intended to promote Kink, was played to a welcoming and, despite the venue's chicken-in-a-basket seating arrangement, receptive crowd. The club also provided the first hearing for many of 'Unfinished Business', a track destined, Dave announced, for a compilation album he had coming out soon. Other rarities included an emotive airing of 'Imagination's Real', from Dave's first solo album, plus 'Misty Water', from The Great Lost Kinks Album, played over the PA system prior to Dave taking the stage. Largely, though, the set remained as earlier: starting with 'I Need You' and ending with 'You Really Got Me'. Most impressively, after so many years on the sidelines, Dave remained on top form as your host for the evening, a point praised by music critics.

"Garage rock epiphany" was what Chuck Crisafulli, reviewing in The LA Times, claims he witnessed at Dave's gig at the Galaxy. Amusingly comparing the guitarist's position as the id in The Kinks, versus his brother's long established superego, Crisafulli marvels at the ambitious and experimental set list which included the likes of 'Susannah's Still Alive', 'Strangers' and the mighty 'Get Back In Line'. Of course, the encores featured the first two hits plus a storming 'David Watts', but for American Kinks fans more used to safer fare in recent years, the overall choice was refreshing, as was, for the reviewer, Dave's "about to pop" vocal style. In short, a stunning solo debut in this particular part of America.

In all, six southern Californian shows took place before the act moved on to Chicago. From there it was scheduled to stop at Pontiac, Philadelphia, Boston, NYC, Providence, Asbury Park and New Haven, but all were cancelled. More dates were lined up for the end of the year, but the original venues were not included.

24 STORIES

While Dave's first solo tour was under way, Ray's seemingly neverending one-Kink show was going from strength to strength. March 1997 saw it kick off in London's prestigious Queen Elizabeth Hall, then cross to take in the USA and Canada over the next two months before a triumphal return to where, in its current form, the show had started: the Edinburgh Festival.

1 April, though, found him at California's Irvine Barclay Theater. While being in a small show means Ray has the flexibility to alter his set at will, apparently not all parts of his tour are so responsive. Almost a year after the TV broadcast, advertisements for the show still called it *20th Century Man*. Inside the auditorium, however, official T-shirts and souvenirs were more commercially labelled with "Storyteller".

The show itself was pretty much what everyone had come to expect by now, only sharper. Just 15 minutes shy of three hours, it had reached its natural length after a year of evolution, and the book was playing less of a role than Ray's memory. Rather than read passages, he was able to tell the stories unabetted, although *X-Ray* was still prominent – "if you want to read the racy bits, turn to pages 239-253," he advised.

Far less esoteric than Dave's shows of the same time, Ray stuck largely to the hits with 'Powerman', 'The Money-Go-Round' and 'Americana' the obvious exceptions. 'Two Sisters' continued to be a pivotal song / anecdote combo, while 'Waterloo Sunset' was again the perfect curtain closer. For veteran followers, however, a highlight of the night was an apparently unscheduled encore of 'Come Dancing', wistful and bluesy, as performed on the VH1 show.

The same song put in an appearance a month later at New York's Colden Auditorium in Flushing, but in many ways that was the only similarity between the two gigs.

A large concert hall dwarfing the two performers plus a sizeable gulf between them and the audience meant that Ray looked in anxious humour from the start. The traditionally rousy – and, it has to be said, largely inebriated – New York crowd didn't on this occasion cheer him up. Many of the audience didn't seem to grasp that a show called "Storyteller" would involve anecdotes between the songs; perhaps the tour's billing as *20th Century Man* could be blamed here. So, as Ray tried to regale one and all with tales of his father's sayings or his sisters' loves, many saw this as the perfect opportunity to heckle, chat or request other songs. As flexible as the production is, there is undoubtedly a tightly woven structure at its core; the stories are irrevocably linked with the songs. If nothing else, after so long honing the presentation and its content, it's debatable whether Ray actually has the ability to engage in a full-on rock show any more.

The answer to the last point was going to be discovered. After one interruption too many, one more poorly judged lighting cue and another erroneous blast of pre-recorded music through the PA system, Ray stormed off stage. The omens hadn't been good: Ray had been hitting occasional bum notes and Pete's guitar had needed to be swapped mid one song. There had also been a louder than usual cheer when Dave's name had been mentioned, causing Ray to caustically remark, "If you keep this up, I'll walk off." Which he did.

Suddenly initiated into the world of the real Kinks, and not just a secure spin-off, lone stage dweller Mathison eventually shuffled off to join his boss. Once again, it was time to expect the unexpected.

The fans needn't have worried. Dispersing with his prompts as much as possible, stopping to relay only a few of the rehearsed speeches, Ray returned to the stage in a mood to rock. "This is what rock 'n' roll is all about," he promised as he moved speakers and tested the microphones. And then he proved it. Two hours of solid singing, straight through, with few interludes, followed, with 'Animal Farm', 'Animal', 'Fancy' and 'Celluloid Heroes' the standout inclusions.

Minds were understandably cast back to the volatile days of The Kinks. Whether it was at Brentwood in 1994, Washington in 1993 (where they barely managed an hour's worth of music before storming off) or the Nassau Coliseum in 1981 which saw Dave and Mick at the height of their destructive powers, the history of The Kinks has enough colour to alert any fan to the constant possibility of the unscripted moment. Perhaps to those who had come to Ray's gig knowing only his VH1 performance, it was a shock; but for die-hard Kinks lovers, as bizarre as the evening was, it was probably like welcoming back an old friend.

Speaking of which, 17 August 1997 saw Ray return to the incubator of *Storyteller*, the Edinburgh Festival, for a 15-night run. In sparkling fettle, he relayed tales which, although well-bedded in the show these days, wouldn't have been heard in that embryonic earlier version. How the Kray brothers had once tried to manage The Kinks; how John Lennon had roundly put the band in its place; Streatham Ice Rink, recording contracts, green amps; the variety was as boundless as the songs.

Taking to the stage at midnight (entertainment laws in that city are particularly generous), Edinburgh Assembly Rooms beheld marvel after marvel during the slightly abridged (just under two hours) set. Just as the first acoustic version of 'Shangri-La' had been previewed there two years earlier, so they were introduced to more new pieces, 'Back In The Front Room' the obvious pick. On the opening night, a stunning version of 'It's Alright' was also to be cherished, along with seminal renditions of 'The London Song', 'Art School Babes', 'Julie Finkle', 'X-Ray' and 'Stop Your Sobbing'. Sadly, due to the shorter time, stalwarts 'Days', 'Animal' and 'Two Sisters' had to make way.

Dwelling on the show's length, *The Scotsman* newspaper explained how Ray's truncated effort allowed him to play virtually two different sets across two nights, either going into detail about the histrionics and the hell-raising of The Kinks, or focusing more on their '60s contribution to music. Suspecting it as a ruse to draw you back another night, it recommends both versions. "Witty and intimate, this is a show of nostalgic reflections, humorous insights and unbeatable music." Shame about the singalongs...

The acclaim continued in the *Edinburgh Evening News*. Promoting Ray's work as the equal of any of his generation – "more scathing than Pete Townshend, as piercing as Jagger and Richards at their best, and as direct and melodic as Lennon and McCartney" – the newspaper recommends universal attendance. "When you mix Davies' finely crafted songs with a laugh-a-minute stand-up routine, a dollop of nostalgia and lashings of rock 'n' roll, you've got one of the best shows at the festival. Sell your granny to see him."

The casual nature of Edinburgh during the festival meant that many were treated to further slices of Ray after the show. Sometimes pushing the landlords' patience to extremes, Ray and Pete could be found in the bar most nights, chatting with fans, discussing the performance, explaining future plans and revealing new songs.

Whereas Edinburgh had, two years ago, seen the first incarnation of a show based around *X-Ray*, Glasgow was now to be treated to its own book-based event, as part of a mini-promotional tour. Ray's writing project for the previous year, and early 1997, had been a work of fiction called *Waterloo Sunset*. A collection of short stories, in many ways it appeared to be a retelling of his autobiography, with many of the same devices employed. In particular, its tactic of manipulating time is extremely familiar to anyone who has read *X-Ray*.

Published in hardback in September in the UK by Viking (a Penguin subsidiary, and the same publisher as the "unauthorised autobiography"), the book explored post-modernism writing as it toyed with accepted formats. One chapter, 'Celluloid Heroes', appears as a screenplay while 'My Diary', as its title infers, takes the form of entries in a daily journal.

"This is a concept album on paper" is how the book's jacket text describes it, "whose interlinking narratives are held together by Richard, who is helping an ageing rocker to make a comeback; by a sinister character from one of the songs; and by deeper chords that are resonant of the struggle to retain identity amid the confusion between pretence and reality. It's still a rock 'n' roll world, and whether the mood is fantastic, laconic, exuberant, witty or moving, like his music, the words of Ray Davies still cut to the bone."

The text also states how "the inspiration behind those classic songs has come alive again", which is a surprise to those who hadn't realised it had died. But, given some of the stories' apparent drawing on Kinks material, you can see the publisher's point. Less of an indication of a creative rebirth, however, is *Waterloo Sunset*'s similarities with the content in *X-Ray* (some would argue there's more of the real Ray here than in his autobiography). Central figure Les Mulligan, a writer, could, for many, be Ray himself. He suffers the same romantic twists as his creator and, in another instance, is sadly abroad when his mother dies, forever afterwards carrying the feeling of guilt at a goodbye unsaid. Similarly, the passages where he describes the anguishes and the practices of songwriting are keenly reproduced opinions that could only be the creation of a master craftsman in this field. Most tellingly, though, are Les' struggles to please the global corporation charged with releasing his records – Sony comes to mind more than once. Other characters, Lucien and Donna, suffer the sorts of emotional trials that you only normally read about...in Kinks biographies.

Since *X-Ray* finished in 1973, it's deceptively tempting to read *Waterloo Sunset* as just a straight continuation, but there is far more to it than that. Stepping outside the familiar, a number of the stories touch upon conceits that one hopes the author has had little or no experience of. In 'Voices In The Dark', he portrays the shabby, grotesque but all too real world of the vagrant, as Muriel, a character who had flitted silently around the Mulligan chapters, is given her own space to reveal the anguish of a mute observer to a world at odds with itself. 'Mr Pleasant', touching on ground and mood familiar to fans of 'Sunny Afternoon' and 'Dedicated Follower', tells of an accountant nearing his career's end who, considering a dalliance with a dominatrix, is forced to reconcile the heartlessness of his existence. Closing the book in powerful, if disturbing, style, though, is 'Return To Waterloo', a brilliant and chilling study of a serial rapist and misogynist crying out for respect.

As with another piece of Ray's recent work, *To The Bone*, there were problems transferring the UK release of *Waterloo Sunset* to America. When it did emerge three years later, for Hyperion in 2000, it was as a reworked piece. For some, the new version was an improvement; tellingly, for Ray himself, it appears it was less so. Speaking in 2001, Ray's manager, Deke Arlon, admits that "*Waterloo Sunset* didn't turn out the way we hoped. Somewhere down the line publishers changed and so the concept that he'd set out with was altered. It was a successful book anyway, but not quite what he envisaged."

The US edition comprised two sections, 'Waterloo Sunset' and 'Stories'. Helpfully, if you were of a mind that this was pure autobiography, the first bundled together the various Les Mulligan pieces. Despite the different time settings, it was now easier to read as one larger tale. The second half compiled the "other" character stories. The new layout made the book less of a jumble than the earlier edition, but it also focused the reader's mind on one section or the other, in effect forcing a preference between what was, effectively, two mini-collections.

Verdicts from reviewers were mixed. *Kirkus Reviews* describes the Mulligan escapades as "a mixed up, unfinished mess" and the latter half "as surprising and unique as the song lyrics he wrote decades ago".

Stephanie Zacharek at salon.com found what was, for many, the stand-out story – 'Return To Waterloo' – "muddled and overwrought, as if Davies had tripped over himself in trying to be writerly and profound". But, overall, she finds the use of lyrics, personal experience and prose devices "engaging instead of gimmicky" and "if Davies gets his observations of people down on paper only half as well as he's able to crystallise them in a song, he's still doing pretty damn good".

Joe Hartlaub at bookreporter.com found the experience a pleasing one. Sympathising with Ray / Les for asking the question "at what point does a contemporary recording artist become a parody of himself?", he concludes that, despite the intrinsic nature of his life in the work, you don't need to know anything about Ray to enjoy it: "Davies is a fine wordsmith and he has an ability to communicate, to gently and subtly touch multiple nerves with a few words. Recent commercial failures notwithstanding, he is too talented to be considered a failure in any medium, whether it be music, literature or whatever other form his art may take in the future. *Waterloo Sunset* is proof of this."

As another art form, Ray's music also played a role in the story collection, as *The Songs Of Waterloo Sunset*, the album, emerged in 1997 to support the book.

A mixture of new songs and Kinks numbers, it was, to varying degrees, the soundtrack of its printed companion. The album and the book had their origins at the same time, although which came first is as straightforward as anything to do with Davies Senior. Writing in the lyric booklet to Castle's double package (*Waterloo* on one disc, *The Singles Collection* on the other disc), however, Ray explains: "Some of the short stories on which this album is based were written in note form at the time I was writing the lyrics (these include 'A Rock And Roll Fantasy', 'Scattered', '32 Bar Bridge' and 'Celluloid Heroes')." Others are less linked.

As a consequence, many themes are shared from lyric to page. For example, "'Million-Pound Semi-Detached' was written around the time of the property boom in 1988 and was later made into a short promotion video, but the project never got off the ground," Ray says, whereas "'Holiday Romance' was simply adapted from the lyrics of the song, although many of the incidents that occur in 'Still Searching' took place long after the song was written."

'Art Lover' and 'Afternoon Tea' were songs first and stories later. Confusingly, the book version of 'Afternoon Tea' was originally called 'The Cake' – which itself was the name of a song later written by Ray ("it would have been too confusing to include it in this collection"). Adding more intrigue, the punk from 'Return To Waterloo' is reprised in 'Art Lover'. "He's given extended life as Lucien," Ray explains. "All the other connected characters in this story are deliberate."

'Return To Waterloo', of course, "started as a song, then turned into a film script which was shown on Channel 4 in 1984". By 1997, though, there had been another transformation when it appeared as a piece of fiction. "The notes for the short story version," Ray says, "were written while I was editing the film." With the actor's face running through the editing machine again and again, Ray found himself constantly seeing new things in the face, a theme pursued in the lyrics and the dark, thought-provoking short story.

The book / song connections are exploded with 'The Shirt'. Arguably an anti-drug song ('Reefer Madness' was its original name), it was as much an anti-MOR song, with Ray keen to prove the type of versatility that Arista's Clive Davis would have railed against. Setting out to attain a certain sound, instructing Mick Avory to strive for "a Gene Krupa style jazz drum solo to give the feel of 1940s film noir". Either way, as Ray pointedly assures, "I must emphasise that the song itself has no bearing or relevance to the short story 'The Shirt'. That's why the lyrics are not included in the book." Whatever its origins, the song is a fine album opener, strong on jazz vibe, courtesy of Mick and the underplayed, stark acoustic accompaniment. Ray's voice soars lightly and with a purity that wouldn't be embarrassed in a venue like Ronnie Scott's (performing its more usual repertoire, rather than the Kinksman's catalogue).

The bulk of the tracks are known quantities from various stages of The Kinks' career. 'Mister Pleasant' is the first, a track from 1967 originally intended as a single in the UK before it was replaced by 'Waterloo Sunset'. It was released in the States, but UK fans had to wait until it appeared on the B-side of 'Autumn Almanac'. 'Celluloid Heroes', 'Holiday Romance', 'Still Searching', 'Afternoon Tea', 'Drivin'' and 'Scattered' complete the set of known versions, although 'Waterloo Sunset' itself appears in its stereo mix.

The lyric of 'A Rock 'N' Roll Fantasy' inspired the story of the same name. The live version on record is a creditable and credible portrayal of an artist coming to terms with his own anachronisticism, admitting that he's been through a lot, hasn't changed one iota and is lucky to still be going. Strongly led by Ray's acoustic, but with full band accompaniment, it tells the tale of a guy living on the edge of reality who, whenever the world gets too much, just turns up the volume on his record player. Distancing himself, the singer doesn't want to live the same life of fantasy.

'Voices In The Dark' was originally written for the *Return To Waterloo* project, initially intended to play over the closing credits. Like a lot of the material on that soundtrack, it featured singing from Ray's daughter Louisa, but ironically met its Waterloo in *Return*, dropped from the film and first cropping up on *Sunset*. The remix on this album is tight, haunting, slightly Enya-ish in places with the female vocal, and worthy in content of the short story that shares its name. Lyrics about lonely cries, a voice without a face and a soul lost on the subway relate it to the book, but the catchy chorus (despite the irritating vocoder sound effects) gives it a life in its own right.

'Art Lover' is a remix, while 'Return To Waterloo' appears in its unreleased demo form. The long-awaited 'Million-Pound Semi-Detached' and new song 'My Diary' complement the mix. The former, beginning with a cuckoo clock, sees The Kinks busk their way through a standard tale of newly-weds subsumed by suburbia, with the usual mentions of national service, pebble dash houses and misplaced consumer pride. An 'Autumn Almanac' for the '90s (although written in the housing boom atmosphere of the '80s), it takes a turn for sadness with its closing refrain looking back wistfully.

'My Diary' sees a journal stacked with appointments too important to break but a life devoid of content since the leaving of a loved one. Told in almost country style, the lyric switches between spoken discussion and melodic invention on the chorus. Mentions of a "lonely one-man play" hint that the story is more heart-felt than its flippancy at first indicates, as the narrator bemoans how a packed itinerary is no substitute for a worthwhile relationship.

'My Diary' was one of the tracks premiered by Ray at the readings which took place to support the book in the UK. Manchester's Deansgate on 10 September, followed on consecutive days by Glasgow's Royal Concert Hall and London's Virgin Megastore, saw him explain the characters from *Waterloo Sunset*, then back them up with the songs that support them, played throughout on his trusty Ovation acoustic. An entertaining question and answer session plus the obligatory signing opportunity in each venue guaranteed happy punters. And the fact that ticket prices could be deducted from the price of the book meant that even the product plugged was suitably subscribed to, so even the publishers were happy.

While Ray was launching and promoting his book and CD, 1997 also witnessed the release of a musical of the same take to the road in the UK.

Centred around the characters Terry and Julie reuniting after 20 years, the show features a live band playing Kinks tunes. By dint of its existence, it was taken that Ray had given his blessing; there were also rumours that he would appear in the show when it played at Glastonbury.

That diversion aside, the creativity of autumn also presaged an outbreak of cancellations and postponements. First, the release of Dave's forthcoming UK solo anthology was put back due to licensing delays (in the States it went ahead as a shorter, eleven-track effort on Velvel, including material from his solo albums); next, Ray cancelled a swathe of gigs in Holland, citing the fact that he was in a recording studio working on new material. Finally, Castle Communications announced that the planned reissue of the Pye catalogue, complete with bonus tracks, would now take place next year, allowing them to concentrate on *The Singles Collection* double CD. On a happier note, both Dave and Ray were able to resume their American solo tours for the last months of the year, but with Dave's dates beginning ominously ten days after Ray's had ended. The USA is a big country, but it might have met its match in two Davies boys crossing over.

25 EVERYBODY'S A SOLO STAR

Since its inception in 1993, the Boston Rock Opera has been bringing to the stage full-scale theatrical representations of classic concept albums. *Jesus Christ Superstar*, *The Rocky Horror Show* and The Beatles' *Sgt Pepper* have all got the treatment to increasing acclaim. In its first year, the troupe – founded by Eleanor Ramsay and Mick Maldonado – performed a one-off night of *Preservation Act II* at the Middle East in Cambridge, Massachusetts and in 1998, five years later, they announced an ambitious run of the full *Preservation* show as Ray Davies had intended it.

How did they know his intentions? Because after years of trying, the BRO finally won Ray's cooperation and blessing to perform the show. Considering that, since The Kinks performed the show in America and briefly in London in 1974, Hollywood, European companies and even Dave Davies have supposedly asked to present it, only to receive a negative response from its creator, for the Boston outfit to get the go-ahead was some achievement.

"I've known about this company's work for several years," Ray says. "They've been very persistent in trying to get *Preservation* put on properly, and they believe in the piece."

While billed as supplying "author's notes", Ray's involvement required little else. "I've given them my blessing to do the production as they see fit," he said at the time. "I feel they have a genuine affinity for the piece and its music."

Given his reputation for hands-on control, Ray was surprisingly accommodating about the changes the new production demonstrated.

Despite the fact that there is no dialogue in the show, as in true opera, Ramsay successfully dropped five songs plus occasional passages and verses. So keen was he to see the show performed that Ray actually suggested further cuts.

"I went up to see Eleanor a few times when I was in Boston," Ray says. "I gave her my blessing because it's good she's got the energy to keep going with it. I stopped by to see a staging and I was quite impressed. But it's their production. Not to be confused with me doing a Pete Townshend."

"Ray was filled with ideas," Ramsay admits. "There were some changes and he encouraged us to go with some ideas we were unsure of."

At the time of the show, both *Preservation* albums had just been re-released, along with other Kinks back catalogue, by the Velvel label. The public mood was as ready as it had been in more than 20 years.

For all its extravagance, the production was deemed a success in all quarters, despite a few technical difficulties. Writing for *The Boston Globe Online*, Jim Sullivan opined that "it seems like a cast of thousands (23 in fact) and it takes some work to keep everyone straight. Occasionally the miking was erratic. The first act is a rather long table-setter – most of the drama, conflict and best songs come in the second act. But taken either bit by bit or as a whole, *Preservation* is a delight. It's a mess out there in the village, but it sure feels good in the audience."

The problem with staging *Preservation*, Ray told *The Boston Globe*, is that 1) it wasn't written for the stage; and 2) it was in fact written under pressure. "I didn't have time to sit around, do workshops, and get fancy directors in," he admits. "You just have to put the thing on and go out. But I'm amazed at how the music carries the story."

The *Boston Herald*'s Dean Johnson made the point that the village may as well be Washington DC and that the common man is played by the Tramp. Again, the paper picked up on the technical hitches. "Dead mics, missed lighting cues, unbalanced singers vs band sound levels apart, it was a fun night, especially for Kinks fans.

"Davies' original tunes range from feisty pop and raging rock to English dance hall ditties, with a little country and western thrown in. The music, particularly ensemble numbers such as 'Here Comes Flash',

'He's Evil' and 'Money Talks', holds up well. Jane Bulger's choreography and Eleanor Ramsay's direction add enough action and visual appeal to flesh out the story. But like any opera, the music carries the real message."

The *Boston Phoenix*'s Jonathan Perry found the whole show an eye-opening experience. "Not only has BRO's production done satisfying, faithful justice to Davies' darkly brilliant vision, in some ways it outshines the original albums. As grandly ambitious as they were, save for a smattering of classic and should-be-classic songs, *Acts I* and *II* were, on album at least, ultimately uneven projects – inferior to works like 1969's *The Kinks Are The Village Green Preservation Society*, which served as the blueprint for a subsequent Davies rock opera. In BRO's hands, the songs, dialogue, and characters leap from dusty obscurity to vivid, three-dimensional life, at once funny and sad and tragic, with all of Davies' original intentions intact."

Northeast Performer Magazine's Scott Chesley wrote that "the songs comprising *Preservation* run the gamut from the pastoral ditty 'Sitting In The Midday Sun' to the flat-out rock of Flash's 'Demolition', to the countrified blues duet of Belle and Tramp's 'Scrapheap City'. With many strong ensemble numbers and exceptionally inspired individual performances from Mick Maldonado, Marty Barrett (The Vicar) and Peter Moore, whose teetering town drunk repeatedly stole the show, the BRO breathed a vibrant life into Davies' exceptionally relevant rock commentary."

And Ray's opinion after the quarter of a century gap between productions? "It was worth the wait."

All in all, a theatrical success then. And possibly, the added spur for Ray persisting with the dramatisation of his stage project, *Come Dancing*, threatened and rumoured throughout the late '90s but never venturing out of the talks stage. According to a spokesman, the show "should be out next year". A nation holds its breath...

The US success of *Preservation* was a surprise to many, not least Ray. Like a protective parent, he normally refuses to let others meddle with his work unless he can oversee. For that reason, most requests for permission to work on similar projects are refused.

"A lot of offers come in every year for theatre companies to do *Schoolboys In Disgrace* or *Preservation* or the other rock operas or concept albums Ray's written," explains manager Deke Arlon. "Normally it's for festivals, sometimes films, even animated films. We don't usually allow them to go forward, though. Generally it's because the people who say, 'Can we do this?' haven't really come up with a good enough idea, they haven't really thought it through. They don't really understand enough about the subject to convince Ray to trust them to go ahead. He can't do everything himself – although he tries – but he does want to be involved, he does want to know what's going on and why.

"It's only when he feels that the people offering to do it really understand what it's about that we would consider it. Nobody in my time has come in with a ballpark plan that's made Ray go, 'Oh yes, absolutely, what a fantastic idea. You've added to my idea and taken it somewhere which is very exciting.' That hasn't happened. They tend to come to him and explain something he already knows. They're just reiterating what's in black and white before them. To be a film director or a record producer or a book editor, you have to have a little more than what's in front of you." All the more reason, then, for *Come Dancing* to be something special – or, at least worth the wait.

Speaking of waiting, after almost four decades in The Kinks, Dave had finally amassed, by 1998, enough material, certainly over enough time, for a career retrospective. He'd already released, as a limited edition, an eleven-track CD called *Unfinished Business: Solo Kronikles 1980-1997* in the US to coincide with the second leg of his 1997 tour, but this was the definitive album he'd been working at for some time. Entitled *Dave Davies Anthology: Unfinished Business 1963-1998*, the double CD emerged to virtually no acclaim but was a worthy release none the less. Comprising some Kinks classics, some Dave Davies favourites plus several of his overlooked band contributions and a couple of new songs, the album offered a surprisingly varied collection of songs. (Sadly it didn't feature two demos on its shorter American predecessor, 'I'll Get Over' and 'When The Wind Blows [Emergency]'.) It wouldn't be a Kinks project if it was totally straightforward, however; due to the legal wrangles which had already seen the album delayed, Dave had to re-record various Kinks tracks, the original versions of which were embargoed. The hits and the perennial 'Death Of A Clown' aside, 'Lincoln County', 'Strangers', 'Living On A Thin Line', 'Changing Hands' and even the title track stand out. Unusual for many stars, Dave admitted to us that the successful singles are his favourites, too.

"Obviously I like 'You Really Got Me' and the early hits because there probably would have been no Kinks without those riffs and those hits to be fair," he says. "I like all the obvious songs, of course, but I also like all the funny little things, like 'Climb Your Wall', which I like the roughness and innocence of. And although it's a new song, I'm particularly pleased with 'Unfinished Business', and I'm glad the record company fancy it as a single. It also shows the ongoing process; the album's not all about nostalgia and reflection, it's meant to be something that's current. The whole project really is unfinished business, and I kind of like the vibe of that.

"There's a song on the album called 'Eastern Eyes' that I've always liked but I don't think would ever have been a hit. Apart from some heavy riffs at the back there's very little guitar on it. I particularly like my vocal performance on that one, and it shows that I do have a vocal range and that it's not all just rock 'n' roll."

That being so, the album ably demonstrates that Dave has always been better suited than Ray, vocally at least, to the heavier songs. A couple of tracks on *Unfinished Business* are reminiscent of 'Paranoid' era Ozzy.

"I think that comes down to who my influences have been," he suggests. "I guess it comes of growing up listening to Eddie Cochran and blues people like Muddy Waters and Big Bill Broonzy and all the greats who inspired our whole generation."

As an album title, "Unfinished Business" seemed to indicate both a tidying up before embarking on the next big project, but also an amount of resentment that so many things were still hanging.

"As far as The Kinks are concerned, I still regard it as unfinished business. But in my own work as a creative person, in some ways I feel like I've only just started. As you go through life you take on different attitudes and you do different things, and I feel more creative now than I ever did when I was younger. I want to branch out and do different things. I've worked on some soundtracks for a few films which I really liked doing, so I very much regard myself as an ongoing, unfinished 'work in progress' type thing."

The track 'Unfinished Business', recorded at Konk in 1996 and featuring Dave's son Simon on drums, is the perfect example of Dave's songwriting technique.

"I like to get titles first. [*sings*] 'Unfinished business' – or like for 'Perfect Strangers'. Once I'd got that part I'd written the chorus straightaway and that shaped the rest of the song. 'Eastern Eyes' I got the title for first – I don't know why I keep going on about that really obscure song of mine, but I suppose it's one of my favourites. The words sort of sing the title.

"I write on guitar, obviously, but sometimes I like to write on keyboards because I don't always know quite what chords I'm playing and I find that helps a lot. When you're on a guitar messing around you have a kind of fluidity about it, because you know where everything is. But playing an instrument you're not that conversant with, you think you've invented a chord and that's really inspiring. But you play it on a guitar and it's, 'Oh, that's Aminor7.' I like that vibe because I like to keep that spontaneity.

"I stop doing it when the writing gets difficult. I don't like it when it gets painful, whereas I think that Ray gets to that pain barrier and starts to enjoy it; I think you've got to be a bit of a masochist to be creative anyway. Torture's part of the enjoyment, almost. It depends how inspired you get. Sometimes in the studio you can be on a high for a couple of tracks so you're working twelve-, 14-, 16-hour days until after four days you collapse in a heap and can't understand what's happened. But when it's not going well, two hours seems like a lifetime.

"Writing's always been a problem, a struggle and a fight. It was very difficult in the early days because stuff used to just come out. Songs used to just appear which was weird in a way; it was a very spontaneous period in the early days. Particularly the first year, it was like everything was on automatic, it just seemed so easy. Probably the easiest things that ever happened to me, happened in that first year or two. It was when I started to realise it was becoming like hard work that it became a bit of a problem. I've always been writing, but I was a lazy writer whereas for Ray it became his craft; he was a craftsman. I could never sit down long enough to write something I didn't want to write, I was too impatient, too busy doing other things.

"Later on I realised the importance of it and really enjoyed doing it. Once I focused myself and said, 'Oh, this is great, I really like doing this,' it became more important."

Despite the arguments, despite the sibling rivalry, and despite their closeness, Dave can still judge objectively the best of his brother's work.

"There's so many songs to choose from," he says. "I think 'Young And Innocent Days' is one of my favourites, because it's kind of timeless; 'This Time Tomorrow' too. I like a lot of the songs that were overlooked because they kind of have a sadness about them. I've always liked songs that sound melancholic but are joyous as well. Like 'Shangri-La'. I thought that was going to be a smash hit, but I think people thought we were taking the mickey out of the middle classes: 'Oh, we're not going to play that.' I thought 'Shangri-La' – and the whole concept of *Arthur* – was really caring, thoughtful and musically accomplished.

"'Waterloo Sunset' and all the singles are always going to be there, though. But I think all the little overlooked things actually have more passion, more feeling. 'Waterloo Sunset' is like a little icon, isn't it? Obviously 'You Really Got Me' has got to be my most favourite track because of that guitar sound, that I created in my mum's front room. I bought a little ten-watt amplifier and carved the speakers up with razor blades. I plugged it in, thinking it wouldn't make a noise, and it came out with this amazing sound. I suppose that's got to be the most important record, hasn't it?"

Unfinished Business was released in the UK by Castle. They, after all, owned most of the rights, including the lucrative Pye songs. Now part of Sanctuary Records, Label Manager Steve Hammonds reveals the album's genesis. "It was a double CD set, so we used all the Pye tracks but some of them we licensed in from other labels," he explains, indicating the area where the delay crept in. "Some of the things were from Dave's solo records, and there was an unreleased track called 'Unfinished Business'. Confusingly, the album in the States called *Unfinished Business* [which came out in 1997] was different. The US collection was called *Kronikles*. I don't know if Dave actually picked the tracks in the end, but the list was certainly run by him."

Reviews of the anthology were mixed – sometimes conflicting on the same website. John Bitzer, reviewing the US version of the album for CDNOW – entitled *Dave Davies Kronikles 1963-1998: Unfinished Business* – insists that Dave has a point to prove because, despite The Kinks being his band, brother Ray had stolen the limelight. Pointing out that, due to the older songs being tied up in litigation, Dave had re-recorded the older songs for the second disc, he concludes: "with less than pleasant results. Anyone familiar with his gorgeous, plaintive ballad 'This Man He Weeps Tonight' will be saddened by the sterility of this 1998 rendition." 'Death Of A Clown' and the original 'You Really Got Me' save the day.

Anthony DeCurtis, also on CDNOW, suggests that the album "gives this often overshadowed Kink his well-earned moment in the spotlight". Mourning that it wouldn't be The Kinks if it didn't live up to its talents, he concludes that "*Unfinished Business* provides compelling plot elements of a story that continues to fascinate as it continues to unfold".

For VH1 Online, the guitarist could do little wrong, for one reason: "Dave Davies invented metal." Everyone from Led Zeppelin to Spiñal Tap, it suggests, has Dave's guitar playing to thank for their success. Listing highlights as the new version of 'Love Gets You', 'Unfinished Business' and 'Hold My Hand', the review is congratulatory throughout: "You might think Dave is just another older rock 'n' roll star, but his back-to-basics ethic doesn't require an arena-sized spectacle."

More of that back-to-basics ethic was evident on Dave's spring tour, once again staying in America and again used to plug his anthology. Highlights of the dozen dates included another night at New York's Bottom Line, on 23 May.

Daringly, the obligatory US leg of a three-month world tour from

Ray strayed dangerously close to Dave's pan-American path, with the elder brother's NYC date his penultimate gig on 25 May. Beginning on 27 March at the Derby Assembly Rooms for a ten-date UK leg which included a couple of nights at the prestigious Theatre Royal in London's Drury Lane, the storyteller took his tales around Holland, Belgium, Sweden, Norway and Germany before the American adventure began.

The penultimate show from the British section took place at the Pavilion Theatre in Glasgow on 10 April. 'Lola' and 'Dead End Street' duly provided the welcome that the chill Scottish night required, but few in the audience could have expected these to be followed by 'Strange Effect', a back catalogue obscurity penned for 1960s star Dave Berry. 'Apeman' concluded the warm-up, then onto the show proper, through 'Victoria', '20th Century Man', 'Black Magic', 'See My Friends', *et al.* The by now customary sight of Ray balancing a pint of stout on his head in memory of his father seems more touching than usual, as the strains of 'Minnie The Moocha' drift from 'Stop Your Sobbing'. 'Julie Finkle', 'Back In The Front Room', 'Waterloo Sunset' and 'You Really Got Me' take the show through to its natural conclusion. Songs now deemed surplus to requirement on this tour, to make way for new material and fresher excerpts from *X-Ray*, included 'Days' and 'Harry Rag'. But, as any attendee knows, there really is no telling with Ray's capricious nightly set building.

A highlight of the new show was the introduction of new song 'Storyteller', a title begging to be used since the VH1 broadcast and beautifully played by Pete and Ray, on his trademark – but rarely used – National steel guitar. By the time the show hit Los Angeles a fortnight later, it was well bedded into the set. New additions at the Wadsworth Theatre from Ray's last Stateside trip included 'A Rock 'N' Roll Fantasy', that Lennon-esque ('God' period) wistful take on ageing rockers, and its companion from the *Waterloo Sunset* collection, the seminal 'Celluloid Heroes', making a surprise appearance *after* the traditional encore closer, 'You Really Got Me'. As if that wasn't the perfect place to end, a boisterous yet bluesy 'Come Dancing' rounded off the evening.

From California to Arizona to Denver to Kansas to Texas and eastwards, culminating in East Hampton, New York. Fans at Atlanta's

Variety Playhouse would have noticed that the show was filmed, quite ostentatiously by one of the on-stage cameraman, for inclusion on a later project. Rumour in 2001 was that it was for a DVD.

Unlike Dave's slightly more hit-and-miss approach, Ray's tour was explicitly timed to promote his new album, a live recording of the show that had been doing the rounds for the last three years. *Storyteller* the album was released in the UK in March, a month earlier than in the States, both dates allowing Ray to tie in CD signings in major towns prior to his gigs. Before the Wadsworth Theatre show, he was to be found signing CDs at the Virgin Megastore in Burbank, happy to chat to the queueing fans and, against the store's wishes, to sign posters and photographs as well as the new album.

Consisting of 30 tracks, including dialogue excerpts of the show's key stories – 'My Name', 'My Big Sister', 'Dad And The Green Amp', 'The Front Room', 'Hunchback', 'Art School Babes', 'Writing The Song', 'When Big Bill Speaks', 'Managers', 'The Kinks' Name', 'Julie Finkle' and 'The Third Single' – it also presented the first recorded appearance of the title track, breaking it in for those at the forthcoming concerts. Another highlight was the bonus inclusion of a studio version of 'London Song', notably different to the version played most nights live (also included).

The dialogue parts aside, as a representative taster for the concerts themselves, *Storyteller* is slightly misleading. Only six of its songs were singles, and certainly as a greatest hits package it misses the mark. There's no room for 'Lola', 'Waterloo Sunset', 'Dedicated Follower Of Fashion', 'Dead End Street', 'Stop Your Sobbing', 'I'm Not Like Everybody Else', 'Celluloid Heroes' and 'Come Dancing' – although all of them appeared on the tour that followed. Clearly that wasn't Ray's intention with the album (although maybe it would have suited EMI / Capitol who released it); what remains is a true reflection of the spoken part of *Storyteller* and their supporting songs, which connoisseurs of the show would appreciate.

This is a fact not lost on UK music magazine, *NME*, although it's not something their reviewer applauds. Awarding the album just 5/10, and calling Ray a "jingoistic former cockney rebel", it accuses him of ageing disgracefully with this release exposing a vast gulf between his deserved reputation as a great songwriter and his perceived shamelessness in exploiting and denigrating that talent on *Storyteller*. Perversely, the criticism comes from a position of admiration for what Ray has already achieved. Castigating him for tarnishing his legacy with such fare, it does accept that "Davies has enough gravitas, mordant wit and self-belief to spin a good yarn. Not only that, but he's blessed with the gift to casually shift moods from pathos to working-class consciousness to snickering humour", even praising 'Art School Babes' for predating Pulp's 'Common People' by decades.

Fans might universally disagree with the *NME*, but most would have mixed feelings about another of Ray's ventures in 1998. British pop singer Cathy Dennis had recorded a cover version of 'Waterloo Sunset' and, amazingly, Ray was persuaded to appear in the video. Earlier in the year, he had revealed that old friend and *Absolute Beginners* director Julien Temple had asked him to participate. At the time, "I'm trying to be philosophical about it," was Ray's line. A couple of months later and he was seen playing the cab driver giving Ms Dennis a tour of London including, of course, Waterloo Bridge and its dirty old river. For the record, it's not a bad attempt on the song, but realistically, who could expect to achieve more? To its credit, as acts like Van Halen (whose Kinks cover was heavily rotated on US TV commercials that year), The Jam and The Pretenders had done, the new single exposed a new generation of music listeners to a classic song written, performed and perfected years before they were born. If it turned a couple of young heads towards hunting down the original, it had been worth it.

In a year that saw the release of albums from both brothers – although still no sign of the fabled "solo" album or *Come Dancing* from Ray – 1998 was also when Castle's long awaited reissue series came to public fruition. Having bought the Pye catalogue in the mid '80s, the company had already taken the step of putting out one series of CDs for its biggest act, The Kinks. According to Sanctuary Label Manager Steve Hammonds (Castle was acquired by Sanctuary in 2000), the CD releases were out of necessity.

"The first thing Castle put out was a single CD called *The Kinks Collection*," he recalls, "but then we started on the individual Pye albums: *Kinks, Kinda Kinks, The Kink Kontroversy, Face To Face, Something Else By The Kinks, Village Green Preservation Society, Lola Versus Powerman And The Moneygoround, Percy, Arthur* and *Live At Kelvin Hall.*

"At the time, it was just a case of getting something out there because people were hunting around, just trying to get anything on CD which was a new format. In those days they didn't remaster CDs; you either took them straight from the tapes or from the discs. Either way, they weren't remastered in the sense that we remaster stuff now. There was no real packaging on the reissues, either. They were basically four-side booklets with just the tracklistings on. There were no rare or unreleased tracks, just the original albums. Later on, people started to get a lot cleverer with the packaging, but the first runs of The Kinks' albums were basically just reissues of the vinyl versions."

With more time to assess what they actually owned, 1998 saw Castle move forward with the next phase of work on The Kinks' catalogue. "This was effectively the second wave of The Kinks' material," Steve Hammonds says, "the first being your bog-standard reissues – in fact, I wouldn't even call them reissues, they were just issues. My predecessor, Mick Carpenter, was responsible for this project, which saw all the albums reissued with expanded booklets and bonus tracks. In some cases there were more bonus tracks than actual original tracks on the album."

The inclusion of the new material shows how groups can lose control of their own work once they sign publishing deals early in their careers. Fortunately for Ray, his management had renegotiated a deal with Castle which allowed him some say in their decisions.

"The bonus tracks were already in our vaults, but we had to get Ray Davies and the band's permission to use them," Steve explains. "Somewhere along the line Castle did a new deal with Ray to allow us to exploit the catalogue with his consent. Before that I don't think it was with his consent, because catalogue is bought and sold all the time."

As Steve says, some of the albums are almost dwarfed by their bonus content. *The Kinks* benefited from twelve bonus additions: 'Long Tall Sally', 'You Still Want Me', 'You Do Something To Me', 'It's Alright', 'All Day And All Of The Night', 'I Gotta Move', 'Louie, Louie', 'I Gotta Go Now', 'Things Are Getting Better', 'I've Got That Feeling', 'Too Much Monkey Business' and 'I Don't Need You Anymore'. The penultimate track was an unreleased alternative take, while the last song was previously unreleased.

Kinda Kinks was just as generously endowed with fresh material: 'Set Me Free', 'Everybody's Gonna Be Happy', 'Who'll Be The Next In Line', 'I Need You', 'See My Friends', 'Never Met A Girl Like You Before', 'Wait Till The Summer Comes Along', 'Such A Shame', 'A Well Respected Man', 'Don't You Fret' and an unreleased demo version of 'I Go To Sleep'.

The Kink Kontroversy had just a third of its original twelve-track content as extras: 'Dedicated Follower Of Fashion', 'Sittin' On My Sofa', 'When I See That Girl Of Mine' (unreleased demo recording) and 'Dedicated Follower Of Fashion' (an unreleased alternative stereo take).

Face To Face carried six extra pieces: 'I'm Not Like Everybody Else', 'Dead End Street', 'Big Black Smoke', 'Mister Pleasant', 'This Is Where I Belong', 'Mr Reporter' (stereo, previously unreleased EP track) and 'Little Women' (stereo, previously unreleased backing track).

1967's *Something Else By The Kinks* was boosted by eight additional tracks: 'Act Nice And Gentle', 'Autumn Almanac', 'Susannah's Still Alive', 'Wonderboy', 'Polly', 'Lincoln County', 'There's No Life Without Love' plus a previously unreleased alternative stereo take of 'Lazy Old Sun'.

Live At Kelvin Hall had no extra tracks, but it was released with both mono and stereo versions of the songs.

Village Green Preservation Society featured alternative versions of most of the album, making it easier to list those not featured: 'Last Of The Steam Powered Trains', 'Big Sky', 'Sitting By The Riverside', 'Animal Farm' and 'All Of My Friends Were There'. On top of that, there were two versions of 'Days' plus 'Mr Songbird'.

Additions to *Arthur* were equally plentiful. There were stereo and mono versions of 'Plastic Man', 'Mindless Child Of Motherhood' and

'This Man He Weeps Tonight', plus mono versions of 'Drivin'', 'She Bought A Hat Like Princess Marina' and 'King Kong' and a stereo, previously unreleased 'Mr Shoemaker's Daughter'.

By *Lola*, the extras had dwindled. The single version of the title track, complete with "cherry cola" lyric is the pick, but also featured were demo versions of 'Apeman' and 'Powerman'.

The final Pye album, *Percy*, is similarly light on new material, including instead mono versions of songs as they appeared in the film: 'Dreams', 'Moments' and 'The Way Love Used To Be', the latter in three versions, all mono with two instrumental.

"There's always been the demand for us to put the bonus tracks out there," explains Steve Hammonds, "because the fans and people like Russell Smith at The Kinks' fan club know they exist, and a lot of them have appeared on bootlegs. A lot of it's just a case of finding the original tapes. With *Percy* and *Kelvin Hall* there were just basically mono and stereo versions, so not really bonus tracks as such, but the rest of the albums all have extra songs on."

The subject of bonus tracks is a moot one if you're The Kinks' manager. Charged as he is with creating the best environment for his artists, Deke Arlon knows that protecting a band's back catalogue will bring long-term respect if not short-term gain. "When Castle and Koch did their series of reissue CDs," he says, "there were unreleased tracks on those which made them very collectable. One of the discussions we have all the time with record companies is about unreleased tracks. I normally go back to them to say that if The Kinks had wanted those songs on that album, they would have gone on that album originally. Generally, if a song wasn't used originally on the album, it was because the band didn't feel it was good enough, so why is it good enough now?

"Another argument we have with record companies is about track listings. Just because a company owns a few Kinks albums, it doesn't mean it has the right to mix and match the songs on these albums. We don't allow companies to take a couple of songs from one album and add a few from another to get a completely new album that never existed. As far as I'm concerned that's conning the public with an album containing songs they will already own. We've never done the definitive greatest hits box set collection of Kinks songs, as far as I'm concerned, but we will do it in our own time."

In the USA, Rhino had taken the same path as Castle in 1986 by releasing their Kinks catalogue onto CD as soon as they were able. Similarly, like Castle, the new copyright owners, Koch / Velvel, undertook a significant CD reissue campaign in 1998, albeit with slightly emptier vaults to search from.

Their first album, *Muswell Hillbillies*, saw a brace of new songs in 'Mountain Woman' and 'Kentucky Moon'. *Everybody's In Show-Biz* added 'Till The End Of The Day' and 'She Bought A Hat Like Princess Marina' to its live disc. *Preservation Acts I* and *II* added single edits, 'One Of The Survivors' and 'Mirror Of Love' respectively, with the latter album also including 'Slum Kids'. While *Soap Opera* included four new tracks in 'Everybody's A Star (Starmaker)' (mono mix) and live versions of 'Ordinary People', 'You Make It All Worthwhile' and 'Underneath The Neon Sign', *Schoolboys In Disgrace* was not reissued.

Sleepwalker again had four extra tracks: 'Artificial Light', 'Prince Of The Punks', 'The Poseur' and 'On The Outside'. Single edits dominated *Misfits*, the final reissue from Velvel in 1998, with 'Black Messiah', 'A Rock 'N' Roll Fantasy' and 'Live Life' appearing, the latter two as their US edits. 'Father Christmas' also appeared.

The end of the year saw Dave pick up his US tour again, filling October with new dates around Washington State, California, Arizona and Nevada, where he played at Vegas' Arizona Charlie's. Ray, meanwhile, limited himself to the Norfolk and Norwich Festival, where he premiered his first classical composition, 'Flatlands', a choral piece written for the event. A film of the festival produced by Anglia Television and Ray won Best Regional Documentary at the following year's TV Awards. The classical interlude out of the way and it was business as usual with a couple of festivals in Belgium and Germany.

Not content with his anthology release, 1998 also saw Dave embark on a new venture with the release of his first internet-only album. Called *Purusha And The Spiritual Planet* and credited to Crystal Radio, it is a concept piece telling the story of a 13-year-old collector of ancient artefacts who comes across a strange pendant which changes his life forever. As if the release medium and concept approach weren't departure enough, Crystal Radio is actually, for the first time, a collaboration between Dave and his son, Russell T Davies. Far more esoteric than his standard work, the album draws on Dave's passion for classical music and his experience of writing film scores. Complemented by classically-influenced Russell's interest in ambient, trance and dance music, the result is, according to the sleeve notes, "a musical landscape that is both exploratory as well as inspirational".

All eleven tracks – among them 'Kochan', 'Mysterious Love', 'Dance Of The Azuras' and 'One Energy' – were recorded, arranged and produced during the summer. Impressively, the album was pressed and ready for release only a few months later, in October 1998, on US label Meta Media Records.

There's definite merit in selling direct and exclusively from the internet but pitfalls as well, as Dave's manager Deke Arlon points out. "If a major artist is making a pound in recouperable royalties per record," he explains, "and you sell a million copies, by the time you take out marketing and packaging costs, that's not a lot left. Then if you go out and tour to promote the record and somebody subsidises the tour, by the time you've paid back the subsidy you're lucky if you're going to make any money out of it. If you do it via the website, however, you can make a lot more than a pound out of every record that you put out, but then you don't get the added benefit of marketing.

"Because you just market it through the website itself, the people who believe in you and like you will buy it, so you're winning the battle to get people to listen to your music; financially you're making more money per records than otherwise, but you're hitting a smaller, focused area, and you're not marketing to casual buyers or larger potential buyers. If you go out on tour to promote an album put out by Sony, the hou-ha that goes with it may be in the long term beneficial to you – you're building a name in the marketplace, you're extending your career – but in the short term you're unlikely to make much money from it. I'm told that Aimee Mann, for example, sells an unbelievable amount of records through her website. However, she hasn't really broken through."

26 DAVE'S GOT HIS READING GLASSES ON

The release of a third album called *Unfinished Business* in as many years occurred in January 1999. *Dave Davies Kronikles (1963-1998): Unfinished Business*, to give it its full title, was the American edition of its Castle counterpart, but with nine fewer tracks and many variations (an indication of the problems with licensing for the UK edition) including live versions and new recordings. (See the section on the English release in the previous chapter for fuller comment and reviews.)

Dutifully, and predictably, Dave embarked on another tour of America in January, this time focusing more on the east coast (but with the obligatory California date to end, thus getting him virtually home). His European duck was nearly broken with the announcement of four shows in Denmark; sadly these were cancelled. Not to worry, come summer and it was time to spend June and July once again on the road in the States.

Ray's movements, by contrast, were considerably less energetic. An appearance at the Midem show in Cannes in January, three European summer festivals and a night in Dublin amounted to the quietest year for the storyteller since 1995.

Release-wise, Dave had another Meta Media internet album available by the end of the year. The first in the company's series of demo albums, *Fortis Green* was recorded, once again, mainly at his son Russell's home studio in north London. One of the exceptions was the title track, already a concert veteran, which was recorded in Los Angeles during August 1999 at the home studio of David Nolte, featuring Jim Laspesa on drums. The song itself was inspired by the early passages from *Kink* about Dave's early days. "Every Saturday night there were parties in our house," he recalls. "There were always lively and colourful characters around." In 1998, *Rolling Stone* reviewer Richard Skanse had pleaded for it to be recorded, and here it was: "An incestuous marriage of The Beatles' 'Strawberry Fields Forever' and 'Penny Lane' crashed by The Kinks' 'Autumn Almanac', this whimsical nostalgia trip through Dave's childhood could have been a standout track on 1968's *Village Green Preservation Society*, which is to say, it could have been a classic." Praise indeed.

Given the more controversial content of the book, the tracks 'Voices' and 'Listen To The Spirit' may also have drawn its roots from the later pages of the same source.

Less obviously, considering his instrument of fame, there is little guitar on the album. A neat funk riff on 'Voices', though, and the solo on 'Love In The World' remind listeners that its absence is through choice and not necessity. Overall, the drawing of numerous influences, including Indian and American Indian, make this Dave's most ambitious work yet. Impressively, his well-known rock vocal range comes out well tackling the new styles and adventurous arrangements.

Adventurous is how most music business insiders would describe Dave's honesty when it comes to his views on spirits, religion and more otherworldly aspects of human existence. In particular, his dedicated website Spiritual Planet (part of www.davedavies.com) provides a forum and a chatroom for like-minded or interested people to meet and discuss their views on those parts of the world unknown to the majority. It is an ambitious project, but one which has earned its own rewards. Surely, the most remarkable honour ever bestowed upon a rock musician is the Marian College Theology Department's Faith In Dialogue Award. Part of the award was a plaque, which featured the legend: "music that raves, rocks, sings, tells the truth, and helps bring healing in the spiritual planet."

The presentation ceremony was an unexpected part of a scheduled event. Perhaps inspired by his brother's show (not that he had seen it), Dave was booked to speak and perform a one-man show at Marian College on 6 October when he was surprised by the tribute. That aside, the show saw him take questions from the audience after a show split into two parts. The first half featured readings of extracts from his autobiography, anecdotes and songs played on acoustic guitar (his first and last songs were played on an electric), all focused around his early years, the time of The Kinks' success and life as a young rocker. Considering it was a world premiere, it was thoroughly entertaining. Dave's openness accounted for much of the audience's enjoyment of the evening, but the funny stories, self-mocking manner and downright charm played their part.

In sharp contrast with Ray's more controlled shows, the second part of Dave's "act" saw him venture into the realms of the dark and spiritual. Painfully frank about his near breakdown in the 1970s, he also explained his thoughts on the psychic rebirth which pulled him through and the manner in which his spiritualism had helped him. To end? What else but 'I'm Not Like Everybody Else'?

For those not fortunate enough to be at the free show at the Marian, a recording of the night was released – as *Solo Live* – in June 2000, once again via the internet by Meta Media. Featuring ten full songs among its 19 tracks, including the above mentioned encore, 'You Really Got Me', 'Long Tall Shorty', 'Death Of A Clown', 'Susannah's Still Alive', 'This Man He Weeps Tonight' and 'Living On A Thin Line', the remaining cuts feature three read pieces from *Kink* plus various spoken pieces. 'Fortis Green' and 'Unfinished Business' didn't make the final version, though. A pity, because Dave had ascribed its genesis to an incident around his 50th birthday (and not, as usual, growing up). He's told the same story before, normally without the 'Fortis Green' reference. "Ray threw a surprise party for me in London for my 50th birthday," he explains. "It was a really nice thing for him to do so I hugged him and thanked him and kissed him on the cheek. He hated that. So he trod on my birthday cake."

Despite the brotherly pain, when asked on the night about the future of The Kinks, Dave was honesty itself: "If Ray calls and wants to do something, I'll be there in a minute." Perhaps the next millennium would hold further luck, because as the 20th century drew to a close, there seemed little chance that Ray's solo commitments – and, who would argue, his priorities – would allow much time. There was still the matter of the first proper solo album plus the much rumoured *Come Dancing* had yet to make an appearance.

In lieu of new material, April 1999 saw Velvel continue its programme of remastering and refurbishing The Kinks' back catalogue. *Low Budget* was improved by the addition of the US extended single mix of 'A Gallon Of Gas', the original extended mix of 'Catch Me Now I'm Falling' and the extended disco mix of '(Wish I Could Fly Like) Superman'. For the live album *One For The Road*, a new disc was added featuring the same songs but with enhanced video capabilities. *Give The People What They Want* failed to do so, unless the people only wanted a straightforward remastered CD. *State Of Confusion*, though, made up for it with its quartet of extra songs: 'Don't Forget To Dance' (original extended edit), 'Once A Thief', 'Long Distance' and 'Noise'. *Word Of Mouth*, the final album in the Velvel series, featured extended versions of 'Good Day' and 'Summer's Gone'.

As was becoming the trend, 2000 was another year bisected by the incredible touring brothers. Ray kicked off proceedings with January dates in Spain, followed by an April-June tour of northern Europe (excluding the UK). Dave's spring tour consisted of two dates on the west coast of America in April before his summer tour began in August, this time covering the north-east territories. A fortnight after Dave's New York appearance, Ray was in town for a string of gigs at the Jane Street Theater.

With such concentration on touring in the USA, it was no surprise that Dave brought out his second live album of 2000 in June (the web-sold *Solo Live* being the first). Recorded at New York's Bottom Line club over four nights in November 1997, the album *Rock Bottom* represented accurately the show that Dave had been touring for three years, although with obvious differences. Solo oldies like 'Imagination's Real' and a healthy complement of Kinks favourites dominate, but there are a few occasions where the singer is allowed to speak, one amusingly entitled 'Dave's Got His Reading Glasses On'. The rockers do as expected, but the quality of Dave's vocals on tracks like 'Strangers' and 'Love Gets You' is stunning. Ably abetting Dave at the

Bottom Line that Thanksgiving was the familiar line-up – Jim Laspesa, Dave Jenkins and Andrew Sandoval – but with Kristian Hoffman on keyboards. (The US version of *Unfinished Business* had already included several songs from the Bottom Line tapes as a way of getting around the licensing problems with the anthology: 'Strangers', 'A Gallon Of Gas' and 'Lincoln County'.)

Reviewing for classicrock.com, Shawn Perry avers that listening to the album makes you consider that Dave really has always been the sound of The Kinks. But Ray will always have one use in the band: "The only thing that really drags this CD through the mud is when Dave bellies up to the mic between numbers and attempts to be witty and brazen. There's a reason why Brother Ray fronts the Kinks. Brother Dave should stick to his guitar and be content to be the riffmeister that he is."

As if to underline his skills as a frontman, Ray ended the year by hosting a programme for BBC Radio 2. Commencing on 23 November, *The Davies Diaries* saw its host waxing lyrical about the year 1964 across as six-part series. Ray proved a pleasant and comfortable host, clearly benefiting from the years of anecdotal performances on the road with *Storyteller* which was itself becoming more ambitious as a piece of theatre each night.

"You see that Ray really is a fine comedy actor," sums up Deke Arlon . "He plays all the parts himself on stage, sometimes doing all the accents. You see his great sense of humour and you realise what a great actor he is."

The year 2000 ended with the news that the proposed double album, *The Songs We Sang For Auntie*, a collection of recordings made for various BBC programmes over the years, would be postponed from November 2000 to February 2001. Who would bet that, like the first studio solo album from Ray, and his musical *Come Dancing*, it stood a good chance of ever appearing?

27 THE SONGS WE SANG FOR AUNTIE

2001 saw a new level activity from Kink central. 22 January heralded the latest Meta Media internet release from Dave, a new album of demos from the last 20 years called *Fragile*. Tracks like 'Astral Nightmare', 'Violet Dreams' and 'No More Mysteries' trod further down the path of spiritual exploration which Dave had made his own. 'I'm Sorry', 'Lost In Your Arms', 'Hope' and 'Long Lonely Road' gave the impression of a man at odds with his own happiness, while 'Bright Lights' and 'Give Something Back' gave a glimmer of future pleasures. 'Long Lonely Road', replete with choppy riff guitar, had in fact been the first song written for the *AFL1 3603* album, although never used. Here it sounded fresher than its age permitted. By contrast, the subtleties of 'Wait', one of the softer ballads on display, reached out to places yet to be probed by the singer. Rounding off the pot pourri of styles, a country feel to 'No More Mysteries', the pop influence on the upbeat 'Give Something Back' and the jazz edge to 'Violet Dreams' showed Dave in a stronger and more versatile light than just some past-it '60s rocker. If the kids want choice, look no further.

As far as songwriting goes, listeners to 'Bright Lights' will not understand how it failed to make the grade on *UK Jive*; it did, in fact, creep onto the cassette and CD versions, but the LP went without. A shame, if this demo is to be judged. Finally, attentive listeners will realise that the interesting 'Open Up Your Heart' actually shares its tune and structure, plus some lyrics with 'Look Through Any Doorway'; as evidenced here, it's interesting how demos become real songs, often in quite radically different guises.

The next news from the Davies camp, albeit of a more personal nature, was that Ray's daughter Natalie (mother: Chrissie Hynde) had signed for a major modelling agency. Her career in the spotlight, like those of her parents, was about to begin.

While almost immediately at the start the year, the release of *Auntie* was put back to March, two tribute CDs were championed in press releases from their respective record companies. The Seattle label BurnBurnBurn had amassed a bill featuring northwest artists such as Mark Lanegan, Mudhoney, The Fastbacks, Neko Case and her boyfriends and Murder City Devils for its album of Kinks kovers. Praxis, meanwhile, promised the slightly more mainstream assortment of Wilco, Jonathan Richman, Aimee Mann, Matthew Sweet, Fastball and Ron Sexsmith for its CD of Davies tributes. Both were listed for autumn 2001, so the pressure was on each to deliver first.

The other news of note for the start of the year was the announcement of the DVD / VHS *One For The Road*. Recorded back in 1980, it was the first occasion when The Kinks Inc had exploited the medium *du jour*. For those with DVD capabilities, it offered interactive options and a menu of songs for ease of use in these modern, time-pressured days. Most provocatively, it featured an hilarious commentary track from Dave, plus a film of him recording it, a tour of Kinks London and a trivia game. Almost as a bonus, it included the actual concert: a hard hitting, post-concept rock show as nature intended.

As nature intended is pretty much how the Dave Davies live experience could be summed up. 2001 would be a big year, tour-wise, for both brothers, but Dave was first out of the blocks with three dates in California – where else? – during February. Summer and autumn tours were booked for elsewhere, with even the rumour that Europe might get its first sniff of the show that had so far stayed on US soil.

Ray's never-ending tour had no such travel limitations and February and March saw it take in a full exploratory of the UK. Lest regular attendees tired of the act, it reverted in places to the version of the show which had been around a year or two earlier; notable, for the inclusion of tracks like 'A Well Respected Man', 'Days' and 'Sunny Afternoon'. Keeping the show fresh for fans who probably had seen it before, and in particular, trying to keep the spoken parts interesting for those on their third or more visit, was a problem Ray seemed to be aware of as he took *Storyteller* towards new ground. But, as Deke Arlon points out, keeping one step ahead while keeping true to the show's intent is Ray's forte. "The show's changed a lot over the years," he says. "Different songs have come and gone, different countries get slightly different versions, new songs are introduced in different places. There are some anchor points that have to remain, but those gaps between the anchor points can vary enormously.

"The successful thing about *Storyteller* which never changes, though, is that you end up knowing who Ray is at the end of it."

February saw Ray reveal to Manchester's *Evening News* that fans could expect three albums in the near future: the *Auntie* collection, the solo album (of course) and "an instrumental album from a show he created last year". Could 2001 be the year of delivery for *Come Dancing*?

As far as delivery went, there was a snag for the *Auntie* album which would see its release held back. In their infinite wisdom, the BBC denied Sanctuary Records the right to use "Auntie" as part of the record's name, as Label Manager Steve Hammonds recalls. "The album was going to be called *The Songs We Sang For Auntie*," he says, "but the BBC wouldn't allow us to use the word 'auntie' in that connection. We weren't even allowed to use the word 'Beeb'. In the end it came out as *The BBC Sessions*, although some of the early press mentions the earlier title."

In March, Ray made an appearance, and lectured, at the South By Southwest Music Conference in Cleveland. As well as giving the keynote address, he sang a number of songs, including 'Starstruck', while backed by a band called The New Pornographers. Back in the UK a few days later, he was forced to cancel a number of shows through illness.

Speaking of which, Canada-dwelling Pete Quaife was at the centre of a health scare in June. Rumours abounded on net forums and gossip pages that the former Kink had had a heart attack, but this was far from the truth. While undergoing straightforward dialysis treatment, too much liquid was taken and he suffered a heart-related spasm. "It punched me hard, in the middle of the chest to let me know not to do that again," Pete explains. "I won't. Of course, everyone screamed, 'Heart attack,' but a spasm is all it was. No damage." As a result of the check-ups that followed, however, Pete was found to have two slightly clouded arteries which he opted to have repaired. Used to obsessive Kinks fans' behaviour even though he left the band decades earlier, he joked, "I will have the operation taped and will send a copy to whomever wants to watch."

With the first ever full CD release (in Japan) of Dave's first solo album, *Dave Davies / AFL1-3603* in July, spring finally saw *The BBC Sessions 1964-1977*, to give it its approved title, released on Sanctuary Records. A double CD featuring "35 previously unreleased digitally remastered klassiks", according to the sleeve, it really was worth the wait – but that wait could have been longer.

"*The BBC Sessions* had been knocking around for ages," Steve Hammonds says. "One day, our Commercial Operations Officer, Roger Semon, asked me to get it going. So I got it all cleared with the BBC – that sounds a bit easy, but it wasn't – got permission from the band and then we went ahead. But it had been in the works for years."

"This has been in the pipeline for some time now," Dave says, "but it's taken a while to get hold of and collate all the tapes. Ray formatted it all in London and it's a bit of history."

Ray's close involvement was thanks to a deal arranged by his manager, Deke Arlon.

"Ray was heavily involved in the *BBC Sessions* album," Deke says. "He oversaw the mastering and was involved in selecting the tracks and picking the mixes. One of the first things I did when I joined up with The Kinks was to revisit their deals with the various record companies that own the Kinks catalogue. Of all the albums The Kinks have recorded, there are now only three that we don't have some kind of control over. One of those record companies, Castle – now Sanctuary – owns the first eight Pye albums as were, so we struck a deal with them whereby Ray and Dave get a say in what the company puts out. This way, we as company can monitor and control everything that gets released into the markets around the world. So, for example, we can say to a company like Koch in Germany, 'Don't release that, because we're releasing this in the UK. Wait three months and then we'll be able to promote it,' etc. It also means that, as with the Sanctuary deal, we have time for Ray to oversee projects if he wants to, and contribute. It makes sense for everyone to have him onside, so the deal we have means they build Ray into their plans when they're at discussion stage, and we take each project from there."

In the case of *The BBC Sessions*, Ray took a hands-on approach, supervising the mastering, which was done by Andy Pierce at Masterpiece. Despite Ray's reputation for protracted perfectionism, the biggest problems were caused by the quality of the original tapes.

"We had loads of material to choose from," Steve says, "and there was tons we couldn't use. On a lot of them the quality wasn't good enough because the BBC didn't have the original tapes – they threw a lot of them out. In the end the tracks came from people's tapes, some vinyl interview transcription discs and a multitude of sources.

"Ray obviously had a lot of control of the quality and the tracks that went on. There was a great version of 'David Watts' but we just couldn't find a tape of decent enough quality to use. He was quite keen for that to go on there at one stage, but without the right tapes there was nothing else we could do with them."

That aside, the album pleased its prodigiously taxing creator: "Ray liked it," Steve admits. "He wasn't the only one. It got brilliant press. There wasn't one bad review for it, from *Rolling Stone* to *Q* to *Mojo* who did a whole page on it. Every major magazine reviewed it and they all seemed to be singing from the same hymn sheet."

The end result is a marvel of modern production, coaxing some stirling performances from decidedly suspect-quality sources. For those unfamiliar with the concept, BBC radio – starting as the Light Programme in the late '60s before becoming Radio 1 – would invite artists to perform live at various venues in London, recording them for national radio broadcast; quite revolutionary when it first began, and a much coveted stamp of public approval of an act's success. The songs would then be featured on a dedicated show, like *Top Gear*, *Top Of The Pops* (before it transferred to television), *The Old Grey Whistle Test* (ditto) or *Saturday Club*, or be part of a DJ's normal music show (included here are tracks premiered by Dave Lee Travis and, more of a kudos symbol than the self-styled hairy cornflake, John Peel).

"I've always been a bit nervous about the sessions and if anyone asked me to have a listen, I always said, 'No!'" Dave admits. "But now I think they fit into an era: the excitement of it all; rushing into the BBC; quick rehearsal. It very much depicts the feel of that time. We never used to spend a lot of time in the studio anywhere and it was a good way of doing it because they sound very spontaneous and wild. Even with all the new digital technology, I don't think it takes away from the recording."

Recorded at 18 separate sessions from the Playhouse Theatre on 7 September 1964 to Christmas Eve at London's Rainbow Theatre, *The BBC Sessions* shows not only the diversity of The Kinks' material, but also their tightness as a live band (whether featuring Pete Quaife or replacement John Dalton on bass) and their ability to perform live some intricate studio arrangements. Renowned for his occasionally perverse and masochistic sense of humour, it seems apposite for Ray to have included some of the original links, interviews and introductions from the various announcements on the BBC programmes, most of them courtesy of the cheesemaster general, Brian "you're tuned to Britain's grooviest radio show, *Top Of The Pops*" Matthew. The opening piece sees us introduced to "five more representatives of the shaggy set" and it doesn't get much better, with a brief question-and-answer session with the band beginning with the poser "why do you wear your hair so long, lads?". To their credit, The Kinks of 30 October 1964 respond in far more charitable fashion than would their '70s or later counterparts.

"He liked to get his two-pennyworth in," Dave recalls. "Why did he do it? But he was great, a really nice guy. Him and Pete Murray were my favourite jocks at the time. Really nice people."

Contemporary criticisms of what was groundbreaking four decades ago apart, the music is a revelation. Disc one's highlights include a rare outing for 'This Strange Effect', written by Ray for crooner Dave Berry, a beautiful rendition of 'Days' and a masterly arrangement of 'Waterloo Sunset'. Perhaps most endearing of all, however, is a powerful trilogy of consecutive tracks performed by Dave Davies: Solo Artist (although backed by the rest of the band on two of the tracks; just live stalwart Nicky Hopkins accompanies the guitarist on 'Good Luck Charm'). Sadly, 'Death Of A Clown' is presaged by an excruciatingly painful interview in which Dave struggles to acquit himself well in the face of Matthew's inane probes (intentional cruelty in the control room from Ray?), but 'Love Me Till The Sun Shines', described by the host as "nice noise", is stunningly performed.

Apart from the rarities, those tracks which originally appeared on some of the better – or more elaborately – produced albums get a chance on this compilation to stand up as raw songs. Devoid of studio trickery, it's comforting to realise just how powerful 'The Village Green Preservation Society' (from "the first album with an embracing theme") and 'Celluloid Heroes' are. Disc two proves this point in spades.

The second batch also proves that, for sheer variety, Kinks songs can be rarely bettered. The searing penetration of 'Mindless Child Of Motherhood' kicks off the latter set. Recorded at Aeolian Hall on 18 May 1970 and first broadcast on *The Dave Lee Travis Show* 13 days later, Dave's (Davies) soul-searching vocal propels the song through tortured waters, setting the tone, if only for contrast, for what follows. A flimsy version of 'Holiday' provides that contrast, but a gutsy 'Demolition' quickly adds more teeth to the album. Stunning versions of 'Mirror Of Love', 'Celluloid Heroes', 'When I Turn Off The Living Room Lights' and 'Skin And Bone' add to the enjoyable mix of the second disc's '70s review.

The BBC Sessions wasn't the only back catalogue project from Sanctuary. July also saw the release of *The Marble Arch Years*, a box set of three compilation CDs: *Well Respected Kinks*, *Sunny Afternoon* and *Kinda Kinks*. "We couldn't release them individually because they were all compilations," Steve Hammonds says, "but they had a worthwhile historical interest so we put them out like this. They were all basically mid-price reissues which Pye put out. They appeared on CD years ago, but only in Europe, but they're very rare now. These versions have booklets, with the CDs in little wallets, but no extra tracks."

Classic Rock magazine was glowing in its appreciation of the triple set, pointing out that not only did London band The Kinks have the ability to come up with one good song after another, but unlike "out of town" rivals like The Animals, The Move and The Troggs, they had that "certain hip style and attitude" that attracted the eye as well as the ear. Awarding *Well Respected Kinks, Sunny Afternoon* and *Kinda Kinks* four stars (out of five), three stars and four stars respectively, reviewer Paul Henderson concludes that, "taken as a whole, *The Marble Arch Years* offers a valuable overview of one of the true icons of the swinging '60s".

Since it acquired the Pye catalogue, and with it The Kinks, Sanctuary / Castle have pursued a policy of republishing the best of their catalogue's tracks on collectable formats. "Sanctuary's remit is to exploit the catalogue by releasing reissues," Steve Hammonds explains. "The catalogue area of the market is enormous. With the advent of CD, it makes it easier to exploit because obviously people are looking to replace their vinyl with CDs. But there's a demand for everything we put out, for all the new versions, and they all do very well. We use Russell Smith, who runs the Kinks fan club, for sleeve notes and cover research, so everything we release is what the fans would want."

Feeding the fans' desires for new versions of their favourite band's music is what this division of Sanctuary Records is geared towards. "When Sanctuary – Castle as was – acquired Pye about 15 years ago," Steve says, "they paid £3 million and obviously The Kinks was one of the major assets and one of the main reasons for buying it. Buying the Pye catalogue really gave Castle the impetus to start moving into the area of catalogue exploitation where they are now."

Having put out the original Pye CDs in 1986 and the revamped versions with bonus tracks in 1998, Sanctuary embarked on the third wave of reissues in summer 2001. The unique selling point of the new editions was their miniature format. "These are all the original albums done as CDs with miniature Japanese-style covers," Steve explains. "Rather than just put out the normal packaging, we've used rare foreign sleeves on the front of each one, so they're all collectable in themselves. They've only just come out but they're selling really well."

Another factor which separated the new versions from their

predecessors was the mix: where possible they are different to the 1998 editions and they have all been remastered direct from the original production masters. A box set containing all eleven albums plus a possible bonus CD is planned for 2002.

The first batch of new releases was unveiled on 20 August. *Kink Size*, featuring its Japanese cover and a stereo mix, was the album known to UK fans as The Kinks' first LP. *The Kinks*, a German mono edition, was the new version of *Kinda Kinks*. *The Kink Kontroversy* came out as its Italian counterpart, *United Kinkdom*, in a mono mix. The Greek *Face To Face* was stereo; the French *Kelvin Hall* mono; and the Japanese *Something Else* was stereo. In each case the new packaging looked superb.

For the second phase in September, *Village Green* was a twelve-track Italian stereo edition; *Arthur* a Dutch mono; *Lola* was stereo and British, as was *Percy*. Also slated, but yet to appear, was The Kinks' *Black Album* in mono.

"The *BBC Sessions* project was the biggest thing we've done with The Kinks," Steve Hammonds says. "The bonus track campaign of two or three years ago was the last big push. To be honest, I don't think there's much else we can put out because of the quality."

28 A COMING OF AGE KIND OF THING

The World Trade Center in downtown Manhattan, dominated by the Twin Towers, has been used for many things since its construction in the 1970s, but in summer 2001 it was a concert venue, hosting a series of Tuesday Lunchtime Rock Shows by acts like Mountain, Herman's Hermits and The Box Tops. Conceived as two 40-minute sets, free of charge to see if you happened to be passing or were working in the Center complex, the Tuesday shows were woken a little by their main act of 31 July. Dave Davies, halfway through his east coast tour, arrived ready to rock, lunchtime or not.

In case New Yorkers were in any doubt, Dave asked them: "Are you like everybody else? I know I'm not." The song which followed needed no introduction. Neither did the stunning 'Living On A Thin Line' which, although a great number in its own right, had special resonance to the local crowd following its recent repeated use in gangster series *The Sopranos*. Top that? He tried, with the countrified 'Young And Innocent Days' and 'This Man He Weeps Tonight', plus 'Fortis Green' and 'Mysterious' for the cognoscenti, and even 'Father Christmas' for the perverse.

As he spent an hour or so signing and chatting to fans after the gig inside One World Trade Center, Dave was as oblivious as the rest of the world to the horrors that would befall the proud building and its twin less than two months later. Like the rest of us, he can take some comfort from the fact that if anywhere can recover from such atrocities, it is New York. The city will be different after 11 September, but its spirit will remain unbowed.

Ray's New York dates were scheduled to take place a week after that fateful Tuesday. He considered cancelling the whole tour but in the end just postponed the obvious east coast gigs, hoping that by going ahead with his business as Mayor Giuliani had advocated, he could actually help the grieving country. "My role is to keep people focused on some semblance of normality," he told John Soeder at *The Cleveland Plain Dealer*. "If going to concerts is normality…"

Fans at the American shows that did go ahead will have heard Ray pepper *Storyteller* with a few numbers not featured last time round. If you were at Chicago's Vic Theater in October you would have heard 'Australia', a rare treat and further evidence that Ray is becoming less anxious about being known only as a "former" writer of great songs.

"Ray went through a period of not acknowledging the success of his back catalogue," Steve Hammonds says. "Some people don't like looking back too much, they'd rather accentuate the new. He's more comfortable now. When he does his *Storyteller* tour he still plays all the old songs, so I'm sure he is very comfortable with it."

With the world already in a state of flux in late 2001, what could seem more likely than a Dave Davies tour outside America? It happened though, with 20-plus dates booked throughout Germany, Austria and the UK. At the first gig in Aschaffenburg, Germany, 'Father Christmas' was still in the set; whether it would be dropped as soon as it threatened to become seasonal, would be seen. What was already clear, though, was that Dave had been away from Europe for too long. Barnstorming nights at Glasgow's famous King Tut's and London's Dingwalls rang bells throughout the industry that here was a talent that hadn't sloped off to easy retirement in the States.

As if proof of that were needed, *Rock Bottom* was finally released in the UK in September, a year after its US launch and four years after it was recorded. "The album was recorded at the Bottom Line in New York in 1997," Steve Hammonds explains. "Koch have already released the album in America and we've picked up the rights for the UK and Europe. We're also providing some tour support for Dave while he's in Europe. We're helping fund the tour and we're getting quite a good response about the album."

Not stopping at releasing four-year-old projects, Sanctuary has plans for an even older album. "In 2002 we're doing *The Great Lost Dave Davies Album*," Steve reveals. There may even be more collaborations, considering how comfortable working with Dave is. "He's a really decent guy and very easy to work with...compared to Ray. Having said that, I found Ray fine to work with on the *BBC* album. Maybe that was a bit of toadying to him. I think I probably got him on a good day. But it's always good to try and interview him when there's a woman around. He's a very good performer when there's women around."

While Dave was surprising everyone with his transatlantic tour itinerary, for Ray watchers it was business as usual at the end of 2001. The solo album, much rumoured, much worked on and much demo'd, has still to see the light of day. It's not for the want of trying though, it seems, since two weeks had been spent writing material in New Orleans, and most recent studio compadres were Yo La Tengo (the New Jersey alt rock combo he'd last worked with at the Jane Street Theater gigs) and Mick Avory, who played drums on four demos.

After years of teasing, Ray has admitted that a finished product isn't even close due to its unusually protracted recording system. "The solo project is weird," he states with some understatement in *The Plain Dealer*. "I talked to the record company and we decided I would make demos of everything I'd been writing for the past five or six years. That took a year, but while I was making those demos, I wrote a lot more material, so I spent the summer doing more demos." And so, it seems, it goes on. The good news is that at least *Storyteller*-goers have a chance of hearing new pieces. "Maybe I'll try out a few pieces here and there."

Deke Arlon is more phlegmatic than most fans when it comes to the album's reluctance to emerge. "Most record companies would like to have a timeline on their artist's delivery of an album," he says, "but Ray won't make the album and he won't deliver it until he believes that he has all the dozen or so songs that he thinks he needs to make it the album he wants. There's a record deal in place with Capitol / EMI, but when they make a deal with someone like Ray, they expect these sorts of delays. Obviously there will be contractual safeguards on their part, but they appreciate that you don't get the best work out of artists of this calibre by pressuring them. It's not like a pop act; we're here to make an album for you and, basically, you'll get it when it happens.

"It is unbelievable to think that there has never been a Ray Davies solo album, though. I've heard a number of songs that have been written with his solo album in mind, some of which are just fantastic, but I'm not – and possibly even Ray is not – in a position to say which are going to make it onto the album. There are a number of people he wants to work with, some of them famous, some not, but as long as they're talented and have an understanding of what he's trying to achieve he'll consider them."

When The Kinks were casting around for new management in the mid '90s, at Ray's behest they weren't just seeking a straightforward rock impresario. Ray had plans for media outside pop venues and he needed a manager with expertise in more than one field. He mentioned this to his friend, wit, producer, writer and broadcaster Ned Sherrin (whom he had worked with on *Virgin Soldiers*) and Ned recommended his own manager, Deke Arlon.

A former juvenile star himself and protégé of the legendary Joe Meek, Deke hosted his own TV show *For Teenagers Only* and starred in leading UK TV soap *Crossroads* before rejoining the music business as a successful music publisher and manager. Responsible in some part for the success of songs like Louis Armstrong's 'What A Wonderful World', 'Hey Joe' and 'Everybody's Talkin'' and theatrical productions *Fiddler On The Roof* and *Side By Side By Sondheim*, Deke seemed a perfect match for Ray's requirements.

"Ray said to Ned, 'I need a manager who understands books, plays, theatre, music and rock 'n' roll – and I want one person to do it all,'" Deke recalls. "I was managing many major artists at the time, and I've managed all the various strands of Ned's career – theatre, writing, journalism, wit, etc – so he suggested me. I met with Ray, we had lunch, but nothing happened. Then five or six years ago he came back and we spent about a year discussing things. We never really talked about his career. We met in pubs and coffee bars and all kinds of places, and I would turn up and be auditioned, as it were, and eventually he asked me to be The Kinks' manager. This was around the beginning of what was then called the *20th Century Man* tour, which later developed into *The Storyteller*, which Ray is still touring with six years later."

The timing of the appointment gives some indication of how long another project of Ray's has been in the pipeline. After several false starts, however, a 13 July 2001 statement from the Official Kinks Fan Club website carried the following statement: "At long last Ray is in the process of wrapping up the production deal for the *Come Dancing* musical." Deke is more precise: "*Come Dancing* is coming together nicely. It's in its second re-write phase and we're talking to substantial producers about putting it on the stage in 2002. We need to find the right director and the right ensemble of people to make sure it's absolutely right.

"One of the reasons Ray came to me was because I have the background in the theatre, managing Ned Sherrin and Elaine Paige. I've produced a lot of stage shows and musicals myself, so I know how it works. *Come Dancing* is a great piece of work, it's got a fabulous score of completely new songs – apart from 'Come Dancing' which is used. There'll be a cast soundtrack album but at the moment Ray hasn't cast himself in an acting role. The show itself is a look at a time in history that he's very familiar with and his observations of what was going on around him then. He's focused incredibly well on it in his normal unbelievable capacity. We've done a few workshops on it and the first time I saw it, a few years ago, my comment was, 'It's a complete snap shot of the era.' He's taken a photograph of the era.

"It's Ray's concept, Ray's story, Ray's lyrics, Ray's music, but Paul Syrret has worked with Ray on the dialogue, on the libretto. He's done a tremendous job, with Ray, of highlighting the nuances of the characters and the period, and of marking the change in society at the time they're writing about, from the pre-pop era into the pop era."

According to an interview Ray gave with staunch Kinks supporters *The Boston Globe* back in 1996, *Come Dancing* is mainly based on the lives of a couple of his sisters. Like the song of its title, it's a story of a time when there used to be dance halls, before Ray's generation came along. His sisters and their friends would go to the dance halls and hear the big bands. In many ways, he says, "it's a coming of age kind of thing".

Set at the end of the '50s and the beginning of the '60s, in other words just before Ray's generation came and took it over, it depicts the rise of youth as a force to be reckoned with – or at least acknowledged – in society. "The establishment was crumbling at the time – just before the Christine Keeler and Profumo scandal," he says, "but it hadn't gone yet. There was still an old order, we had the West Indian influx of immigrants and the conflict there. It was a time when the British Empire was going through a time of change, just before the fall."

Like a lot of the work associated with The Kinks, it's also about London – "but not tied down to London, in the sense that it's about people and the problems they can relate to, wherever they live, really".

Deke's words augur well for a 2002 premiere but, as long-suffering fans are too aware, another year of delays won't be a total shock.

29 THANK YOU AND GOODNIGHT

"I could tour with this show forever," Ray says of *The Storyteller*. "I've been all over the world with it. I've been to a lot of non-English-speaking territories and it goes over very well there, too."

"When we're in Japan and he sings 'Muswell Hillbilly', there's just as much applause in Osaka as there is in north London," confirms Deke Arlon. "He's taken his English lyrical background all over the world. Whatever language they speak, everyone's excited by the things and places he sings about. He is one of the world's great songwriters, one of the true troubadours. He writes about the world he lives in, like Paul Simon does; like Neil Diamond used to; Dylan; James Taylor. Paul McCartney is a great pop writer who wrote some amazing songs, but his were about love whereas John's were about what angered him, what made him think. Most of Ray's songs are about the world he sees around him. The streets, the people, what's behind the curtains, the politics of the situation, his love of England. Without wishing to sound grand, he's a poet. In 100 years' time you'll be able to read his lyrics or listen to his songs and picture the world he lived in.

"As a music publisher for 40 years, what impresses me most is always the lyrics – for me, that's the difference between a good song and a great one. Tunes are very important, of course, but it's the words that can attack you and make you think, 'I wish I'd said that.' Ray Davies does that more than most people. He makes you stand back and think about the words. The image of 'Waterloo Sunset' is amazing, and on 'The Money-Go-Round' he summed up the business of music publishing in 36 bars. He's a great painter of pictures, he's a Dylan

Thomas. You get more from Ray Davies than just a melody and a pretty lyric. You get an environment, a way of life, you can place the whole thing in time. He's a pop writer too, and he's happy being that. He's written some great rock songs, he's written some great ballads, but his important songs sum up 1964 onwards."

"The Kinks were one of the quintessential British bands of all time, along with The Beatles and The Rolling Stones," Steve Hammonds agrees. "They've had a longevity combined with a bit of dignity as well. 'Sunny Afternoon' was Number One when England won the World Cup and Ray was one of the first, great English songwriters, behind Lennon and McCartney."

"I've been working with The Kinks for approximately six years and it's amazing," Deke continues. "Whatever area I walk into – film, television, radio, theatre – anywhere in the world, I say that I'm proud to represent The Kinks and people are so impressed. Ray is a huge influence on people: there's not a movie director in Los Angeles that isn't aware totally of Ray's contribution to the world of music and drama and words. He's a huge icon and deservedly so.

"When Ray appeared on *Later With Jools Holland*, one of the other acts that night was Reef, who he really loved. When it was Ray's turn to perform, he thought it would be great to have some more percussion so he got Reef's drummer to come over. They couldn't move his drum kit, so he brought his sticks over and played on some flightcases. The guy was just blown away to be asked, but Ray knew that it would add something to the song. He has this affinity with things to just know what's right. It's an overused word, but I guess that's something you could put down to his 'genius'. If people are allowed to have that title, and I'm not sure they are, then Ray certainly has greater claim to it than most."

As a result of the TV show, Reef have become one of the many young bands to record at Konk Studios. In fact, Ray surprises even his manager with his knowledge of new bands.

"He stays up to date with what's going on," Deke says. "For example, my son's a young, budding rock 'n' roll artist and when I played some of his stuff to Ray, he immediately said, 'That's great. You should get him to work with the guy who produces Ben Folds Five' – and I'd never heard of Ben Folds Five. I'm pretty up to date, but at the time I'd never heard of them, and Ray had their CD which he'd either bought or someone had sent to him. But for one reason or another, he probably knew before anybody else in this country who they were. Whether he continues to enjoy them, I don't know, but he's extremely up to date on new music."

He's up to date on new technology too. "Ray's work recently has been putting together a DVD version of *Storyteller* from various areas of the world where he shot the show," Deke says. "He doesn't just do the live show on the disc, it's far more exciting than that."

The results should be unveiled in 2002 along with some other Kinks product from the ever industrious Sanctuary Records. "There is material from *The Great Lost Kinks Album* which we've never put out," Steve Hammonds explains. "One day we'll get round to doing it. It's a combination of tracks that didn't make it onto different albums, and they've never been on CD before, only vinyl. I'm also at this moment putting together another Kinks project which will be ready for 2002.

"We're in contact with all members of the band, not just Ray. Dave we speak to when we have to, but mostly decisions are made by Ray. They do talk, and I have met them both, but not in the same room. Ray has the consent on all the projects. Dave's more the silent partner in it. Ray basically has control, even when it comes to Dave's songs."

However silent a partner Dave has been in most aspects of The Kinks' history, Deke Arlon, for one, is convinced that there would be no band as we know it today without him. Whether you take the press' early fixation with his image as the "star" of the group, or his ground-breaking guitar sound, there's no doubt that The Kinks, for all of Ray's acclaim, is at the very least a two-man concern.

"Ray's name, of course, comes up a lot because he wrote the majority of the hits," Deke explains, "but Dave's influence has been enormous, too. As well as writing some great songs himself and, of course, forming the band in the first place, no one was playing the kind of guitar he was playing before he came along. He's influenced everyone from Jimmy Page onwards, and he pretty much invented heavy metal guitar. Also, when The Kinks first started, Dave was the star. This young teenager, dressed in outrageous clothes and long hair, living the rock 'n' roll lifestyle, he was the one that the papers were interested in. It's like with Wham!. George Michael had the songwriting skills, but Andrew Ridgeley had a lot to offer in the early days, too. He dropped away a bit towards the end, but in The Kinks, Dave continued to be important. Musically he's contributed a hell of a lot.

"He's currently on tour at the moment, and people who've seen him are impressed with what a great showman he is. Standing alongside Ray all these years, perhaps he hasn't got the credit he deserved, but as the lead singer with his own band, Dave puts on a great show and gives the audience an amazing time. He has a great rapport with a crowd and really knows how to have a fun evening. He's singing some of his own songs plus some of the Kinks songs he's written, plus a few of their classics. He's written some fabulous songs, and in most bands he'd be the main songwriter. Unfortunately for him, he happens to be in a band with Ray Davies, who most people would have trouble matching. Dave understands all about melody, though, and how to communicate with his music, and as a guitar player he's fantastic."

All the songwriting skills in the world won't see a new Kinks album materialise without both brothers' attention, so in the meantime fans of esoteric collectables might be advised to invest in a Finnish version of *Soap Opera* available through Poko Records. Not only that, but January / February 2002 will also see a new musical based on *Schoolboys In Disgrace* at the Arroyo Grande High School Eagle Theater in California.

Equally restricted in its reach if not its appeal was a small moment of music history in September 2001. Customers at Filthy McNasty's pub in Islington, north London, would have been pleased to see former Sex Pistol Glen Matlock run through a rousing and faithful version of 'Dedicated Follower Of Fashion' to mark a book reading of new fashion / music tome *The Look*. With other luminaries in the audience including Man In Black Hugh Cornwell and Dexy's frontman Kevin Rowland (who also performed), the entertainment was eclectic. To a man, though, the highlight of the night was the trip down Ray's memory lane.

On the subject of memories, Pete Quaife, health fears assuaged, continues his work as an artist and, recently, a writer in Canada. He has completed a book called *Veritas*, which, he told us, "deals with the lives of four boys in the early '60s as they form a group. (Go figure, eh?) The book is accompanied with a CD that (supposedly) is the band in the book, showcasing their greatest hits. There are also several lithographs of the illustrations in the book.

"These days I work from home in my downstairs studio as a freelance illustrator. I also teach classical guitar at the local college and I am president of the local astronomy club." He is not averse to the occasional appearance alongside Dave at the Bottom Line, however, and most famously turned up to the Hall of Fame gig.

Mick Avory, quite uniquely for an ex-Kink, continues to work occasionally with Ray and can be found at Konk as and when. He can also be found playing in several other bands, recently depping for an absent player in John Dalton's occasional Kinks tribute outfit, along with John Gosling and sometimes Andy Pyle. ("We appeared at a fan club convention in 1994, when we were called The Juices," Dalton explains. "Then we got back together and called ourselves The Kast Off Kinks after The Bootleg Beatles.")

At various times over the last 35 or so years The Kinks have swayed between being England's green and pleasant band and her most cynical and downright unpleasant. Whatever the future holds, the past has been indelibly touched by their existence. There has never been another band like them. And the reason? For all their obvious talents, the chemistry of family has a lot to answer for.

"Being brothers I'm sure gives them an edge," Deke Arlon insists, "despite the fact they spend half their time trying to disown each other. Ray had this wonderful comment that 'I was brought into this world to make Dave's life really uncomfortable, and so far I think I've done a good job', but there's real brotherly love there, of course there is."

So much love that the world may yet see the band reunited if Ray's tease to Cleveland's *Plain Dealer* in September 2001 is to be believed. "The Kinks are under contract to do another album," he admitted. "Once I finish my solo record, a band record could come quite quickly.

But I'd only do it if the music warranted a get-together; not for nostalgia. And I'd only do it if I can get my brother on it."

Somehow, one doubts that, should the mythical solo album ever see fruition, and despite everything that's gone before, Dave's contribution would be in doubt.

"Personally, I'd really like The Kinks to make a new album," he told us. "I would hate to think that this was actually 'thank you and goodnight'."

DISCOGRAPHY

The Kinks' official album releases in full (UK dates), not including record company compilations.

The Kinks
(Pye NPL 18096)
Released October 1964
Produced By Shel Talmy

1. Beautiful Delilah
2. So Mystifying
3. Just Can't Go To Sleep
4. Long Tall Shorty
5. I Took My Baby Home
6. I'm A Lover Not A Fighter
7. You Really Got Me
8. Cadillac
9. Bald Headed Woman
10. Revenge
11. Too Much Monkey Business
12. I've Been Driving On Bald Mountain
13. Stop Your Sobbing
14. Got Love If You Want It

Kinda Kinks
(Pye NPL 18112)
Released February 1965

Produced by Shel Talmy
1. Look For Me Baby
2. Got My Feet On The Ground
3. Nothin' In The World Can Stop Me Worryin' 'Bout That Girl
4. Naggin' Woman
5. Wonder Where My Baby Is
6. Tired Of Waiting
7. Dancing In The Street
8. Don't Ever Change
9. Come On Now
10. So Long
11. You Shouldn't Be Sad
12. Something Better Beginning

The Kink Kontroversy
(Pye NPL 18131)
Released February 1966
Produced by Shel Talmy
1. Milk Cow Blues
2. Ring The Bells
3. Gotta Get The First Plane Home
4. When I See That Girl Of Mine
5. I Am Free
6. Till The End Of The Day
7. The World Keeps Going Round
8. I'm On An Island
9. Where Have All The Good Times Gone
10. It's Too Late
11. What's In Store For Me
12. You Can't Win

Face To Face
(Pye N(S)PL 18149)
Released November 1966

Produced by Shel Talmy

1. Party Line
2. Rosy Won't You Please Come Home
3. Dandy
4. Too Much On My Mind
5. Session Man
6. Rainy Day In June
7. House In The Country
8. Holiday In Waikiki
9. Most Exclusive Residence For Sale
10. Fancy
11. Little Miss Queen Of Darkness
12. You're Looking Fine
13. Sunny Afternoon
14. I'll Remember

Something Else By The Kinks

(Pye N(S)PL 18193)

Released September 1967

Produced by Shel Talmy, except Waterloo Sunset produced by Ray Davies

1. David Watts
2. Death Of A Clown
3. Two Sisters
4. No Return
5. Harry Rag
6. Tin Soldier Man
7. Situation Vacant
8. Love Me Till The Sun Shines
9. Lazy Old Sun
10. Afternoon Tea
11. Funny Face
12. End Of The Season
13. Waterloo Sunset

Live At Kelvin Hall

(Pye N(S)PL 18191)

Released January 1968

Produced by Shel Talmy

1. Till The End Of The Day
2. A Well Respected Man
3. You're Looking Fine
4. Sunny Afternoon
5. Dandy
6. I'm On An Island
7. Come On Now
8. You Really Got Me
9. Medley: Milk Cow Blues; Batman Theme; Tired Of Waiting For You

The Kinks Are The Village Green Preservation Society

(Pye N(S)PL 18233)

Released November 1968

Produced by Ray Davies

1. The Village Green Preservation Society
2. Do You Remember Walter?
3. Picture Book
4. Johnny Thunder
5. Last Of The Steam Powered Trains
6. Big Sky
7. Sitting By The Riverside
8. Animal Farm
9. Village Green
10. Starstruck
11. Phenomenal Cat
12. All Of My Friends Were There
13. Wicked Annabella
14. Monica
15. People Take Pictures Of Each Other

Arthur (Or The Decline And Fall Of The British Empire)

(Pye N(S)PL 18317)
Released October 1969
Produced by Ray Davies
  1. Victoria
  2. Yes Sir, No Sir
  3. Some Mother's Son
  4. Drivin'
  5. Brain Washed
  6. Australia
  7. Shangri-La
  8. Mr Churchill Says
  9. She Bought A Hat Like Princess Marina
  10. Young And Innocent Days
  11. Nothing To Say
  12. Arthur

Lola Versus Powerman And The Moneygoround, Part One
(Pye N(S)PL 18359)
Released November 1970
Produced by Ray Davies
  1. Intro
  2. The Contenders
  3. Strangers
  4. Denmark Street
  5. Get Back In Line
  6. Lola
  7. Top Of The Pops
  8. The Money-Go-Round
  9. This Time Tomorrow
  10. A Long Way From Home
  11. Rats
  12. Apeman
  13. Powerman
  14. Got To Be Free

Percy
(Pye N(S)PL 18365)
Released March 1971
Produced by Ray Davies
1. God's Children
2. Lola
3. The Way Love Used To Be
4. Completely
5. Running Round Town
6. Moments
7. Animals In The Zoo
8. Just Friends
9. Whip Lady
10. Dreams
11. Helga
12. Willesden Green
13. God's Children - End

Muswell Hillbillies
(RCA SF8243)
Released November 1971
Produced by Ray Davies
1. 20th Century Man
2. Acute Schizophrenia Paranoia Blues
3. Holiday
4. Skin And Bone
5. Alcohol
6. Complicated Life
7. Here Come The People In Grey
8. Have A Cuppa Tea
9. Holloway Jail
10. Oklahoma USA
11. Uncle Son
12. Muswell Hillbilly

Everybody's In Show-Biz, Everybody's A Star
(RCA DPS 2035)
Released August 1972
Produced by Ray Davies
Studio tracks

1. Here Comes Yet Another Day
2. Maximum Consumption
3. Unreal Reality
4. Hot Potatoes
5. Sitting In My Hotel
6. Motorway
7. You Don't Know My Name
8. Supersonic Rocket Ship
9. Look A Little On The Sunny Side
10. Celluloid Heroes

Live tracks

11. Top Of The Pops
12. Brain Washed
13. Mr Wonderful
14. Acute Schizophrenia Paranoia Blues
15. Holiday
16. Muswell Hillbilly
17. Alcohol
18. Banana Boat Song
19. Skin And Bone
20. Baby Face
21. Lola

Preservation Act 1
(RCA SF 8392)
Released December 1973
Produced by Ray Davies

1. Morning Song
2. Daylight

3. Sweet Lady Genevieve
4. There's A Change In The Weather
5. Where Are They Now?
6. One Of The Survivors
7. Cricket
8. Money & Corruption/I Am Your Man
9. Here Comes Flash
10. Sitting In The Midday Sun
11. Demolition

Preservation Act II
(RCA LP2 5040)
Released June 1974
Produced by Ray Davies

1. Announcement
2. Introduction To Solution
3. When A Solution Comes
4. Money Talks
5. Announcement
6. Shepherds Of The Nation
7. Scum Of The Earth
8. Second Hand Car Spiv
9. He's Evil
10. Mirror Of Love
11. Announcement
12. Nobody Gives
13. Oh Where Oh Where Is Love?
14. Flash's Dream (The Final Elbow)
15. Flash's Confession
16. Nothing Lasts Forever
17. Announcement
18. Artificial Man
19. Scrapheap City
20. Announcement
21. Salvation Road

(Note: Rhino's *Preservation – A Play In Two Acts* reissue includes the non-LP single, 'Preservation', as a prologue to the albums.)

Soap Opera
(RCA SF 8411)
Released March 1975
Produced by Ray Davies

1. Everybody's A Star (Starmaker)
2. Ordinary People
3. Rush Hour Blues
4. Nine To Five
5. When Work Is Over
6. Have Another Drink
7. Underneath The Neon Sign
8. Holiday Romance
9. You Make It All Worthwhile
10. Ducks On The Wall
11. (A) Face In The Crowd
12. You Can't Stop The Music

Schoolboys In Disgrace
(RCA RS 1028)
Released November 1975
Produced by Ray Davies

1. Schooldays
2. Jack The Idiot Dunce
3. Education
4. The First Time We Fall In Love
5. I'm In Disgrace
6. Headmaster
7. The Hard Way
8. The Last Assembly
9. No More Looking Back
10. Finale

Sleepwalker
(Arista SPARTY 1002)
Released February 1977
Produced by Ray Davies
 1. Life On The Road
 2. Mr Big Man
 3. Sleepwalker
 4. Brother
 5. Juke Box Music
 6. Sleepless Night
 7. Stormy Sky
 8. Full Moon
 9. Life Goes On

Misfits
(Arista SPART 1055)
Released May 1978
Produced by Ray Davies
 1. Misfits
 2. Hay Fever
 3. Live Life
 4. A Rock 'N' Roll Fantasy
 5. In A Foreign Land
 6. Permanent Waves
 7. Black Messiah
 8. Out Of The Wardrobe
 9. Trust Your Heart
 10. Get Up

Low Budget
(Arista SPART 1099)
Released September 1979
Produced by Ray Davies
 1. Attitude
 2. Catch Me Now I'm Falling

3. Pressure
4. National Health
5. (Wish I Could Fly Like) Superman
6. Low Budget
7. In A Space
8. Little Bit Of Emotion
9. A Gallon Of Gas
10. Misery
11. Moving Pictures

One For The Road
(Arista DARTY 6)
Released October 1980
Produced by Ray Davies

1. Opening
2. Hardway
3. Catch Me Now I'm Falling
4. Where Have All The Good Times Gone
5. Lola
6. Pressure
7. All Day And All Of The Night
8. Misfits
9. Prince Of The Punks
10. Stop Your Sobbing
11. Low Budget
12. Attitude
13. Superman
14. National Health
15. Till The End Of The Day
16. Celluloid Heroes
17. You Really Got Me
18. Victoria
19. David Watts

Give The People What They Want

(Arista SPART 117)
Released January 1982
Produced by Ray Davies

1. Around The Dial
2. Give The People What They Want
3. Killer's Eyes
4. Predictable
5. Add It Up
6. Destroyer
7. Yo-Yo
8. Back To Front
9. Art Lover
10. A Little Bit Of Abuse
11. Better Things

State Of Confusion
(Arista 205 275)
Released June 1983
Produced by Ray Davies

1. State Of Confusion
2. Definite Maybe
3. Labour Of Love
4. Come Dancing
5. Property
6. Don't Forget To Dance
7. Young Conservatives
8. Heart Of Gold
9. Cliches Of The World (B Movie)
10. Bernadette

The cassette of the album also included: 'Noise' and 'Long Distance'. Some early pressings contain a listing for 'Once A Thief', originally intended for the album but never included.

Word Of Mouth
(Arista 206 685)

Released November 1984
Produced by Ray Davies
Associate Producer: Dave Davies

1. Do It Again
2. Word Of Mouth
3. Good Day
4. Living On A Thin Line
5. Sold Me Out
6. Massive Reductions
7. Guilty
8. Too Hot
9. Missing Persons
10. Summer's Gone
11. Going Solo

Think Visual
(London LONLP 27)
Released November 1986
Produced by Ray Davies

1. Working At The Factory
2. Lost And Found
3. Repetition
4. Welcome To Sleazy Town
5. The Video Shop
6. Rock 'N' Roll Cities
7. How Are You
8. Think Visual
9. Natural Gift
10. Killing Time
11. When You Were A Child

The Kinks Live The Road
(London LONLP 49)
Released May 1988
Produced by Ray Davies

1. The Road
2. Destroyer
3. Apeman
4. Come Dancing
5. Art Lover
6. Clichés Of The World (B Movie)
7. Think Visual
8. Living On A Thin Line
9. Lost And Found
10. It (I Want It)
11. Around The Dial
12. Give The People What They Want

UK Jive
(London 828-165-1)
Released October 1989
Produced by Ray Davies, except + produced by Dave Davies
1. Aggravation
2. How Do I Get Close
3. UK Jive
4. Now And Then
5. What Are We Doing
6. Entertainment
7. War Is Over
8. Down All The Days (To 1992)
9. Loony Balloon
10. Dear Margaret
11. Bright Lights+
12. Perfect Strangers+

Phobia
(Columbia 472489 2)
Released March 1993
Produced by Ray Davies
1. Opening

2. Wall Of Fire
3. Drift Away
4. Still Searching
5. Phobia
6. Only A Dream
7. Don't
8. Babies
9. Over The Edge
10. Surviving
11. It's Alright (Don't Think About It)
12. The Informer
13. Hatred (A Duet)
14. Somebody Stole My Car
15. Close To The Wire
16. Scattered

To The Bone
(Konk Grapevine KNKCD 1)
Released October 1994
Produced by Ray Davies

1. All Day And All Of The Night
2. Apeman
3. Tired Of Waiting
4. See My Friends
5. Death Of A Clown
6. Waterloo Sunset
7. Muswell Hillbilly
8. Better Things
9. Don't Forget To Dance
10. Autumn Almanac
11. Sunny Afternoon
12. Dedicated Follower Of Fashion
13. You Really Got Me

INDEX